LAMB *of* GOD

7th EDITION

VERWALTER DES UMHANGS

AuthorHouse™
1663 Liberty Drive
Bloomington, IN 47403
www.authorhouse.com
Phone: 833-262-8899

Because of the dynamic nature of the Internet, any web addresses or links contained in this book may have changed
since publication and may no longer be valid. The views expressed in this work are solely those of the author and do
not necessarily reflect the views of the publisher, and the publisher hereby disclaims any responsibility for them.

Any people depicted in stock imagery provided by Getty Images are models,
and such images are being used for illustrative purposes only.
Certain stock imagery © Getty Images.

This book is printed on acid-free paper.

ISBN: 978-1-7283-7300-3 (sc)
ISBN: 978-1-7283-7301-0 (hc)
ISBN: 978-1-7283-7299-0 (e)

Library of Congress Control Number: 2020917141

Print information available on the last page.

Published by AuthorHouse 02/09/2021

authorHOUSE®

Title:

LAMB OF GOD

Presentation:

LAMB OF GOD

The Truth Behind the World's Most Mysterious Mysteries of Deceased, Present Lasting and Forming a New of Society's.

Contents:

Reserved

Prologue

Among the scriptures written within the Holy Bible are the breathed words of the Holy Ghost. The scriptures unveil the encrypted seal to eternal life through the salvation offered by the Messiah. Truth is unveiled, within the prophesies by the chosen prophets within the writings of the scriptures. Within the Holy Bible scriptures, the pathway to the Kingdom of Heaven is encrypted for those who present a mustard seed of faith. Book title "HOLY BIBLE" decoded is an acronym HOLY means He Only Left You. BIBLE means Basic Instructions Before Leaving Earth. Decoding of encrypted messages within the scriptures are clear for the true to God.

Souls are given their own free will, the open minds of believers, faithful to the Messiah with their soul shall endeavor to persevere the seal upon their forehead. Further, to be most effective the scripture must be read out loud by the believer with their tongue from the book of life unchanged scripture held in the believer's hands while the book is open. The way to receive the insight to the encrypted decryption of the seal is given in vision by the Messiah Incarnation Jesus Christ. This may be achieved, while holding the book of life open while reading from the indoctrination of the seal as delivered by the ordained Apostles, indoctrinated by the Messiah Lord and Savior Messianic King Jesus Christ.

Others due to their ignorance of truth, agnostics, atheists, satanists, non-believers who attempt to read the encryption will be unable to endeavor this decryption to the code, as written in scripture Revelation 22. Until the unveiling of the veil by the root of David all are blinded from viewing the evil, corruption and pollution among the surroundings of this world. Blinded from the understanding within the encoded encryption.

Ultimately, achieving balance in connection with God creator of all will institute knowledge of the encryption decoding. This may be revealed through the connection achieved with the prophesied Messiah who alone is the way.

Revelation 7: 1 – 3
"7 And after these things I saw four angels standing on the four corners of the earth, holding the four winds of the earth, that the wind should not blow on the earth, nor on the sea, nor on any tree.2 And I saw another angel ascending from the east, having the seal of the living God: and he cried with a loud voice to the four angels, to whom it was given to hurt the earth and the sea,3 Saying, Hurt not the earth, neither the sea, nor the trees, till we have sealed the servants of our God in their foreheads."

رؤيا 7 :3-1
"7 وبعد هذا رأيت أربعة ملائكة واقفين على اربع زوايا الارض ممسكين اربع رياح الارض، ان الرياح لكي لا تهب على الأرض، وبعد ان ختم الله الحي tree.2 وأنا رأى آخر تصاعدي ملاك من الشرق، ولا على البحر ولا على أي فنادى بصوت عظيم إلى الملائكة الأربعة، الذين أعطوا أن يضروا الأرض والبحر، 3 قائلا لا تضروا الأرض ولا البحر ولا الأشجار، حتى نختم عبيد الهنا على جباههم".

ruyaan 7: 1-3
" 7 w baed hdha ra'ayt arbet malayikatan waqifin ealaa arbe zawaya al'ard mumsikin arbe riah al'ard , 'ann alrriah likay la tahib ealaa al'ard , wala ealaa albahr wala ealaa 'ay tree.2 wa'ana

ra'aa akhar tasaeudi malak min alshrq , wabaed 'an khatam alllah alhay , fnada bisawt eazim 'iilaa almalayikat alarbet , alladhin 'uetuu 'ann yadurru al'ard walbahr , 3 qaylaan la tadarru al'ard wala albahr wala al'ashjar , hatta nakhtim eubayd alhna ealaa jibahuhum ".

Revelation 22: 17
"17 And the Spirit and the bride say, Come. And let him that heareth say, Come. And let him that is athirst come. And whosoever will, let him take the water of life freely."

الوحي 22: 17
"17 والروح والعروس يقولان تعال. واسمحوا له ان يسمع ويقول تعال. والسماح له ما جاء عطشان. واراد ان، دعه يأخذ ماء الحياة بحرية ".

alwahy 22: 17
" 17 walrruh w alerus yaqulan tueal . w aismahu lah 'an yasmae wayaqul taeala. walssamah lah ma ja' eatshan . w 'arad 'an, daeah yakhudh ma' alhayat bahria ".

Revelation 21: 9 – 10
"9 And there came unto me one of the seven angels which had the seven vials full of the seven last plagues, and talked with me, saying, come hither, I will shew thee the bride, the Lamb's wife.10 And he carried me away in the spirit to a great and high mountain, and shewed me that great city, the holy Jerusalem, descending out of heaven from God,"

رؤيا 21: 9-10
"9 وهناك جاء لي واحد من السبعة الملائكة التي كان لها سبعة قوارير المملوءة من السبع الضربات الاخيرة وتكلم معي الخروف وذهب بي بالروح إلى جبل عظيم عال، وأراني المدينة wife.10 ،قائلا: تعال إلى هنا، وأنا أريك العروس العظيمة أورشليم المقدسة نازلة من السماء من عند الله "

ruya 21: 9-10
" 9 w hunak ja' li wahid min alssabeat almalayikat alty kan laha sabeat qawarir almamlu'at min alsbe alddarbat al'akhirat w takallam maei qayla: taeal 'iilaa huna , wa'ana 'urik aleurus , wife.10 alkhuruf wadhahab bi bialrruh 'iilaa jabal eazim eal , w 'arani almadinat aleazimat 'uwrishlim almuqaddasat nazilatan mmin alssama' mmin eind alllah

Galatians 4: 26
"26 But Jerusalem which is above is free, which is the mother of us all."

غلاطية 4: 26
"26 ولكن القدس التي هي فوق هو الحرة، والتي هي أم لنا جميعا ".

ghalatiat 4: 26
" 26 walakann alquds alty hi fawq hu alhuratu, wallati hi 'umm lana jamyea. "

John 6: 27 – 28
"27 Labour not for the meat which perisheth, but for that meat which endureth unto everlasting life, which the Son of man shall give unto you: for him hath God the Father

sealed. 28 Then said they unto him, what shall we do, that we might work the works of God?"

يوحنا 6: 27-28

"27 اعملوا لا للطعام البائد، ولكن لأن اللحوم التي تصبر إلى الحياة الأبدية، ويقوم ابن الانسان إعطاء لكم: له حرم الله يختم الأب. 28 فقالوا له ماذا نفعل، حتى نعمل أعمال الله؟"

ywhna 6: 27-28

" 27 aemaluaan la lil taeam albayid , walakan l 'ann allluhum alty tasbir 'iilaa alhayat al'abadiat , wayaqum abn al'iinsan 'iieta' lakum : lah harram alllah yakhtim al'ab . 28 faqaluu lah madha nafeal , hatta naemal 'aemal alllah ? "

John 6: 53 – 56

"53 Then Jesus said unto them, Verily, verily, I say unto you, except ye eat the flesh of the Son of man, and drink his blood, ye have no life in you. 54 Whoso eateth my flesh, and drinketh my blood, hath eternal life; and I will raise him up at the last day. 55 For my flesh is meat indeed, and my blood is drink indeed. 56 He that eateth my flesh, and drinketh my blood, dwelleth in me, and I in him."

يوحنا 6: 53-56

"53 فقال لهم يسوع الحق أقول لكم: إن لم تأكلوا جسد ابن الإنسان وتشربوا دمه، عندكم فليس لكم حياة فيكم. 54 من يأكل جسدي ويشرب دمي فله حياة أبدية. وأنا أقيمه في اليوم الأخير. 55 لان جسدي اللحوم في الواقع، ودمي مشرب حق. 56 من يأكل جسدي ويشرب دمي يثبت في وانا فيه."

ywhna 6: 53-56

" 53 faqal lahum yasue alhaqq alhaqq 'aqul lakm: 'iin llam takuluu jasad abn al'iinsan w tashrabuu dammah , eindakum falays lakum hayat fikum . 54 min yakul jasdi w yashrab dami falah hayatan 'abadiatan . wa'ana 'aqimuh fi alyawm al'akhir . 55 li'ann jusidi allluhum fi alwaqie , wadumi mushrib haqq . 56 min yakul jasdi w yashrab dumi yuthbit fi wa'inna fih . "

Matthew 26: 17 – 19

"17 Now the first day of the feast of unleavened bread the disciples came to Jesus, saying unto him, where wilt thou that we prepare for thee to eat the Passover? 18 And he said, go into the city to such a man, and say unto him, The Master saith, My time is at hand; I will keep the Passover at thy house with my disciples. 19 And the disciples did as Jesus had appointed them; and they made ready the Passover."

متى 26: 17-19

"17 الآن في اليوم الأول من عيد الفطير تقدم التلاميذ إلى يسوع قائلين له اين انت الذبول أن نعد لك لتأكل الفصح؟ 18 فقال اذهبوا الى المدينة لمثل هذا الرجل، وقل له: المعلم يقول وقتي قريب. وسأبقي الفصح في بيتك مع تلاميذي. 19 ففعل التلاميذ كما أمرهم يسوع. وأعدوا الفصح."

mataa 26: 17-19

" 17 alan fi alyawm al'awwal min eid alfatir taqaddam alttalamuydh 'iilaa yaswe qayilayn lah 'ayn 'ant aldhdhubul 'ann naeudd lak l takul alfush ? 18 faqal adhhabuu 'iilaa almadinat l mithl hdha alrrajul , waqul lh: almaelam yaqul waqati qryb. wasa'abaqi alfash fi baytik mae tlamydhi . 19 fafeal alttalamuydh kama 'amrihim yasue . w 'aeaduu alfash "

Matthew 26: 26 – 28
"26 And as they were eating, Jesus took bread, and blessed it, and brake it, and gave it to the disciples, and said, Take, eat; this is my body. 27 And he took the cup, and gave thanks, and gave it to them, saying, Drink ye all of it; 28 For this is my blood of the new testament, which is shed for many for the remission of sins."

متى 26: 26 - 28
"26 وفيما هم يأكلون أخذ يسوع الخبز وبارك وكسر وأعطى لتلاميذه، وقال: خذوا كلوا. هذا هو جسدي. 27 وأخذ الكأس، وقدم الشكر، وأعطاه لهم، قائلا اشربوا منها كلكم منه. 28 لأن هذا هو دمي الذي للعهد الجديد الذي يسفك من أجل كثيرين لمغفرة الخطايا ."

mataa 26: 26 - 28
" 26 wafima hum yakulun 'akhadh yaswae alkhubz wabarak wakasr wa'aetaa l talamidhih , waqal: khudhuu klu. hadha hu jusdi . 27 w 'akhadh alkas , w qaddam alshshukr , wa'aetah lahum , qayla aishrabuu minha klkum minh . 28 li'ann hadha hu dami aldhy lil eahid aljadid aldhy yusfik min ajl kthyryn lamaghfirat alkhataya "

Leviticus 23: 4 - 5
"4 These are the feasts of the Lord, even holy convocations, which ye shall proclaim in their seasons. 5 In the fourteenth day of the first month at even is the Lord's Passover."

لاويين 23: 4-5
"4 هذه هي أعياد الرب، حتى الدعوات المقدسة، التي تشكون ناد في أوقاتها. 5 في اليوم الرابع عشر من الشهر الأول حتى في غير فصح للرب ."

lawiyn 23: 4-5
" 4 hadhih hi 'eyad alrrab , hatta alddaeawat almuqaddasat , alty tashkun nad fi 'awqatiha . 5 fi alyawm alrrabie eshr min alshshahr al'awwal hatta fi ghyr fush lilrrab " .

Revelation 5:1-5
5 And I saw in the right hand of him that sat on the throne a book written within and on the backside, sealed with seven seals.
2 And I saw a strong angel proclaiming with a loud voice, who is worthy to open the book, and to loose the seals thereof?
3 And no man in heaven, nor in earth, neither under the earth, was able to open the book, neither to look thereon.
4 And I wept much, because no man was found worthy to open and to read the book, neither to look thereon.
5 And one of the elders saith unto me, Weep not: behold, the Lion of the tribe of Judah, the Root of David, hath prevailed to open the book, and to loose the seven seals thereof.

رؤيا 5: 1-5
5 ورأيت في اليد اليمنى من الجالس على العرش سفرا مكتوبا من داخل ومن وراء، مختوما بسبعة ختوم.

2 ورأيت ملاكا قويا ينادي بصوت عظيم من هو مستحق أن يفتح السفر ويفك ختومه؟

3 فلم يستطع أحد في السماء ولا على الأرض ولا تحت الأرض، وكان قادرا على فتح الكتاب، ولا أن ينظر إليه.

4 فصرت أنا أبكي كثيرا، لأنه لم يوجد أحد مستحقا أن يفتح ولقراءة الكتاب، ولا أن ينظر إليه.

5 واحدة من يقول شيوخ لي، لا تبك هوذا قد غلب الأسد الذي من سبط يهوذا، أصل داود، ساد هاث لفتح الكتاب، ويفك الأختام سبعة منها.

ruya 5: 1-5

5 wara'ayt fi alyad alyumnaa min aljalis ealaa alearsh sifarana maktubana min dakhil wamin wara'a, makhtumana bisbeat khutum.

2 wara'ayt malaka qawiaan yunadi bisawt eazim man hu mustahaqq 'an yaftah alssafar wayafakk khutumah?

3 falam yastatie ahd fi alssama' wala ealaa al'ard wala taht al'ard, wakan qadiraan ealaa fath alkitabi, wala 'ann yanzur 'iilayh.

4 fasart 'ana 'abki kathirana, li'annah lm yujad ahd mustahaqqaan 'an yaftah walaqara'at alkitabi, wala 'ann yanzur 'iilayh.

5 wahidat min yaqul shuyukh llia, la tabik huadha qad ghalab al'asad aldhy min sabt yahawdha, 'asl dawud, sad hath lifath alkitab, wayafik al'akhtam sbetan minha.

Baptism by Salt Water

Water of Life	Messianic King Jesus Christ	All knees will bend to His Holiness King Christ	Born again in Him	It is in Him all life will flourish	In Him eternal salvation eternal life

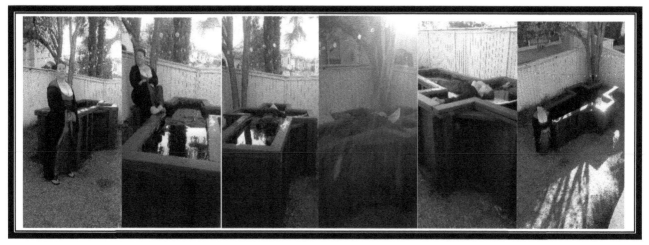

Holy Water	We must give ourselves entirely to the Messiah	All tongues will confess of His Holiness Messianic King Jesus Christ	Eternal life He is in me and I in Him	Outside of Him all life withers even the blades of grass, within Him all life will flourish gardens of everlasting life	All life will live through Him in His Holiness of Living Water there will never again be thirst

Reserved

LAMB OF GOD

7th Edition

Chapter 1

Introductory Narrative

John 3 Verse 16

" For God so loved the world that He gave His only begotten Son, that whosoever believeth in Him should not perish, but have everlasting life."

John wanted his readers to experience life in the name of Jesus. Jesus offered humanity the water of life, the bread of life and the light of life. He came to give his people full, rich, joyful lives and admonished those who refused to accept that life. We come to the Father through Jesus in order to obtain God's grace-filled gift of eternal life.

Further exploitation of Jesus; allow us to understand the many blessings given us beneath the Canopy of Heaven, that the grace we are recharged with, this God in Man Jesus experience of the atonement by the Lamb of God reinforces our many gifts of blessings we are already provided freely by Yahweh God, Abba Father through the Jesus God in flesh of Man experience.

Lifting us into Faith beneath the Canopy of Heaven our God given home final destination through this earth experience in the flesh of Man. Therefore, we are led out of the wilderness by Jesus God in the Flesh of Man experience.

As also, the Jews were led out of the desert wilderness with the Ten Commandments given onto Moses by Yahweh God, and crossing the river of the parting sea, and by Yahweh God onto Joshua with also the Holy of most Holy the first five books of the Old Sanctuary (Old Testament) the Hebrew Tora The Ark of the Covenant.

Then and by Joshua, through the land of Cannon and into Jerusalem. Wherein there and since we are given this gift of the Christ. There forth, we are also not left behind also lead out of the desert wilderness in the formation of the Christian Church through the atonement one-time sacrificial offering by Abba Father through the blood and passion of the Yahweh God, Abba Father, and Holy Ghost Jesus Christ Man experience on the cross for all of humanity. Amen

Anointed One

1 Kings 19:16 New King James Version (NKJV)

"Also, you shall anoint Jehu the son of Nimshi as king over Israel. And Elisha the son of Shaphat of Abel Meholah you shall anoint as prophet in your place."

Anointing serves at least four purposes in the Bible: to make oneself beautiful, to promote healing, to prepare the dead for burial and to dedicate an object or a person to the service of God.

Prophets, priests and kings were all anointed; one of the titles for a king was "the Lords anointed."

The most important anointing in the Bible is that of Jesus, the Messiah, and the Christ. (The Anointed One). Jesus' anointing, prophesied in the Old Testament, was marked by the descent of the Holy Spirit on Him at His baptism. During His life He functioned as Prophet, Priest and King. (Acts 17:3 "explaining and demonstrating that the Christ had to suffer and rise again from the dead, and saying, "This Jesus whom I preach to you is the Christ").

Christians also are anointed with the Holy Spirit, suggesting that we must live in the power of the Spirit as prophets who boldly proclaim Gods message of grace and life, as priests who offer ourselves as "living sacrifices" committed to obedient service, and as kings who sensitively rule over creation on Gods behalf. (Romans 12:1-2 "I beseech you therefore, brethren, by the mercies of God, that you present your bodies a living sacrifice, holy, acceptable to God, which is your reasonable service. 2 And do not be conformed to this world, but be transformed by the renewing of your mind, that you may prove what is that good and acceptable and perfect Will of God.")

Sanctification is closely allied to holiness (Leviticus 11:45 "For I am the Lord who brings you up out of the land of Egypt, to be your God. You shall therefore be holy, for I Am Holy"). And justification (Romans 3:24 "being justified freely by His grace through the redemption that is in Christ Jesus,"). It expresses both a state in which Christians exist and a process of becoming holy that takes place throughout life. This process of sanctification, whereby we gradually become more holy, follows justification. Sanctification is possible only in the Father, in Christ and in Holy Spirit. These who are sanctified are called "saints."

Some feel it is possible for us to be fully sanctified in this life and so attain perfection. Others feel that our sanctification will not be completed until after death.

In passages referring to headship, there are two basic meanings to the word "head": (a) A source or origin; for example, Christ is the source (head) of all creation and of the church, and the source of spiritual growth in the church. (b) Particularly in dispute are those passages that compare the headship of Christ to the headship of male over female. Some interpret man's role as a loving servant of his wife, just as Christ lovingly serves the church. Others prefer to emphasize man's authority over woman, so that she must submit to him as Christ did to God. (Colossians 1:18 "And He is the head of the body, the church, who is the beginning, the firstborn from the dead, that in all things He may have the preeminence").

As well, in Genesis 17:7 conveying one of the nine covenants of God expresses the importance of salvation both individually for the family and household.

Narrative

Salvation both individually for the family and household is explained in latter pages of this document including all nine Covenants of God with men who could not sustain their Covenants in this corrupt world. Until the arrival of Jesus Christ Messiah of the poverty struck village of Nazareth, no Covenants had been sustainable in mankind. Jesus arrives inhabiting Yahweh God within His flesh of Man body experience - through His Baptism the Holy Ghost Yahweh God Abba Father inhabited Jesus' body fulfilling biblical prophecy. He is Rabbi, Priest, Lord King Savior, of which He holds the Covenant for all of humanity in Yahweh God, this Covenant held by Him cannot be broken.

Thereunto, we are at the sixth millennia marked from the covenant with Noah. The Ark is located and under excavation proving the Bible is a true book. (According to the Bible, Noah was 9 generations after Adam 4004 B.C. – 3074 B.C. which is about 3500 B.C. and Jesus' resurrection sum 2021 A.D. years ago. Noah living to 500 years of age and Jesus' Ministry about 30 years of age at 33 trial, flogging, crucified and on the third day resurrected as written in scripture).

Henceforth, the headship of Christ and to institute good leadership with their voices restored, the men must accept King Christ as their "head" wherein the women can have faith restored in their men that they are men being led by the head of King Christ the Anointed One. This is the obligation of Men to bring salvation forward as head go before the alter of the Lord, bend your knee and bow your head, gather together share in reading scripture as it is written. The woman will have no fear of your headship in Christ.

Therein, Christ the head your leadership will not stagger. Where brethren is restored brethren and sistren restored sistren unified in fulfillment of the Lord. Drinketh His blood of the Holy Grail, this is good drink indeed. Eateth of His body the bread of life. This is good eat indeed. Share in the Eucharist. For His flesh is of our flesh and His blood is of our blood. Do all of this in thanksgiving and in all that you do, show gratitude unto Christ Jesus.

The Priestly Blessing

Numbers 6:22-27

"The Lord bless you and keep you; The Lord make His face shine upon you and be gracious to you; The Lord lift up His countenance upon you and give you peace."

Thanksgiving

Giving Thanks With Gratitude to Our Lord Savior King Jesus

Thanksgiving in the Bible is the giving of thanks to God for everything that we receive at his hand. We receive from him our lives and the food and drink to sustain us. Every good thing in our lives comes ultimately from God and we owe Him thanks for all.

Acts 17:25 seeing He giveth to all life, and breath, and all things; Under the Law of Moses an offering of thanksgiving could be made to God via the priest.

It is described in Leviticus 7. Leviticus 7:12 If he offer it for a thanksgiving, then he shall offer with the sacrifice of thanksgiving unleavened cakes mingled with oil, and unleavened wafers anointed with oil, and cakes mingled with oil, of fine flour, fried. It was a voluntary offering as we might expect. God does not compel us to gives thanks; it is our free response to Him.

Leviticus 22:29 and when ye will offer a sacrifice of thanksgiving unto the Lord, offer it at your own will.

1 Thessalonians 5:18 in everything give thanks: for this is the will of God in Christ Jesus concerning you.

Christmas

The Most Important Birthday of Each Year, Acknowledgement of Messiah Jesus Christs Arrival

Narrative

The Birth of Our Messianic Christian King His Holy Royal Majesty King Jesus Christ Our Lord Our Savior the Lamb of Lambs the one-time Atonement Blood Sacrifice for all of humanity.

Mass of Christ

The word "Christmas" means "Mass of Christ" or, as it later became shortened, "Christ-Mass." It came to us as a Roman Catholic Mass.

The historic record of the birth of Christ can be found in Matthew 1:18-25 and Luke 2:1-20.

Unlike any other baby, the one born that night in Bethlehem was unique in all of history. He was not created by a human father and mother. He had a heavenly pre-existence (John 1:1-3, 14). He is God, the Son - Creator of the universe (Philippians 2:5-11). This is why Christmas is called the Incarnation, a word which means "in the flesh." In the birth of Jesus, the eternal, all-powerful and all-knowing Creator came to earth in the flesh of mankind.

Easter

The Fulfillment of Scripture the Resurrection of His Holy Royal Majesty Our Christian King Jesus Christ Our Lord.

Christians believe, according to Scripture, that Jesus came back to life, or was raised from the dead, three days after his death on the cross. As part of the Easter season, the death of Jesus Christ by crucifixion is commemorated on Good Friday, always the Friday just before Easter. Through his death, burial, and resurrection, Jesus paid the penalty for sin, thus purchasing for all who believe in him, eternal life in Christ Jesus.

In Western Christianity, Easter marks the end of Lent, a 40-day period of fasting, repentance, moderation and spiritual discipline in preparation for Easter. Lent begins on Ash Wednesday and ends on Easter Sunday. Eastern Orthodox churches observe Lent or Great Lent, during the 6 weeks or 40 days preceding Palm Sunday with fasting continuing during the Holy Week of Easter. Lent for Eastern Orthodox churches begins on Monday and Ash Wednesday is not observed.

The biblical account of Jesus' death on the cross, or crucifixion, his burial and his resurrection, or raising from the dead, can be found in the following passages of scripture: Matthew 27:27-28:8; Mark 15:16-16:19; Luke 23:26-24:35; and John 19:16-20:30.

The well-known Old Testament Passover story centers on Gods deliverance of Israel from Egypt through ten miraculous plagues. These included how the death angel would "pass over" all the houses where the Israelites lived. They were instructed to put blood over their doorposts to ensure that only the firstborn of Egypt would die. In this first Passover, it was only the blood of the slain lamb that protected each Israelite home.

While Egypt suffered the plague of death, the Israelite firstborn were delivered by blood. By obeying Gods command and by faith in His promise to protect them, they were spared from death.

The Passover account is found in Exodus 12:12-14. Verse 14 states that the Passover ceremony was commanded by God to be an annual memorial feast to be kept by Israel "forever." (This command is repeated in Leviticus 23:5.) Exodus 12:15 introduces the seven-day festival called the Days of Unleavened Bread (also repeated in Leviticus 23:6-8), which was to immediately follow the Passover feast each year.

This is why Acts 12:3 states, "Then were the days of unleavened bread," before mentioning the Passover in the next verse. These days were always kept in conjunction with one another.

If the Passover was instituted forever, then New Testament instruction for its observance should be clear. This instruction is found in I Corinthians 5:7-8: "Purge out therefore the old leaven, that you may be a new lump, as you are unleavened. For even Christ our Passover is sacrificed for us: Therefore, let us keep the feast (of unleavened bread, which always followed Passover, as explained above) …"

Christ, as the Lamb of God (John 1:29; Acts 8:32; I Peter 1:19; Rev. 5:6), replaced the Old Testament lamb eaten on Passover evening each year.

The New Testament symbols of the bread and wine were instituted so that Christians could eat the body and drink the blood of Christ, the true Lamb of God. Jesus' sacrifice replaced the need to kill a spring lamb. Luke 22:19 shows that Jesus substituted the bread and wine to be taken annually in commemoration of His sacrifice for the remission of our sins—both spiritual and physical.

Chapter 2

The Ancient Roots of Judaism

The ancient roots of Judaism lie in the Bronze Age polytheistic Ancient Semitic religions, specifically Canaanite religion, a syncretization with elements of Babylonian religion and of the worship of Yahweh reflected in the early prophetic books of the Hebrew Bible. During the Babylonian captivity of the 6th and 5th centuries BCE, certain circles within the exiled Judahites in Babylon redefined pre-existing ideas about monotheism, election, divine law and Covenant into a theology which came to dominate the former Judah in the following centuries.

Narrative

Variant spellings YHWH, Jehovah

Yahweh in the Septuagint: kurios - Lord, Master

despotês - Lord, Master, denoting the omnipotence of God (TDNT), despot, absolute ruler.

Meaning and Derivation

Yahweh is the promised name of God. This name of God which (by Jewish tradition) is too holy to voice, is actually spelled "YHWH" without vowels. YHWH is referred to as the Tetragrammaton (which simply means "the four letters"). YHWH comes from the Hebrew letters: Yud, Hay, Vav, Hay. While YHWH is first used in Genesis 2, God did not reveal Himself as YHWH until Exodus 3. The modern spelling as "Yahweh" includes vowels to assist in pronunciation.

Many pronounce YHWH as "Yahweh" or "Jehovah." We no longer know for certain the exact pronunciation. During the third century A.D., the Jewish people stopped saying this name in fear of contravening the commandment "Thou shalt not take the name of the Lord thy God in vain" (Exd 20:7).

As a result of this, Adonai is occasionally a substitute for YHWH. The following compound names which start with "YHWH" have been shown using "Jehovah." This is due to the common usage of "Jehovah" in the English of these compound names in the early English translations of the Bible (e.g., the Geneva Bible, the King James Version, etc.).

Ark of the Covenant

The Ark of the Covenant (Hebrew: אֲרוֹן הַבְּרִית ʾărōn habbrīṯ; Koinē Greek: Κιβωτός της Διαθήκης, romanized: Kībōtós tis Diathíkis) also known as the Ark of the Testimony, and in a few verses across various translations as the Ark of God, is a gold-covered wooden chest with lid cover described in the Book of Exodus as containing the two stone tablets of the Ten Commandments. According to New Testament Book of Hebrews, it also contained Aaron's rod and a pot of manna.

The biblical account relates that, approximately one year after the Israelites' exodus from Egypt, the Ark was created according to the pattern given to Moses by God when the Israelites were encamped at the foot of Mount Sinai. Thereafter, the gold-plated acacia chest was carried by its staves by the Levites approximately 2,000 cubits (approximately 800 meters or 2,600 feet) in advance of the people when on the march or before the Israelite army, the host of fighting men. When carried, the Ark was always hidden under a large veil made of skins and blue cloth, always carefully concealed, even from the eyes of the priests and the Levites who carried it. God was said to have spoken with Moses "from between the two cherubim" on the Ark's cover. When at rest the Tabernacle was set up and the holy Ark was placed in it under the veil of the covering, the staves of it crossing the middle side bars to hold it up off the ground.

Exodus 20:1-26 King James Version (KJV) Ten (X.) Commandments

"And God spake all these words, saying,"

"I am the Lord thy God, which have brought thee out of the land of Egypt, out of the house of bondage."

"Thou shalt have no other gods before me."

"Thou shalt not make unto thee any graven image, or any likeness of anything that is in heaven above, or that is in the earth beneath, or that is in the water under the earth."

"Thou shalt not bow down thyself to them, nor serve them: for I the Lord thy God am a jealous God, visiting the iniquity of the fathers upon the children unto the third and fourth generation of them that hate me;"

"And shewing mercy unto thousands of them that love me and keep my commandments."

"Thou shalt not take the name of the Lord thy God in vain; for the Lord will not hold him guiltless that taketh his name in vain."

"Remember the Sabbath day, to keep it Holy."

"Six days shalt thou labour, and do all thy work:"

"But the seventh day is the Sabbath of the Lord thy God: in it thou shalt not do any work, thou, nor thy son, nor thy daughter, thy manservant, nor thy maidservant, nor thy cattle, nor thy stranger that is within thy gates:"

"For in six days the Lord made heaven and earth, the sea, and all that in them is, and rested the seventh day: wherefore the Lord blessed the Sabbath day, and Hallowed it."

"Honour thy father and thy mother: that thy days may be long upon the land which the Lord thy God giveth thee."

"Thou shalt not kill."

"Thou shalt not commit adultery."

"Thou shalt not steal."

"Thou shalt not bear false witness against thy neighbour."

"Thou shalt not covet thy neighbour's house, thou shalt not covet thy neighbour's wife, nor his manservant, nor his maidservant, nor his ox, nor his ass, nor any thing that is thy neighbours."

"And all the people saw the thundering's, and the lightning's, and the noise of the trumpet, and the mountain smoking: and when the people saw it, they removed, and stood afar off."

"And they said unto Moses, speak thou with us, and we will hear: but let not God speak with us, lest we die."

"And Moses said unto the people, Fear not: for God is come to prove you, and that his fear may be before your faces that ye sin not."

"And the people stood afar off, and Moses drew near unto the thick darkness where God was."

"And the Lord said unto Moses, thus thou shalt say unto the children of Israel, Ye have seen that I have talked with you from heaven."

"Ye shall not make with me gods of silver, neither shall ye make unto you gods of gold."

"An altar of earth thou shalt make unto me, and shalt sacrifice thereon thy burnt offerings, and thy peace offerings, thy sheep, and thine oxen: in all places where I record my name I will come unto thee, and I will bless thee."

"And if thou wilt make me an altar of stone, thou shalt not build it of hewn stone: for if thou lift up thy tool upon it, thou hast polluted it."

"Neither shalt thou go up by steps unto mine altar, that thy nakedness be not discovered thereon."

Narrative

Of all the biblical laws and commandments, the Ten Commandments alone are said to have been "written with the finger of God" (Exodus 31:18). The stone tablets were placed in the Ark of the Covenant (Exodus 25:21, Deuteronomy 10:2, 5).

The Ten (X.) Commandments Short Form

  I.   You shall have no other gods before Me.
  II.   You shall not make idols.
  III. You shall not take the name of the Lord your God in vain.
  IV.   Remember the Sabbath day, to keep it holy.
  V.   Honor your father and your mother.
  VI.   You shall not murder.
  VII. You shall not commit adultery.
  VIII. You shall not steal.
  IX.   You shall not bear false witness against your neighbor.
  X.   You shall not covet.

Chapter 3

Earliest Known Commandments of God

The Law

The First Five Books

The Pentateuch (its Greek name, but also known as the Torah by the Hebrews) consists of the first five books of the Bible: Genesis, Exodus, Leviticus, Numbers, and Deuteronomy.

From Adam and Eve in the Garden, to Noah's Ark, to Moses' parting of the Red Sea, to its conclusion with the death of Moses, the Pentateuch contains some of the most important and memorable stories in Western civilization.

Alternative Names

> Bereshit/Genesis.
> Shemot/Exodus.
> Vayikra/Leviticus.
> Bamidbar/Numbers.
> D'varim/Deuteronomy.

Narrative

We can observe a reference in these first five books as the Hebrew Torah is made of these books in the building as well formation of the Hebrew Nation (Old Testament). Also, Joshua with major victories by the hand of God in battles taking the promised land of Cannon, and the build of the House of the Lord, Solomon's Temple rich flowing with milk and honey within the Holy Land of Israel.

Thereafter, Immaculate conception by the angel of light Messiah Jesus Christ arrives "per scripture", prophesy becomes animated the Christian Nation is formed Christs beloved Church (New Testament). Formed herein, "Nation Under God" (Christendom an act or (Acts) of the hand of God support thereof the Holy Land Israel.) Theretofore, many prophesied events animate recoded in historical media passing of earth time for a duration, behold as prophesied in scriptures by the chosen prophets, His apocalypse, the rapture of His church, the Second Advent Second Coming of Jesus Christ King of Kings (Future Testament of Peace) the continuance of the Holy Bible, refer to the nine recorded Covenants of God found in the Holy Bible scriptures. Prophecies by the chosen Prophets from the Pentateuch throughout the book of the Old Testament and New Testament unto Revelation animating our witness of truth the scriptures recoded words of the Holy Ghost.

Pentateuch

Meaning "Five Books"

The first five books of the Bible are sometimes called the Pentateuch which means "five books." They are also known as the books of the law because they contain the laws and instruction given by the Lord through Moses to the people of Israel. These books were written by Moses, except for the last portion of Deuteronomy because it tells about the death of Moses. These five books lay the foundation for the coming of Christ in that here God chooses and brings into being the nation of Israel. As Gods chosen people, Israel became the custodians of the Old Testament, the recipients of the covenants of promise, and the channel of Messiah (Rom. 3:2; 9:1-5).

Genesis (The Book of Beginnings)

Author

Moses

Date:

1450-1410 B.C.

Name of the Book

The name Genesis is taken from the Septuagint (LXX), the Greek translation of the Old Testament.

Theme and Purpose

Even a casual reading of the Book of Genesis reveals the prominence of the theme of blessing and cursing. For obedience and faith, there is blessing as in the Garden of Eden, but for disobedience, there is cursing. The entire book turns on this theme and its antithetical opposite, cursing. But perhaps the main theme is the choice of a nation through Abraham and the Abrahamic Covenant. Through Abraham God promised to bless the nations (Gen. 12:1-3; 15:1-21).

Key Words

"Generations" or "account."

A key word or phrase is "these are the generations of" or "this is the account of." It is used some eleven times to introduce the reader to the next section which gives the narrative about what happened in connection with the key events and persons of the book from the creation of the heavens and the earth to all the patriarchs of Israel.

Key Idea

Beginnings: Genesis not only means 'beginning', but it is the book of beginnings. The book of Genesis gives us our historical point of reference, from which all subsequent revelation proceeds. In the book of Genesis all the major themes of the Bible have their origin. It is a book of many beginnings: in it we see the beginning of the universe, of man and woman, of human sin and the fall of the race, the beginning of Gods promises of salvation, and the beginning of the nation Israel as the chosen people of God because of Gods special purpose for them as the channel for Messiah and Savior. In Genesis we learn about Adam and Eve, about Satan the tempter, about Noah, the flood, Abraham, Isaac, Jacob, and Joseph and his brothers. But here we also have the beginning of marriage, family, work, sin, murder, capital punishment, sacrifice, races, languages, civilization, Sabbath, the first attempt at a United Nations, and Babylonianism. The Bible is, through and through, a historical revelation. It is the account of Gods activity in history.

Key Chapters

Since the call of Abraham and the promises of blessing to the nations through his seed is the prominent message of Genesis, the key chapters are those relating to the Abrahamic covenant and its reiteration, 12:1-3; 15:1-21; 17:1-9.

Key People

Adam, Eve, Noah, Abraham, Sarah, Isaac, Rebekah, Esau, Jacob, Rachel, Joseph.

Christ as Seen in Genesis

Prophetically: Immediately after the fall, the promise of salvation is given in the seed of the woman (3:15), but then the Messianic links are made clear throughout Genesis: the line of Seth (4:25), the offspring of Shem (9:26), the family of Abraham (12:3), the seed of Isaac (26:3), the sons of Jacob (46:3), and the tribe of Judah (49:10).

Typologically: There are several key types that portray the Savior in Genesis.

I.   Adam is a type of Christ (Rom. 5:14). As Adam is the head of the old creation, so Christ is the head of the new spiritual creation.
II.   Abel's offering of a blood sacrifice points to Christ who would die for us. Abel's murder by Cain may also illustrate Christ's death.
III.   Melchizedek is also a type of Christ (see Heb. 7:3).
IV.   Joseph, who was loved dearly by his father, betrayed by his brothers, and yet became the means of their deliverance typifies Christ.

Outline

The book easily falls into two major sections: Four Events and Four People

I. Four Events (Gen. 1-11)

    1. The creation of the world and man (1-2)
    2. The corruption of man, the fall (3-5)
    3. The destruction of man, the flood (6-9)
    4. The dispersion of man, the nations (10-11)

II. Four People: the election of a nation and the preparation for the redeemer (Gen. 12-50)

    1. Abraham (the father of faith and of the nation Israel) (12-23)
    2. Isaac (the beloved son of promise) (24-26)
    3. Jacob (scheming and chastening) (27-36)
    4. Joseph (suffering and glory) (37-50)

Exodus (The Book of Redemption)

Author

Moses

Date

1450-1410 B.C.

Name of The Book

"Exodus" is a Latin word derived from the Greek exodos; the name given to the book by those who translated it into the Greek Septuagint (LXX). The word means "exit," "departure."

Theme and Purpose

Two themes prevail in Exodus: (1) Redemption as pictured in the Passover, and (2) deliverance from the bondage of Egypt as seen in the Exodus out of Egypt and crossing the Red Sea.

Key Word

"Redeem," used nine times (6:6; 13:13; 15:13; 21:8; 34:20).

After nearly four hundred years of growth in Egypt, Exodus continues the history of God's chosen people, the nation of Israel, and describes their deliverance out of Egypt and their development as a nation, actually, a theocracy under God. It describes the birth, history, and call of Moses by God to lead the people out of their Egyptian bondage and into the Promised Land, the land of Canaan. Through the Passover lamb, the sparing of the firstborn, along with the miracles of the ten plagues, and the crossing of the Red Sea, God showed His people that He was not only more powerful than any Egyptian Pharaoh, but was the Sovereign Lord, Yahweh, the God of redemption and revelation.

Once the people had crossed the Red Sea and arrived in the wilderness or desert, God gave them His righteous law and declared that they were a treasured possession to Him and were to be a kingdom of priests, a holy nation as a testimony to the nations (Ex. 19:4-7). This holy law, including the Ten Commandments, demonstrated Gods Holiness, taught them how to love God and one another, but in the process, it also demonstrated how all fall short of the Holiness of God and need a way of access to God that provides forgiveness. This was provided for in the tabernacle, the sacrifices, and the Levitical Priesthood.

Key Chapters

Chapter's 12-14 record the redemption of Israel from slavery in fulfillment of Gods promises; delivered from slavery by blood (the Passover Lamb) and by power (the parting of the Red Sea).

Key Verses

6:6 Say, therefore, to the sons of Israel, 'I am the Lord, and I will bring you out from under the burdens of the Egyptians, and I will deliver you from their bondage. I will also redeem you with an outstretched arm and with great judgment' (see also 20:2).

19:5-6 'Now then, if you will indeed obey My voice and keep My covenant, then you shall be My own possession among all the peoples, for all the earth is Mine; 6 and you shall be to Me a kingdom of priests and a holy nation.' These are the words that you shall speak to the sons of Israel.

Key People

Moses, Aaron, Miriam, Pharaoh.

Christ as Seen in Exodus

While Exodus contains no direct prophecy of Christ, there are a number of beautiful types of the Savior.

I.   In many ways, Moses is a type of Christ. Deuteronomy 18:15 shows that Moses, as a prophet, anticipates Christ. Both are kinsman-redeemers who were endangered in infancy, renounced their power to serve others, and functioned as mediators, lawgivers, and deliverers.
II.   The Passover is a very specific type of Christ as the sinless Lamb of God (John 1:29, 36; 1 Cor. 5:7).
III. The Seven Feasts, each of which portray some aspect of the Savior.
IV.   The Exodus, which Paul connects with baptism, pictures our identification with Christ in His death, burial, and resurrection (1 Cor. 10:1-2; Rom. 6:2-3).
V.   The Manna and Water are both portrayed as pictures of Christ (John 6:31-35, 48-63; 1 Cor. 10:3-4).
VI.   The Tabernacle portrays the Savior in its material, colors, furniture, arrangement, and the offerings sacrificed there (Heb. 9:1-10:18).
VII. The High Priest quite clearly foreshadows the person and ministry of Christ (Heb. 4:14-16; 9:11-12, 24-28).

Outline

Exodus easily divides into two sections: Redemption and Revelation

I. Redemption from Egypt (1-18)

1. In Bondage (Subjection) (1-12)
2. Out of Bondage (Redemption by blood and power) (12-14)
3. Journeying to Sinai (Education) (15-18)

II. Revelation from God (19-40)

1. The Giving of the Law (19-24)
2. The Institution of the Tabernacle (25-31)
3. The Breaking of the Law (32-34)
4. The Construction of the Tabernacle (35-40)

Leviticus (The Book of Holiness)

Author

Moses

Date

1450-1410 B.C.

Name of The Book

Leviticus receives its name from the Septuagint and means "relating to the Levites." The Levites were the priests who were chosen of God to minister to the nation. The book of Leviticus contains many of the laws given by God to direct them in their work as priests for the worship of God.

Theme and Purpose

Leviticus 11:45 says, "Be holy, because I am Holy." The directives given in the book of Leviticus showed Israel was to walk before God as a holy people. Leviticus was designed to teach Israel (1) how to worship and walk with God and (2) how the nation was to fulfill its calling as a nation of priests. The great theme of Leviticus is holiness. A Holy God can only be approached on the basis of sacrifice through the mediation of a priest.

Key Word

"Holiness."

Key Verses

17:11 For the life of the flesh is in the blood, and I have given it to you on the altar to make atonement for your souls; for it is the blood by reason of the life that makes atonement.

20:7-8 You shall consecrate yourselves therefore and be holy, for I am the Lord your God. 8 And you shall keep My statutes and practice them; I am the Lord who sanctifies you (see also 11:45).

Key Chapter

Chapter 16 deals with the Day of Atonement, which became the most important day in the Hebrew calendar because it was the only day the high priest was allowed to enter into the Holy of Holies in order to make atonement for the people. "… for it is on this day that atonement shall be made for you to cleanse you; you shall be clean from all your sins before the Lord" (16:30).

Key People

Moses and Aaron.

Christ as Seen in Leviticus

Similar to Exodus, a number of types of Christ are evident in Leviticus.

    I.   The Five Offerings all typify the person and work of Christ in His sinless life, submission to the Father that we might have fellowship with God.

    II.   The High Priest as mentioned above is a very prominent type of Christ in Leviticus.

    III.   The Seven Feasts, again, as mentioned, also form a type of the Savior.

Outline

Leviticus falls into two clear divisions: Sacrifice and Sanctification

I. Sacrifice (1-17)

1. The Laws of Sacrifice for Approach to God (1-7)
2. The Laws of the Priests (8-10)
3. The Laws Regarding Purity (11-15)
4. The Laws of National Atonement (16-17)

II. Sanctification (18-27)

1. The Laws of Sanctification for Gods People (18-20)
2. The Laws of Sanctification for Gods Priests (21-22)
3. The Laws of Sanctification in Worship (23-24)
4. The Laws of Sanctification in the Land of Canaan (25-26)
5. The Laws of Sanctification and Vows (27)

Numbers (Wilderness Wanderings)

Author

Moses

Date

1450-1410 B.C.

Name of The Book

Numbers gets its name from the two accounts in chapters 1 and 26 of the numbering or counting of the people of Israel first at Mount Sinai and second on the plains of Moab.

Theme and Purpose

Though Numbers gets its name from the numbering of the people, it is primarily concerned with nearly 40 years of wandering in the desert. A journey which should have only lasted eleven days became a 38-year agony of defeat simply because of the disbelief and disobedience of the people. Numbers, then, shows the consequence of failing to mix faith with the promises of God (see Heb. 3:16-4:2). Further, Numbers teaches us that while life does have its wilderness experiences, Gods people do not have to stay in those conditions. Joshua will illustrate this later.

Another important theme shown throughout the book of Numbers is found in Gods continual care for his people. Over and over again, regardless of their rebellion and unbelief, He miraculously supplied their needs. He provided them with water, manna, and quail. He continued to love and forgive the people even when they complained, grumbled, and rebelled against Him.

Key Word

"Wanderings."

Key Verses

14:22-23 Surely all the men who have seen My glory and My signs, which I performed in Egypt and in the wilderness, yet have put Me to the test these ten times and have not listened to My voice, 23 shall by no means see the land which I swore to their fathers, nor shall any of those who spurned Me see it.

20:12. But the Lord said to Moses and Aaron, "Because you have not believed Me, to treat Me as holy in the sight of the sons of Israel, therefore you shall not bring this assembly into the land which I have given them."

Key Chapters

Chapters 13-14 stand as the key chapters because these chapters record a critical turning point for the nation. Here, at Kadesh-Barnea (32:8), after receiving the evil report from 10 of the 12 spies whom Moses sent to spy out the land, with the exception of Joshua and Caleb Israel focused on the giants in the land, failed to believe God, and refused to enter to possess and conquer the land, a Land that flowed with milk and honey.

Key People

Moses, Aaron, Miriam, Joshua, Caleb, Balak

Christ as Seen in Numbers

I.   Perhaps no place is there a clearer portrait of Christ and His crucifixion than in the serpent lifted up on the standard (cf. Num. 21:4-9 with John 3:14).
II. The rock that quenched the thirst of the people is a type of Christ (1 Cor. 10:4).
III. The daily manna pictures Christ as the bread come down from Heaven (John 6:31-33).
IV. The pillar of cloud and fire portray the guidance of Christ and the cities of refuge certainly portray Christ as our refuge from judgment.

V.   Finally, the red heifer is also a type of Christ (Ch. 19).

Outline

Numbers divides into three sections: Preparation at Sinai, Failure of the Old Generation, and preparation of the New Generation.

I. Preparation at Sinai (Old Generation) (1-10)

1.   The Position and Numbering of the People (1-4)
2.   The Precepts of God and Sanctification of the People (5:1-9:14)
3.   The Pilgrimage toward the Promised Land (9:15-10:36)

II. Failure of the Old Generation (11-25)

1.   Discontent along the Way (11-12)
2.   Disbelief at Kadesh-Barnea (13-14)
3.   Discipline from the Lord (15-25)

III. Preparation of the New Generation (26-36)

1.   Reorganization of Israel (26-27)
2.   Regulation of Offerings and Vows (28-30)
3.   Regionalization of the Land (31-36)

Deuteronomy (Reiteration and Reviewing)

Author

Moses

Date

1410 B.C.

Name of The Book

The English title, which comes from the Septuagint, means "second law-giving" and comes from the mistranslation of 17:18, which actually says "a copy of this law." Deuteronomy is not a second law, but rather a review, expansion, and reiteration of the original law given at Sinai.

Theme and Purpose

Watch yourself lest you forget. After forty years of wandering in the wilderness, the Israelites were on the eve of entering the Promised Land. Before they did, it was necessary (lest they forget what God had done and who they were) that they be reminded about all that God had done for them and about Gods Holy Law which was so vital to their ability to remain in the land and function as Gods Holy Nation and as a kingdom of priests to the nations (Deut. 4:1-8). As a part of this theme or purpose, the book also emphasizes the vital necessity of teaching children to love and obey God. Deuteronomy ends with the renewal of Gods covenant with Israel (chapter 29), Joshua's appointment as the new leader (chapter 31), and Moses' death (chapter 34).

Key Word

"Covenant" (occurring some 27 times)

Key Verses

4:9, 23 Only give heed to yourself and keep your soul diligently, lest you forget the things which your eyes have seen, and lest they depart from your heart all the days of your life; but make them known to your sons and your grandsons. 23 So watch yourselves, lest you forget the covenant of the Lord your God, which He made with you, and make for yourselves a graven image in the form of anything against which the Lord your God has commanded you.

4:31 For the Lord your God is a compassionate God; He will not fail you nor destroy you nor forget the covenant with your fathers which He swore to them.

10:12-14 And now, Israel, what does the Lord your God require from you, but to fear the Lord your God, to walk in all His ways and love Him, and to serve the Lord your God with all your heart and with all your soul, 13 and to keep the Lords commandments and His statutes which I am commanding you today for your good? 14 Behold, to the Lord your God belong heaven and the highest heavens, the earth and all that is in it.

30:19-20 I call heaven and earth to witness against you today, that I have set before you life and death, the blessing and the curse. So, choose life in order that you may live, you and your descendants, 20 by loving the Lord your God, by obeying His voice, and by holding fast to Him; for this is your life and the length of your days, that you may live in the land which the Lord swore to your fathers, to Abraham, Isaac, and Jacob, to give them.

Key Chapters

Chapter 27 is key because in it there is a formal ratification of Israel's covenant as Moses and the Levitical Priests call upon all Israel to take heed and listen, for in verses 9-10 it is declared, "This day you have become a people for the Lord your God. You shall therefore obey the Lord your God and do His commandments and His statutes which I command you today."

Chapters 28-30 are also key because of the promises regarding Israel's near and distant future as it pertains to blessing for obedience or cursing for disobedience.

Key People

Moses and Joshua.

Christ as Seen in Deuteronomy

The statement about Moses in 18:15 is one of the clearest portraits of Christ. It reads, "The Lord your God will raise up for you a prophet like me from among you, from your countrymen, you shall listen to him." Further, Moses, as a type of Christ, is the only figure other than Christ to fill all three of the offices of prophet (34:10-12), priest (Ex. 32:31-35), and king (although Moses was not king, he functioned as ruler of Israel; 33:4-5).

Outline

Deuteronomy divides into three sections:

I. Preamble (1:1-5)

II. Review of Israel's Wanderings—Historical (1:6-4:43)

1. Rehearsal of Israel's Law—Legal (4:44-26:19)
2. Ratification of Israel's Covenant—Motivational (27:1-30:20)

III. Conclusion (31:1-34:12)

Summary: Key Words and Themes to Remember

Genesis	Beginnings	Election of the nation
Exodus	Redemption	Redemption of the nation
Leviticus	Holiness	Sanctification of the nation
Numbers	Wandering	Direction of the nation
Deuteronomy	Review	Instruction of the nation

Chapter 4

Narrative

If I could only show you King Jesus how much I love you and worship you Lord, for all you have achieved for us. I can only kneel in prayer too you Lord to show you Lord my gratitude.

Acknowledged, our Holy Messianic King Lord Jesus Christ came to us here on earth, Incarnation God in the flesh of man. Our young Messianic King Jesus was sold out at age thirty-three for only thirty pieces of silver. And then flogged and crucified in accordance to prophesied scripture. In His sacrifice for our chance to have salvation Christ is the first Judahite from the lineage of Judaism to indoctrinate Christianity theretofore Messianic Judaism begins Christianity. "Judahite meaning, noun Judahite (plural Judahites) A descendant of Judah (the patriarch). A descendant or member of the tribe of Judah. An inhabitant of the ancient kingdom of Judah."

Messianic Judaism is a movement that combines Christianity most importantly, the Christian belief that Jesus is the Messiah with elements of Judaism and Jewish tradition.

The Birth of His Holy Royal Majesty Our Christian King Jesus Christ Our Lord brought animation to prophesy. A synopsis connects the prophesied Messiah with family. Special noting, Mothers love their children, Mother Mary with her heart and soul loved her Son Jesus. As well, worshipped the Christ Messiah.

His Majesty Our Holy Messianic King Jesus Christs Synopsis

Matthew 1

18-19 The birth of Jesus took place like this. His mother, Mary, was engaged to be married to Joseph. Before they came to the marriage bed, Joseph discovered she was pregnant. (It was by the Holy Spirit, but he didn't know that.) Joseph, chagrined but noble, determined to take care of things quietly so Mary would not be disgraced.

20-23 While he was trying to figure a way out, he had a dream. Gods' angel spoke in the dream: "Joseph, son of David, don't hesitate to get married. Marys' pregnancy is Spirit-conceived. Gods Holy Spirit has made her pregnant. She will bring a Son to birth, and when she does, you, Joseph, will name Him Jesus 'God saves' because He will save his people from their sins." This would bring the prophets embryonic sermon to full term: Watch for this a virgin will get pregnant and bear a Son; they will name Him Immanuel (Hebrew for "God is with us").

24-25 Then Joseph woke up. He did exactly what Gods angel commanded in the dream: He married Mary. But he did not consummate the marriage until she had the baby. He named the baby Jesus.

Narrative

Jesus Christ was born circa 6 B.C. in Bethlehem. Little is known about His early life. However, as a Young Man Jesus Christ founded Christianity. Christianity was planted as a seed of faith within Christ Messiahs ministry teachings indoctrination to the crowds animating His Church discipleship. The seed of faith embracing the Rabbis' word of love multiplied the seed of faith. Messiah Rabbi Christs' word grew His Christian Church theretofore one of the world's most influential religions. Messiah Jesus Christs' life is recorded in the New Testament, more a theological document than a biography. According to Messiah Christs' Christians of His Church, Rabbi Jesus Christ is considered the Incarnation of God, and his teachings an example for living a better-balanced spiritual life in connection with God the Father – Holy Ghost. Christians as members of His Church believe Rabbi Christ died for the sins of all people, and rose His body reanimating the living flesh of the Man Messiah Jesus Christ from the dead as recorded it would become from prophesy in scripture referencing the Old Testament Holy Bible. Written within the Old Testament scripture are the prophesies of Messiah who will animate in His coming from the lineage of the root of David. Messiah Jesus Christ brings within Him the New Testament indoctrination of the Father - Holy Ghosts' Epistles to the Apostles the first chosen disciples of the prophesied Messiah Rabbi Jesus Christ Savior for all of humanity.

His Majesty King Jesus Christ Background and Early Life

Most of Jesus's life is told through the four Gospels of the New Testament Bible, known as the Canonical Gospels, written by Matthew, Mark, Luke and John. These are not biographies in the modern sense but accounts with allegorical intent. They are written to engender faith in Jesus as the Messiah and the Incarnation of God, who came to teach, suffer and die for people's sins.

Jesus was born circa 6 B.C. in Bethlehem. His mother, Mary, was a virgin who was betrothed to Joseph, a carpenter. Christians believe Jesus was born through Immaculate Conception. His lineage can be traced back to the house of David. According to the Gospel of Matthew (2:1), Jesus was born during the reign of Herod the Great, who upon hearing of His birth felt threatened and tried to kill Jesus by ordering all of Bethlehem's male children under age two to be killed. But Joseph was warned by an angel and took Mary and the child to Egypt until Herod's death, where upon he brought the family back and settled in the town of Nazareth, in Galilee.

There is very little written about Jesus's early life. The Gospel of Luke (2:41-52) recounts that a 12-year-old Jesus had accompanied his parents on a pilgrimage to Jerusalem and became separated. He was found several days later in a temple, discussing affairs with some of Jerusalem's elders. Throughout the New Testament, there are trace references of Jesus working as a carpenter while a Young Adult. It is believed that He began His ministry at age 30 when He was baptized by John the Baptist, who upon seeing Jesus, declared Him the Son of God.

After baptism, Jesus went into the Judean desert to fast and meditate for 40 days and nights. The Temptation of Christ is chronicled in the Gospels of (Matthew, Mark and Luke (known as the Synoptic Gospels). The Devil appeared and tempted Jesus three times, once to turn stone to bread, once to cast himself off a mountain where angels would save Him, and once to offer Him all the kingdoms of the world. All three times, Jesus rejected the Devils temptation and sent him off.

Our King Jesus's Ministry

Jesus returned to Galilee and made trips to neighboring villages. During this time, several people became His disciples. One of these was Mary Magdalene, who is first mentioned in the Gospel of Luke (16:9) and later in all four gospels at the crucifixion. Though not mentioned in the context of the "12 disciples," she is considered to have been involved in Jesus's ministry from the beginning to His death and after.

Matthew 7:12 King James Version (KJV) Golden Rule

This well-known verse presents what has become known as the Golden Rule. In the King James Version of the Bible the text reads;

12 Therefore all things whatsoever ye would that men should do to you, do ye even so to them: for this is the law and the prophets.

Narrative

Confucius

Similar by Confucius; "Do not impose on others what you do not wish for yourself." (This was one of the guiding principles of life that Confucius taught his followers, (BCE five centuries before Jesus.)

Although, for better understanding of the Golden Rule, the original origin derives of the Middle East. The Golden Rule was prevalent before Jesus Christ the Man existed B.C.E. and was known among the forming of the Hebrew Nation along with the Laws of Yahweh God as indoctrination unto Moses leading the Israelites through the desert wilderness.

Moreover, we can observe the Golden Rule to be emphasized in the Ministry of Messiah Jesus Christ to a much greater level of importance with insight to the light forming perception delivered in ministry by the Messiah Rabbi Jesus Christ - Yahweh God -Holy Ghost in the flesh of this Man Jesus Christ Abba - Father.

In furtherance, Lord King Savior Ministering before the crowds gathered in His presence for the first time ever recoded in biblical scripture presented by anyone, Rabbi Christ presented in His Ministry teaching The First and Great Commandment known currently to be the New Testament scripture consisting of the "word" (love). This has greater importance than all other commandments because it is delivered by the prophesied Old Testament scripture Messiah Jesus Christ in His Ministry teaching. The crowds would build in numbers, discipleships multiplying with astonished persons of faith, Rabbi Christ uplifting their souls by the voice of Messiah Rabbi Christs' preaching the crowds in His presents connecting with Him this Great Commandment of love of the Father – Holy Ghost animated through the Son of Man.

Matthew 22:34-40 King James Version (KJV) The First and Great Commandment

"But when the Pharisees had heard that He had put the Sadducees to silence, they were gathered together."

"Then one of them, which was a lawyer, asked Him a question, tempting Him, and saying,"

"Master, which is the great commandment in the law?"

"Jesus said unto him, thou shalt love the Lord thy God with all thy heart, and with all thy soul, and with all thy mind."

"This is the first and great commandment."

"And the second is like unto it, thou shalt love thy neighbor as thyself."

"On these two commandments hang all the law and the prophets."

His Majesty our King Jesus Christs Chronology

A chronology of Jesus aims to establish a timeline for some of the events of the life of Jesus in the four canonical gospels. The Christian gospels were primarily written as theological documents rather than historical chronicles and their authors showed little interest in an absolute chronology of Jesus. However, it is possible to correlate the New Testament with non-Christian sources such as Jewish and Greco-Roman documents to estimate specific date ranges for the major events in Jesus' life.

Two independent approaches can be used to estimate the year of birth of Jesus, one based on the nativity accounts in the gospels, the other by working backwards from the date of the start of His ministry. Most scholars assume a date of birth between 6 and 4 B.C. Three independent approaches to estimate the dates of the ministry of Jesus are first, the fifteenth year of the reign of Tiberius Caesar, second: the date of the building of the Jerusalem Temple and third, the date of the death of John the Baptist.

Scholars generally estimate that the ministry of Jesus began around 27-29 A.D. and lasted at least one year, and perhaps three years, or more. Diverse approaches have been used to estimate the date of the crucifixion of Jesus. One approach uses the attestations of non-Christian sources such as Josephus and Tacitus. Another method works backwards from the historically well-established trial of Apostle Paul in Achaea to estimate the date of his conversion. Scholars generally agree that Jesus died between 30-36 A.D.

The estimation of the hour of death of Jesus is only based on the New Testament accounts and the timing presented in the gospel of Mark and John have been the subject of debate among scholars.

Narrative

Apostle Marks' Epistle in His Narrative of The Passion Has Three-Hour Segments

Marks narrative of the passion has three-hour segments; in the early part Jesus is before Pilate, the Crucifixion takes place at the third hour 9am in Mark 15:25, darkness appears at the six hour (noon) and Jesus' death at the ninth hour 3pm. However, in John 19:14 Jesus is still before Pilate at the sixth hour.

Scholars have presented a number of arguments to deal with the issue. Raymond E. Brown reviews various approaches that have been presented and suggests that they cannot be easily reconciled. Several notable scholars have argued that the modern precision of marking the time of day should not be read back into the gospel accounts, written at a time when no standardization of timepieces, or exact recording of hours and minutes was available.

Richard L. Niswonger states that in antiquity times were always approximate, and that Johns "about the 6th hour" may be close enough to Marks time because sundials were not accurate. Andreas Köstenberger states that early in the first century time was often estimated to the closest three-hour mark, and hence any time between 9am and noon may have resulted in someone saying that an event occurred at about the third or the sixth hour. Köstenberger then adds; "Marks concern likely was to provide the setting for the three hours of darkness (15:25, 33), while John seeks to stress the length of the proceedings, starting in the 'early morning.'

The earliest followers of Jesus composed an apocalyptic, Second Temple Jewish sect, which historians refer to as Jewish Christianity. The first part of the period, during the lifetimes of the Twelve Apostles, is called the Apostolic Age. In line with the Great Commission attributed to the resurrected Jesus, the Apostles are said to have dispersed from Jerusalem, and the missionary activity spread Christianity to cities throughout the Hellenistic world and even beyond the Roman Empire.

Though Paul's influence on Christian thinking is said to be more significant than any other New Testament author, the relationship of Paul of Tarsus and Judaism is still disputed.

Early Christians suffered sporadic persecution because they refused to pay homage to the emperor as divine. Persecution was on the rise in Asia Minor towards the end of the 1st century, as well as in Rome in the aftermath of the Great Fire of Rome in A.D. 64.

During the Ante Nicene period following the Apostolic Age, a great diversity of views emerged simultaneously with strong unifying characteristics lacking in the apostolic period. Part of the unifying trend was an increasingly harsh rejection of Judaism and Jewish practices. Early Christianity gradually grew apart from Judaism during the first two centuries and established itself as a predominantly gentile religion in the Roman Empire.

According to Will Durant, the Christian Church prevailed over Paganism because it offered a much more attractive doctrine and because the church leaders addressed human needs better than their rivals.

Chapter 5

Deity of The Holy Ghost

de·i·ty

'dēədē,'dāədē'

noun

a god or goddess (in a polytheistic religion).

"a deity of ancient Greece"

synonyms: god, goddess, divine being, supreme being, divinity, immortal; More

divine status, quality, or nature.

"a ruler driven by delusions of deity"

the creator and supreme being (in a monotheistic religion such as Christianity).

noun: Deity; noun: The Deity

Narrative

Although little is known of Lord and Savior Jesus Christs' childhood years, through extensive research of such topic of influence, indeed Rabbi Christs' Ministry teaching may be observed consisting of tremendous knowledge with indoctrination within ever so short of thirty-six months - three years process influencing sanctification in animation of His Ministry. As well, in the

Deity of the Holy Ghost. Indeed, if we are to speak of the deity of God than we cannot allow ourselves to fall short of truth in reference to the Savior Lord King Jesus Christ Messiah. Nor may we leave out the indoctrination process of sanctification of the Apostles in epic short time in animation of the Messiah Rabbi Christs' Ministry. These twelve ordained Apostles by name consist of: Simon, Andrew, James, John, Philip, Thaddeus, Bartholomew, Thomas, James, Matthew, Simon, Matthias. According to the list occurring in each of the Synoptic Gospels (Mark 3:13-19, Matthew 10:1-4, Luke 6:12-16), the Twelve chosen by Jesus. In furtherance of these Apostles of Christ we may endeavor more in depth each by their names in reference to scripture.

Simon: called Peter (Grk. petros, petra; Aram. kēf; Engl. rock) by Jesus of Nazareth, also known as Simon bar Jonah and Simon bar Jochanan (Aram.) and earlier (Pauline Epistles were written first) Cephas (Aram.), and Simon Peter, a fisherman from Bethsaida "of Galilee" (John 1:44; cf. 12:21) Simon / Peter - Andrew's brother (Matthew 10:2; Mark 3:16; Luke 6:14)

Andrew: brother of Peter, a Bethsaida fisherman and disciple of John the Baptist, also the First - Called Apostle. (Matthew 10:2; Mark 3:18; Luke 6:14)

James - John's brother, son of Zebedee, Boanerges, son of Thunder (Matthew 10:2; Mark 3:17; Luke 6:14)

John son of Zebedee, called by Jesus Boanerges (an Aramaic name explained in Mk 3:17 as "Sons of Thunder") - James' brother (Matthew 10:2; Mark 3:17; Luke 6:14) Known as the only Apostle who was not martyred, also has his own Gospel in the New Testament.

Philip: from Bethsaida "of Galilee" (John 1:44, 12:21) (Matthew 10:3; Mark 3:18; Luke 6:14)

Thaddeus: "Judas, son of James", (Matthew 10:3, Acts 1:13, Luke 6:16, John 14:22). Lebbaeus / Judas / Juda -, Simon's brother (Matthew 10:3; 13:55; Mark 3:18; 6:3; Luke 6:16; Jude 1:1)

Bartholomew: in Aramaic "bar-Talemai?", "son of Talemai" or from Ptolemais, some identify with Nathanael. (Matthew 10:3; Mark 3:18; Luke 6:14)

Thomas: also known as Judas Tomas Didymus - Aramaic T'oma - twin, and Greek Didymous - twin (Matthew 10:3; Mark 3:18; Luke 6:15)

James: commonly identified with James the Less - Matthew's / Levi's brother, son of Alphaeus (Matthew 10:3; 27:56; Mark 2:14; 3:16, 18; 6:3; 15:40, 47; Luke 5:27; 6:14-15; 24:18; Acts 1:13; 4:36).

Matthew: the tax collector, some identify with Levi son of Alphaeus - Levi - James' brother (James the less) (Matthew 10:3; 27:56; Mark 2:14; 3:16, 18; 6:3; 15:40, 47; Luke 5:27; 6:14-15; 24:18; Acts 1:13; 4:36) and author of the Book of Matthew

Simon the Canaanite: called in Luke and Acts "Simon the Zealot", some identify with Simeon of Jerusalem -, Thaddeus' brother (Matthew 10:4; 13:55; Mark 3:18; 6:3; Luke 6:15)

Judas Iscariot: the name Iscariot may refer to the Judaean towns of Kerioth or to the sicarii (Jewish nationalist insurrectionists), or to the tribe of Issachar; (Matthew 10:4; Mark 3:19; Luke 6:16) He was replaced as an apostle in Acts by Saint Matthias It should also be noted that while the "Twelve Apostles" refer to the twelve who followed Jesus during his lifetime (and later Matthias in place of Judas Iscariot), Paul (formerly Saul of Tarsus) can be considered as another Apostle. Notably, he begins many of his Epistles with "Paul, an Apostle of Christ Jesus", or some variant.

The original twelve were Apostles sent out to the Jews, whereas Paul has the unique role of being the Apostle to the gentiles after Christ's resurrection and ascent. However, notably with extensive research it is evident espionage most Monarchies involving conspiracy even betrayal to underhandedly betray a King of such Royalty, Jesus Christ being King of Kings Lord of Lords. This spiritual espionage by the adversary uses betrayal of King Jesus Christ Messiah through Judas Iscariot the thirteens disciple of the Christ leading to Judas Iscariots dismissal of his discipleship by the advocacy of King Jesus Christ Messiah. Yet, another disciple being the fourteenth disciple remaining unrecognized because the time of era, region and of women not having recognition of civil standing. Marry Magdalene the fourteenth disciple although not recognized in civil standing, is recognized by King Jesus Christ Messiah for her advocacy in devotion. Nor may we stop short, short of those who love Him our Jesus. Therefore, we cannot allow ourselves to devalue but indeed place significant value onto the works of Mary Magdalene, who worked with The Christ and continued works among the Apostles in the Apostolic Age influencing Christianity including the Holy Roman Apostolic Church infrastructure fallowing the resurrection of Rabbi Jesus Christ Messiah. In addition, the unreleased records preserved of the continuation of The Holy Bible in archives allegedly for their protection and future application by the Roman Catholic Archdiocese of the future Covenant of Peace that will be written after the return of Lord King Jesus Christ during the era of His age the Second Advent.

Deity Short Version

Acts 10:36 King James Version (KJV)

"The word which God sent unto the children of Israel, preaching peace by Jesus Christ: (he is Lord of all:)"

1 Corinthians 2:7-8 King James Version (KJV)

"But we speak the wisdom of God in a mystery, even the hidden wisdom, which God ordained before the world unto our glory:"

"Which none of the princes of this world knew: for had they known it; they would not have crucified the Lord of glory."

John 20:28-31 King James Version (KJV)

"And Thomas answered and said unto him, My Lord and my God."

"Jesus saith unto him, Thomas, because thou hast seen me, thou hast believed: blessed are they that have not seen, and yet have believed."

"And many other signs truly did Jesus in the presence of his disciples, which are not written in this book:"

"But these are written, that ye might believe that Jesus is the Christ, the Son of God; and that believing ye might have life through his name."

1 John 5:1-5 King James Version (KJV)

"Whosoever believeth that Jesus is the Christ is born of God: and everyone that loveth him that begat loveth him also that is begotten of him."

"By this we know that we love the children of God, when we love God, and keep his commandments."

"For this is the love of God, that we keep his commandments: and his commandments are not grievous."

"For whatsoever is born of God overcometh the world: and this is the victory that overcometh the world, even our faith."

"Who is he that overcometh the world, but he that believeth that Jesus is the Son of God?"

1 John 2:22-23 King James Version (KJV)

"Who is a liar but he that denieth that Jesus is the Christ? He is antichrist, that denieth the Father and the Son."

"Whosoever denieth the Son, the same hath not the Father: he that acknowledgeth the Son hath the Father also."

Matthew 19:13-14 King James Version (KJV)

"Then were there brought unto him little children, that he should put his hands on them, and pray and the disciples rebuked them."

"But Jesus said, suffer little children, and forbid them not, to come unto me: for of such is the kingdom of heaven."

Matthew 18:3 King James Version (KJV)

"And said, Verily I say unto you, except ye be converted, and become as little children, ye shall not enter into the kingdom of heaven."

Mark 9:36-37 King James Version (KJV)

"And he took a child, and set him in the midst of them: and when he had taken him in his arms, he said unto them,"

"Whosoever shall receive one of such children in my name, receiveth me: and whosoever shall receive me, receiveth not me, but him that sent me."

Narrative

trin·i·ty

/ˈtrinədē/

noun

the Christian Godhead as one God in three persons: Father, Son, and Holy Spirit.

a group of three people or things.

noun: trinity; plural noun: trinities

"the wine was the first of a trinity of three excellent vintages"

the state of being three.

noun: trinity

"God is said to be trinity in unity"

The doctrine of the deity of Rabbi Christ Messiah, says that Jesus possesses a truly divine nature. It does not deny that he possesses a truly human nature Holy Ghost in the flesh of man Jesus Christ experience. Also, with all of its attendant properties intact and unconfused which is the corresponding doctrine of the hypostatic union or dual natures of Christ. But it affirms that he is as to his deity, in the language of the Nicene Creed, "the only Son of God, eternally begotten of the Father, God from God, Light from Light, true God from true God, begotten, not made, of one Being with the Father." Here listed are the biblical support verses for the doctrine of our Jesus Christs Lord King and Savior prophesied by the chosen Prophets to be the Messiah in accordance with scripture. Here, it is found significantly evident the Holy Ghost is in the flesh Man Jesus experience, the trinity Father, Son, Holy Ghost.

Deity Long Version

Deity of Christ

Jesus Bears The Names And Titles of Deity

"God"

There is only one God.

Deuteronomy 6:4 - "Hear, O Israel: The Lord our God, the Lord is one."

Deuteronomy 4:35 – "To you it was shown that you might know that the Lord is God; there is no other besides him."

Isaiah 43:10 - "You are my witnesses, declares the Lord, and my servant whom I have chosen, that you may know and believe me and understand that I am he. Before me no god was formed, nor shall there be any after me."

Jesus is Called God

John 1:1 – "In the beginning was the Word, and the Word was with God, and the Word was God."

John 1:18 – "No one has ever seen God; the only God, who is at the Father's side, he has made him known."

Titus 2:13 – "Waiting for our blessed hope, the appearing of the glory of our great God and Savior Jesus Christ"

2 Peter 1:1 – "Simeon Peter, a servant and apostle of Jesus Christ, to those who have obtained a faith of equal standing with ours by the righteousness of our God and Savior Jesus Christ"

Isaiah 9:6 – "For to us a child is born, to us a son is given; and the government shall be upon his shoulder, and his name shall be called Wonderful Counselor, Mighty God, Everlasting Father, Prince of Peace."

Romans 9:5 – "To them belong the patriarchs, and from their race, according to the flesh, is the Christ, who is God over all, blessed forever. Amen."

Hebrews 1:8 – "But of the Son he says, Your throne, O God, is forever and ever, the scepter of uprightness is the scepter of your kingdom."

John 20:28-29 – "Thomas answered him, My Lord and my God! Jesus said to him, have you believed because you have seen me? Blessed are those who have not seen and yet have believed."

c.f. Matthew 1:21-23

Jehovah

Narrative

The New Testament cites numerous Old Testament passages about Jehovah and refers them to Messiah Jesus Christ Lord King and Savior. Again, and again throughout the Holy Bible credible witness among doctrinarian writings are translated from original old Egyptian Arabic to Hebrew, Greek, and Latin translation format early King James translations to the many global New International Version translation of the New Testament currently available for the world population to receive the "Word" of the Messiah, Holy Ghost, the Incarnation Lord King and Savior Rabbi Jesus Christ the Anointed One who is Messiah the light the way for all of humanity to receive freedom from their afflictions through salvation of their souls.

Hebrews 1:8-12 - But of the Son he says, "Your throne, O God, is forever and ever, the scepter of uprightness is the scepter of your kingdom. You have loved righteousness and hated wickedness; therefore God, your God, has anointed you with the oil of gladness beyond your companions." And "You, Lord, laid the foundation of the earth in the beginning, and the heavens are the work of your hands; they will perish, but you remain; they will all wear out like a garment, like a robe you will roll them up, like a garment they will be changed. But you are the same, and your years will have no end."

Psalm 102:25-27 – "Hear my prayer, O Lord Jehovah of old you laid the foundation of the earth, and the heavens are the work of your hands. They will perish, but you will remain; they will all wear out like a garment. You will change them like a robe, and they will pass away, but you are the same, and your years have no end."

John 12:36-41 – "When Jesus had said these things, he departed and hid himself from them. Though he had done so many signs before them, they still did not believe in him, so that the word spoken by the prophet Isaiah might be fulfilled:" "Lord, who has believed what he heard from us, and to whom has the arm of the Lord been revealed?" Therefore, they could not believe. For again Isaiah said, "He has blinded their eyes and hardened their heart, lest they see with their eyes, and understand with their heart, and turn, and I would heal them." Isaiah said these things because he saw his glory and spoke of him.

Isaiah 6:1-10 – "In the year that King Uzziah died I saw the Lord sitting upon a throne, high and lifted up; and the train of his robe filled the temple. Above him stood the seraphim. Each had six wings: with two he covered his face, and with two he covered his feet, and with two he flew. And one called to another and said:" "Holy, holy, holy is the Lord Jehovah of hosts; the whole earth is full of his glory!" "And the foundations of the thresholds shook at the voice of him who called, and the house was filled with smoke. And I said:" "Woe is me! For I am lost; for I am a man of unclean lips, and I dwell in the midst of a people of unclean lips; for my eyes have seen the King, the Lord Jehovah of hosts!" "Then one of the seraphim flew to me, having in his hand a burning coal that he had taken with tongs from the altar. And he touched my mouth and said:" "Behold, this has touched your lips; your guilt is taken away, and your sin atoned for." "And I heard the voice of the Lord saying," "Whom shall I send, and who will go for us?" Then I said, "Here I am! Send me." And he said, "Go, and say to this people: "'Keep on hearing, but do not understand; keep on seeing, but do not perceive.' Make the heart of this people dull, and their ears heavy, and blind their eyes; lest they see with their eyes, and hear with their ears, and understand with their hearts, and turn and be healed."

Ephesians 4:7-8 – "But grace was given to each one of us according to the measure of Christ's gift. Therefore, it says," "When he ascended on high he led a host of captives, and he gave gifts to men."

Psalm 68:18 – "You ascended on high, leading a host of captives in your train and receiving gifts among men, even among the rebellious, that the Lord God may dwell there."

1 Peter 2:4-8 – "As you come to him, a living stone rejected by men but in the sight of God chosen and precious, you yourselves like living stones are being built up as a spiritual house, to be a holy priesthood, to offer spiritual sacrifices acceptable to God through Jesus Christ. For it stands in Scripture:" "Behold, I am laying in Zion a stone, a cornerstone chosen and precious, and whoever believes in him will not be put to shame." "So, the honor is for you who believe, but for those who do not believe," "The stone that the builders rejected has become the cornerstone," and "A stone of stumbling, and a rock of offense." (c.f. Luke 2:34)

Isaiah 8:13-14 – "But the Lord Jehovah of hosts, him you shall honor as holy. Let him be your fear and let him be your dread. And he will become a sanctuary and a stone of offense and a rock of stumbling to both houses of Israel, a trap and a snare to the inhabitants of Jerusalem."

Romans 10:9-13 – "Because, if you confess with your mouth that Jesus is Lord and believe in your heart that God raised him from the dead, you will be saved. For with the heart, one believes and is justified, and with the mouth one confesses and is saved. For the Scripture says," "Everyone who believes in him will not be put to shame." "For there is no distinction between Jew and Greek; for the same Lord is Lord of all, bestowing his riches on all who call on him." "For everyone who calls on the name of the Lord will be saved." (c.f. Romans 9:33)

Joel 2:32 – "And it shall come to pass that everyone who calls on the name of the Lord Jehovah shall be saved."

Revelation 1:7 – "Behold, he is coming with the clouds, and every eye will see him, even those who pierced him, and all tribes of the earth will wail on account of him. Even so. Amen."

Zechariah 12:1,10 – "The oracle of the word of the Lord concerning Israel: Thus, declares the Lord Jehovah…" "And I will pour out on the house of David and the inhabitants of Jerusalem a spirit of grace and pleas for mercy, so that, when they look on me, on him whom they have pierced, they shall mourn for him, as one mourns for an only child, and weep bitterly over him, as one weeps over a firstborn."

Mark 1:1-3 – "The beginning of the gospel of Jesus Christ, the Son of God. As it is written in Isaiah the prophet," "Behold, I send my messenger before your face, who will prepare your way, the voice of one crying in the wilderness: 'Prepare the way of the Lord, make his paths straight,'" (c.f. Matthew 3:3; Luke 3:4; John 1:23)

Isaiah 40:3 – "A voice cries: "In the wilderness prepare the way of the Lord Jehovah; make straight in the desert a highway for our God."

Matthew 11:10 – "As they went away, Jesus began to speak to the crowds concerning John:" "What did you go out into the wilderness to see? …" "A prophet? Yes, I tell you, and more than a prophet. This is he of whom it is written," "'Behold, I send my messenger before your face, who will prepare your way before you.'"

Malachi 3:1 - "Behold, I send my messenger, and he will prepare the way before me. And the Lord whom you seek will suddenly come to his temple; and the messenger of the covenant in whom you delight, behold, he is coming, says the Lord Jehovah of hosts."

1 Corinthians 10:9 – "We must not put Christ to the test, as some of them did and were destroyed by serpents."

Numbers 21:5-6 – "And the people spoke against God and against Moses," "Why have you brought us up out of Egypt to die in the wilderness? For there is no food and no water, and we loathe this worthless food." "Then the Lord sent fiery serpents among the people, and they bit the people, so that many people of Israel died."

Luke 4:16-21 – "And He Jesus came to Nazareth, where he had been brought up. And as was his custom, he went to the synagogue on the Sabbath day, and he stood up to read. And the scroll of the prophet Isaiah was given to him. He unrolled the scroll and found the place where it was written," "The Spirit of the Lord is upon me, because he has anointed me to proclaim good news to the poor. He has sent me to proclaim liberty to the captives and recovering of sight to the blind, to set at liberty those who are oppressed, to proclaim the year of the Lord's favor." "And he rolled up the scroll and gave it back to the attendant and sat down. And the eyes of all in the synagogue were fixed on him. And he began to say to them," "Today this Scripture has been fulfilled in your hearing."

Isaiah 61 – "The Spirit of the Lord God is upon me, because the Lord has anointed me to bring good news to the poor; he has sent me to bind up the brokenhearted, to proclaim liberty to the captives, and the opening of the prison to those who are bound; to proclaim the year of the Lord's favor… For I the Lord Jehovah love justice, I hate robbery and wrong; I will faithfully give them their recompense, and I will make an everlasting covenant with them."

Narrative

Special Note: This Isaiah 61 passage is too lengthy to include in its entirety. The diligent Bible reader will readily discern that the speaker in the entire chapter is Jehovah, himself.

c.f. Romans 14:11 of Isaiah 45:22-23, 1 Corinthians 1:30-31 of Jeremiah 9:24, and 1 Peter 2:3 of Psalm 34:8, 2 Peter 3:8 of Psalm 90:4

I Am

"I am" is the covenant name of God, highlighting his timeless self-existence.

Exodus 3:14-15 - God said to Moses, "I am who I am." And he said, "Say this to the people of Israel, 'I am has sent me to you.' "God also said to Moses, "Say this to the people of Israel, 'The Lord, the God of your fathers, the God of Abraham, the God of Isaac, and the God of Jacob, has sent me to you.' This is my name forever, and thus I am to be remembered throughout all generations.

Jesus Identified Himself as "I Am"

John 8:24 – "I told you that you would die in your sins, for unless you believe that I am he you will die in your sins."

John 8:28 - So Jesus said to them, "When you have lifted up the Son of Man, then you will know that I am he, and that I do nothing on my own authority, but speak just as the Father taught me."

John 13:19 – "I am telling you this now, before it takes place, that when it does take place you may believe that I am he."

John 18:5-6 - They answered him, "Jesus of Nazareth." Jesus said to them, "I am he." Judas, who betrayed him, was standing with them. When Jesus said to them, "I am he," they drew back and fell to the ground.

John 8:58-59 - Jesus said to them, "Truly, truly, I say to you, before Abraham was, I am." So they picked up stones to throw at him, but Jesus hid himself and went out of the temple.

Alpha And The Omega

The Alpha and the Omega, the First and the Last is peculiarly the name of God, highlighting His eternal being.

Revelation 1:8 - "I am the Alpha and the Omega," says the Lord God, "who is and who was and who is to come, the Almighty."

Isaiah 44:6 - Thus says the Lord, the King of Israel and his Redeemer, the Lord of hosts: "I am the first and I am the last; besides me there is no god.

Yet Jesus takes the name "the Alpha and the Omega".

Revelation 1:17-18 - When I saw him, I fell at his feet as though dead. But he laid his right hand on me, saying, "Fear not, I am the first and the last, and the living one. I died, and behold I am alive forevermore, and I have the keys of Death and Hades.

Revelation 2:8 - "And to the angel of the church in Smyrna write: 'The words of the first and the last, who died and came to life.

Revelation 22:12-13 - "Behold, I am coming soon, bringing my recompense with me, to repay each one for what he has done. I am the Alpha and the Omega, the first and the last, the beginning and the end."

King of Kings and Lord of Lords

God is the King of kings and Lord of lords.

Deuteronomy 10:17 - For the Lord your God is God of gods and Lord of lords, the great, the mighty, and the awesome God, who is not partial and takes no bribe.

Psalm 136:1-3 - Give thanks to the Lord, for he is good, for his steadfast love endures forever. Give thanks to the God of gods, for his steadfast love endures forever. Give thanks to the Lord of lords, for his steadfast love endures forever.

1 Timothy 6:13-15 - I charge you in the presence of God, who gives life to all things, and of Christ Jesus, who in his testimony before Pontius Pilate made the good confession, to keep the commandment unstained and free from reproach until the appearing of our Lord Jesus Christ, which he will display at the proper time—he who is the blessed and only Sovereign, the King of kings and Lord of lords, who alone has immortality, who dwells in unapproachable light, whom no one has ever seen or can see. To him be honor and eternal dominion. Amen.

Jesus is Called The King of Kings And Lord of Lords.

Revelation 17:14 - They will make war on the Lamb, and the Lamb will conquer them, for he is Lord of lords and King of kings,

Revelation 19:11-16 - Then I saw heaven opened, and behold, a white horse! The one sitting on it is called Faithful and True, and in righteousness he judges and makes war. His eyes are like a flame of fire, and on his head are many diadems, and he has a name written that no one knows but himself. He is clothed in a robe dipped in blood, and the name by which he is called is The Word of God. And the armies of heaven, arrayed in fine linen, white and pure, were following him on white horses. From his mouth comes a sharp sword with which to strike down the nations, and he will rule them with a rod of iron. He will tread the winepress of the fury of the wrath of God the Almighty. On his robe and on his thigh, he has a name written, King of kings and Lord of lords.

"Savior"

While the Bible recognizes occasional national "saviors" raised up to deliver Israel from earthly oppressors, God declares that He is the only Savior of His people in the ultimate and religious sense.

Isaiah 43:11 - I, I am the Lord Jehovah, and besides me there is no savior.

Isaiah 49:26 - Then all flesh shall know that I am the Lord Jehovah your Savior, and your Redeemer, the Mighty One of Jacob.

Hosea 13:4 - But I am the Lord Jehovah your God from the land of Egypt; you know no God but me, and besides me there is no savior.

Yet Jesus is designated the Savior, not occasionally but officially, not nationally but spiritually, and not temporally but eternally.

Luke 2:11 - For unto you is born this day in the city of David a Savior, who is Christ the Lord.

John 4:42 - They said to the woman, "It is no longer because of what you said that we believe, for we have heard for ourselves, and we know that this is indeed the Savior of the world."

Acts 5:31 - God exalted him at his right hand as Leader and Savior, to give repentance to Israel and forgiveness of sins.

Ephesians 5:23 - For the husband is the head of the wife even as Christ is the head of the church, his body, and is himself its Savior.

2 Timothy 1:10 - and which now has been manifested through the appearing of our Savior Christ Jesus, who abolished death and brought life and immortality to light through the gospel

Titus 1:4 - Grace and peace from God the Father and Christ Jesus our Savior.

Titus 3:5-6 - he saved us, not because of works done by us in righteousness, but according to his own mercy, by the washing of regeneration and renewal of the Holy Spirit, whom he poured out on us richly through Jesus Christ our Savior

2 Peter 1:11 - For in this way there will be richly provided for you an entrance into the eternal kingdom of our Lord and Savior Jesus Christ.

2 Peter 2:20 - For if, after they have escaped the defilements of the world through the knowledge of our Lord and Savior Jesus Christ, they are again entangled in them and overcome, the last state has become worse for them than the first.

2 Peter 3:18 - But grow in the grace and knowledge of our Lord and Savior Jesus Christ. To him be the glory both now and to the day of eternity. Amen.

1 John 4:14 - And we have seen and testify that the Father has sent his Son to be the Savior of the world.

Titus 2:13 - waiting for our blessed hope, the appearing of the glory of our great God and Savior Jesus Christ

2 Peter 1:1 - To those who have obtained a faith of equal standing with ours by the righteousness of our God and Savior Jesus Christ

c.f. Matthew 1:21, Acts 13:23, Philippians 3:20, etc.

Jesus Partakes of The Prerogatives of Deity

He Shares God's Glory

God declares that He shares His glory with no one else.

Isaiah 42:8,11 - I am the Lord; that is my name; my glory I give to no other, nor my praise to carved idols. For my own sake, for my own sake, I do it, for how should my name be profaned? My glory I will not give to another.

Yet Jesus shares the Father's glory.

John 17:5 - And now, Father, glorify me in your own presence with the glory that I had with you before the world existed.

John 17:24 - Father, I desire that they also, whom you have given me, may be with me where I am, to see my glory that you have given me because you loved me before the foundation of the world.

c.f. 2 Peter 3:18

He Receives Religious Worship

Scripture is clear that God alone is to be worshipped. Elect angels and holy men reject worship when rendered to them.

Narrative

Meaning of Proskuneo

The New Testament was written in Greek and the most common Greek word translated as worship is "proskuneo." According to Strong's Concordance "proskuneo" means "to kiss" as to kiss the hand of a superior. It is commonly associated with bowing down or lying prostrate on the ground with the idea of kissing the ground before someone. Perhaps we can elaborate into an imaginative understanding in depth to the Garden of Eden as described by the book of Genesis before the sin leading to the fall of mankind where humans were in balance with God's creation uncorrupt, unpolluted, and since that moment of the separation from Gods balance of creation with animals and mankind, God left a few animals with reverence to reach to mankind one of the animals being dog with recognition to (dog spelled in reverse spells God) these animals "proskuneo" worship with such great loyalty their master. Some scholars believe the word "proskuneo" worship actually is derived from the idea of a dog licking its master's hand. The idea is to show profound reverence and submission to our Messianic King, His Holy Excellency Lord and Savior His Majesty King Jesus Christ Lord of Lords King of Kings – Messiah Rabbi Jesus Christ.

Exodus 34:14 - You shall worship no other god, for the Lord, whose name is Jealous, is a jealous God

Matthew 4:10 - Then Jesus said to him, "Be gone, Satan! For it is written, "'You shall worship (proskuneo) the Lord your God and him only shall you serve.'"

Acts 10:25-26 - When Peter entered, Cornelius met him and fell down at his feet and worshiped (proskuneo) him. But Peter lifted him up, saying, "Stand up; I too am a man."

Revelation 19:10 - Then I fell down at his feet to worship (proskuneo) him, but he said to me, "You must not do that! I am a fellow servant with you and your brothers who hold to the testimony of Jesus. Worship (proskuneo) God."

Revelation 22:8-9 - I fell down to worship (proskuneo) at the feet of the angel who showed them to me, but he said to me, "You must not do that! I am a fellow servant with you and your brothers the prophets, and with those who keep the words of this book. Worship (proskuneo) God."

Jesus Accepts Worship

Matthew 2:2 - "Where is he who has been born king of the Jews? For we saw his star when it rose and have come to worship him."

Matthew 2:11 - And going into the house they saw the child with Mary his mother, and they fell down and worshiped him.

Matthew 14:31-33 - Jesus immediately reached out his hand and took hold of him, saying to him, "O you of little faith, why did you doubt?" And when they got into the boat, the wind ceased. And those in the boat worshiped him, saying, "Truly you are the Son of God."

Matthew 28:9 - And behold, Jesus met them and said, "Greetings!" And they came up and took hold of his feet and worshiped him.

Matthew 28:16-17 - Now the eleven disciples went to Galilee, to the mountain to which Jesus had directed them. And when they saw Him, they worshiped him, but some doubted.

John 9:35-38 - Jesus heard that they had cast him out, and having found him he said, "Do you believe in the Son of Man?" He answered, "And who is he, sir, that I may believe in him?" Jesus said to him, "You have seen him, and it is he who is speaking to you." He said, "Lord, I believe," and he worshiped him.

Hebrews 1:6 - And again, when he brings the firstborn into the world, he says, "Let all God's angels worship him."

Revelation 5:11-14 - Then I looked, and I heard around the throne and the living creatures and the elders the voice of many angels, numbering myriads of myriads and thousands of thousands, saying with a loud voice, "Worthy is the Lamb who was slain, to receive power and wealth and wisdom and might and honor and glory and blessing!" And I heard every creature in heaven and on earth and under the earth and in the sea, and all that is in them, saying, "To him who sits on the throne and to the Lamb be blessing and honor and glory and might forever and ever!" And the four living creatures said, "Amen!" and the elders fell down and worshiped.

He Receives Sacred Service

Narrative

(λατρεύω - latreúō) in the Greek concordance of the KJV

I. To serve for hire.
II. To serve, minister to, either to the gods or men and used alike of slaves and freemen.
III. In the New Testament, to render religious service or homage, to worship.
IV. To perform sacred services, to offer gifts, to worship God in the observance of the rites instituted for his worship.
V. Of priests, to officiate, to discharge the sacred office.

Daniel 7:13-14 - "I saw in the night visions, and behold, with the clouds of heaven there came one like a son of man, and he came to the Ancient of Days and was presented before him. And to him was given dominion and glory and a kingdom, that all peoples, nations, and languages should serve (latreuo, LXX) him; his dominion is an everlasting dominion, which shall not pass away, and his kingdom one that shall not be destroyed.

Psalm 2:11-12 - Serve the Lord (Jehovah) with fear and rejoice with trembling. Kiss the Son, lest he be angry, and you perish in the way, for his wrath is quickly kindled. Blessed are all who take refuge in him.

Revelation 22:1-3 - Then the angel showed me the river of the water of life, bright as crystal, flowing from the throne of God and of the Lamb through the middle of the street of the city; also, on either side of the river, the tree of life with its twelve kinds of fruit, yielding its fruit each month. The leaves of the tree were for the healing of the nations. No longer will there be anything accursed, but the throne of God and of the Lamb will be in it, and his servants will worship (latreuo) him.

He is Prayed to And Invocated

John 14:13-14 - Whatever you ask in my name, this I will do, that the Father may be glorified in the Son. If you ask me anything in my name, I will do it.

Acts 1:24-25 - And they prayed and said, "You, Lord, who know the hearts of all, show which one of these two you have chosen to take the place in this ministry and apostleship from which Judas turned aside to go to his own place."

Acts 7:59-60 - And as they were stoning Stephen, he called out, "Lord Jesus, receive my spirit." And falling to his knees he cried out with a loud voice, "Lord, do not hold this sin against them." And when he had said this, he fell asleep.

2 Corinthians 12:8-9 - Three times I pleaded with the Lord about this, that it should leave me. But he said to me, "My grace is sufficient for you, for my power is made perfect in weakness." Therefore, I will boast all the more gladly of my weaknesses, so that the power of Christ may rest upon me.

Acts 9:13-14 - But Ananias answered, "Lord, I have heard from many about this man, how much evil he has done to your saints at Jerusalem. And here he has authority from the chief priests to bind all who call on your name."

Acts 22:16 - And now why do you wait? Rise and be baptized and wash away your sins, calling on his name.

Romans 10:12-14 - For there is no distinction between Jew and Greek; for the same Lord is Lord of all, bestowing his riches on all who call on him. For "everyone who calls on the name of the Lord will be saved." How then will they call on him in whom they have not believed? And how are they to believe in him of whom they have never heard? And how are they to hear without someone preaching?

1 Corinthians 1:2 - To the church of God that is in Corinth, to those sanctified in Christ Jesus, called to be saints together with all those who in every place call upon the name of our Lord Jesus Christ, both their Lord and ours:

c.f. 1 Corinthians 16:22, Revelation 22:20

He is Believed on And Followed

John 3:36 - Whoever believes in the Son has eternal life; whoever does not obey the Son shall not see life, but the wrath of God remains on him.

John 11:25 - Jesus said to her, "I am the resurrection and the life. Whoever believes in me, though he die, yet shall he live,

Acts 16:31 - And they said, "Believe in the Lord Jesus, and you will be saved, you and your household."

John 14:1 - "Let not your hearts be troubled. Believe in God; believe also in me.

c.f. John 10:27

He Forgives Sins

Mark 2:5-7 - And when Jesus saw their faith, he said to the paralytic, "Son, your sins are forgiven." Now some of the scribes were sitting there, questioning in their hearts, "Why does this man speak like that? He is blaspheming! Who can forgive sins but God alone?"

Luke 5:22-25 - When Jesus perceived their thoughts, he answered them, "Why do you question in your hearts? Which is easier, to say, 'Your sins are forgiven you,' or to say, 'Rise and walk'? But that you may know that the Son of Man has authority on earth to forgive sins"—he said to the man who was paralyzed—"I say to you, rise, pick up your bed and go home." And immediately he rose up before them and picked up what he had been lying on and went home, glorifying God.

Jesus Possesses The Incommunicable Attributes of Deity

Independence (AKA Aseity or Self-Existence)

John 5:26 - For as the Father has life in himself, so he has granted the Son also to have life in himself.

c.f. I Am.

Eternality

Micah 5:2 - But you, O Bethlehem Ephrathah, who are too little to be among the clans of Judah, from you shall come forth for me one who is to be ruler in Israel, whose coming forth is from of old, from ancient days.

Isaiah 9:6 - For to us a child is born, to us a son is given; and the government shall be upon his shoulder, and his name shall be called Wonderful Counselor, Mighty God, Everlasting Father, Prince of Peace.

John 1:1-2 - In the beginning was the Word, and the Word was with God, and the Word was God. He was in the beginning with God.

Hebrews 7:3 - He is without father or mother or genealogy, having neither beginning of days nor end of life, but resembling the Son of God he continues a priest forever.

c.f. The Alpha and the Omega

Unchangeableness (AKA Immutability)

Hebrews 13:8 - Jesus Christ is the same yesterday and today and forever.

Hebrews 1:12 - like a robe you will roll them up, like a garment they will be changed. But you are the same, and your years will have no end."

Fullness of Deity

Colossians 1:15 - He is the image of the invisible God, the firstborn of all creation.

2 Corinthians 4:4 - In their case the god of this world has blinded the minds of the unbelievers, to keep them from seeing the light of the gospel of the glory of Christ, who is the image of God.

Colossians 2:9-10 - For in him Christ the whole fullness of deity dwells bodily, and you have been filled in him, who is the head of all rule and authority.

Hebrews 1:2-3 - but in these last days he has spoken to us by his Son, whom he appointed the heir of all things, through whom also he created the world. He is the radiance of the glory of God and the exact imprint of his nature, and he upholds the universe by the word of his power.

Jesus is Attributed With The Works of Deity

Creation

God specifically disclaims any help or agency in creation outside himself.

Isaiah 44:24 - Thus says the Lord, your Redeemer, who formed you from the womb: "I am the Lord, who made all things, who alone stretched out the heavens, who spread out the earth by myself,

c.f. Job 9:8

And yet Jesus is repeatedly attributed with the work of creation.

John 1:3 - All things were made through him, and without him was not anything made that was made.

John 1:10 - He was in the world, and the world was made through him, yet the world did not know him.

1 Corinthians 8:6 - Jesus Christ, through whom are all things and through whom we exist.

Hebrews 1:2 - but in these last days he has spoken to us by his Son, whom he appointed the heir of all things, through whom also he created the world.

Hebrews 3:3-4 - For Jesus has been counted worthy of more glory than Moses—as much more glory as the builder of a house has more honor than the house itself. (For every house is built by someone, but the builder of all things is God.)

Final Judgment

Scripture teaches that God will execute final judgment.

Romans 14:10 - For we will all stand before the judgment seat of God

Yet The Son, Not The Father, Will Judge

2 Corinthians 5:10 - For we must all appear before the judgment seat of Christ

John 5:22 - The Father judges no one, but has given all judgment to the Son

Whatever The Father Does

John 5:19 - So Jesus said to them, "Truly, truly, I say to you, the Son can do nothing of his own accord, but only what he sees the Father doing. For whatever the Father does, that the Son does likewise.

Jesus Claimed Deity

One With The Father

John 10:30-38 - Jesus answered them I and the Father are one." The Jews picked up stones again to stone him. Jesus answered them, "I have shown you many good works from the Father; for which of them are you going to stone me?" The Jews answered him, "It is not for a good work that we are going to stone you but for blasphemy, because you, being a man, make yourself God." Jesus answered them, "Is it not written in your Law, 'I said, you are gods'? If he called them gods to whom the word of God came—and Scripture cannot be broken—do you say of him whom the Father consecrated and sent into the world, 'You are blaspheming,' because I said, 'I am the Son of God'? If I am not doing the works of my Father, then do not believe me; but if I do them, even though you do not believe me, believe the works, that you may know and understand that the Father is in me and I am in the Father."

John 14:9-11 - Jesus said to him, "Have I been with you so long, and you still do not know me, Philip? Whoever has seen me has seen the Father. How can you say, 'Show us the Father'? Do you not believe that I am in the Father and the Father is in me? The words that I say to you I do not speak on my own authority, but the Father who dwells in me does his works. Believe me that I am in the Father and the Father is in me, or else believe on account of the works themselves.

c.f. John 17:11,22

Etc.

Luke 18:18-19 - And a ruler asked him, "Good Teacher, what must I do to inherit eternal life?" And Jesus said to him, "Why do you call me good? No one is good except God alone. (c.f. Mark 10:17-18)

Significance of The Doctrine

1 John 4:1-3 - Beloved, do not believe every spirit, but test the spirits to see whether they are from God, for many false prophets have gone out into the world. By this you know the Spirit of God: every spirit that confesses that Jesus Christ has come in the flesh is from God, and every spirit that does not confess Jesus is not from God. This is the spirit of the antichrist, which you heard was coming and now is in the world already.

John 8:24 - I told you that you would die in your sins, for unless you believe that I am you will die in your sins."

Narrative

In the man physical body Jesus Christ Incarnation experience, the Holy Ghost - God and Jesus Christ are one as prophesied in scripture. In original Holy Bible Greek Translation from Egyptian script - c.f. Granville Sharp's Rule of Greek exegesis, which states that when two nouns which are not proper nouns are connected by the word kai (and), if the article ho (the) precedes the first but not the second, they refer to the same person. This being the Father – Son – Holy Ghost in one man as prophesied by the chosen prophets written within scripture Messiah Rabbi Christ.

The word "he" is not present in the original language. Its addition in our English translations makes the text read more naturally to us but obscures the Old Testament reference that Jesus's contemporaries apparently recognized. Again, reinforcing the truth of the Holy Bible textual writing being Gods breathed words in the Holy Bibles texts the supernatural phenomena is like magic, sorcery, or craft. However, by far better theretofore the source of the light of creation of all in the greatest of divine creationism, emasculate conception, immaculately conceived in the virgin Marry, as well with receiving of the Holy Ghost through baptism in water, the message of the "word" delivered by the living God, the man Jesus Christ is Messiah as recorded in the Testimonies both Old and New Testaments of the Holy Bible.

Chapter 6

Encoded Die Frage XCV

Narrative

During World War II with the failing of the German Army to properly defend Berlin Germany, Fascist Government secret documents were allegedly captured by the invading and conquering United States Army Infantry. These alleged captured documents were SS Nazi intelligence documents with a written code in German. When the alleged SS Nazi intelligence documents were decoded the codes meaning in German Language meant Die Frage. When Die Frage was translated to English Language translation the meaning was found to be "The Question"; with further decoding of the alleged captured Fascist Government secret SS Nazi intelligence document in German Language translation to English Language alleged further elaboration with meaning decoded genocide as a resolve to the Jewish problem. The movement of a genocide of the descendant and relatives of Christ and the disciple's genealogy as well a total destruction of the church administration including the burning of the books would be administered by a smaller allegedly embedded radical organization also the Nazi SS (satans subordinates) certainly rising to their darkness of infrastructure unleashing evil acts, pollution and corruption across the regions ultimately working against God. Satan, also known as the Devil, is an entity in the Abrahamic religions that seduces humans into sin or falsehood. In Christianity and Islam, he is usually seen as either a fallen angel or a genie, who used to possess great piety and beauty, but rebelled against God, who nevertheless allows him temporary power over the fallen world and a host of demons. In Judaism, Satan is typically regarded as a metaphor for the yetzer hara, or "evil inclination", or as an agent subservient to God.

A figure known as "the satan" first appears in the Tanakh as a heavenly prosecutor, a member of the sons of God subordinate to Yahweh, who prosecutes the nation of Judah in the heavenly court and tests the loyalty of Yahweh's followers by forcing them to suffer.

Although, the German people are primarily Roman Catholic, as well, the German Army primarily a Roman Catholic Christian Army and had been sworn on oath to an allegiance with God to protect Germany. This sworn oath of allegiance is recoded as Valkyrie in Norse mythology, a Valkyrie is one of a host of female figures who choose those who may die in battle and those who may live. Germans had been mostly converted to Roman Catholic Christianity during the earlier centuries through Roman Imperial occupation with a rise of the Holy Roman Apostolic Catholic Church an Age of Roman Catholicism. Yet, this SS (satans subordinates) Elite Echelon were placed in positions of power administratively over all other German peoples and German Army oppressively dominating order.

The alleged decoded document consisting of the "Jewish Question", also referred to as the "Jewish Problem", was a wide-ranging debate in 19th and 20th-century European society that pertained to the appropriate status and treatment of Jews. The debate, which was similar to other "National Questions", dealt with the civil, legal, national, and political status of Jews as a minority within society, particularly in Europe during the 18th, 19th and 20th centuries.

The debate was started within western and central European societies by politicians and writers who were influenced by the Age of Enlightenment and the ideals of the French Revolution. The debate's issues included the legal and economic Jewish disabilities (e.g., Jewish quotas and segregation), Jewish assimilation, Jewish emancipation and Jewish Enlightenment.

Wherein founded in 1925, the "Schutzstaffel," German for "Protective Echelon," initially served as Nazi Party leader Adolf Hitler's (1889-1945) personal bodyguards, and later became one of the most powerful and feared organizations in all of Nazi Germany. Heinrich Himmler (1900-45), a fervent anti-Semite like Hitler, became head of the Schutzstaffel, or SS, in 1929 and expanded the group's role and size. Recruits, who had to prove none of their ancestors were Jewish, received military training and were also taught they were the elite not only of the Nazi Party but of all humankind. By the start of World War II (1939-45), the SS had more than 250,000 members and multiple subdivisions, engaged in activities ranging from intelligence operations to running Nazi concentration camps. At the postwar Nuremberg trials, the SS was deemed a criminal organization for its direct involvement in war crimes.

The expression has been used by antisemitic movements from the 1880s onwards, culminating in the Nazi phrase "the Final Solution to the Jewish Question". Similarly, the expression was used by proponents for and opponents of the establishment of an autonomous Jewish homeland or a sovereign Jewish state.

Furthermore, during earlier centuries to be early forming of administrative type governments within Europe had been the regional area of recognizing women leadership through centuries of rule by Queens and Dutch's and men as Kings and Dukes throughout history. Europe was recognized as regional poisoning for Mary Magdalene's great service to the establishing of King Jesus' Monarchy and building the Christian Church by recruiting soldiers for church military service and increasing disciples through conversion to Christianity. Theretofore, Mary Magdalen's sincere devotional worship with love and loyalty to King Jesus Christ Messiah through the devoted works of discipleship in assisting the building of the Christian church for King Christs future Monarchy could render the disciple's relative's genealogy to be present in the reginal area of Europe.

Furthermore, historical not yet released biblical documentation including lineage of the descendants of the Apostles are being archived within the Roman Catholic Archdiocese for their protection and secrecy of the future coming of Christ Second Advent with the continuation of the Testaments of the Holy Bible future Covenant of Peace. These documents remain within the Vatican's allegedly protective preservation in secrecy.

Nation shall rise against Nation as worded in prophesies by the chosen Prophets of the Holy Bible. Theoretically, there can be Three Nations that rise animating by Prophesy of scripture. The Chosen Jewish Nation of Judah – of the Father, The Christian Nation – The Church by the Son of the Father Jesus Christ – Messiah Father Son Holy Ghost, and the Nation of Satanism – The Beast. Yet, with all of the political parties, social groups, titles held in societies there are only decisively two groups of animation, the Adversary of Darkness, or the Advocate of Light. Societies are expressive with the animation by presenting signs, symbols, representing shapes of all sizes consisting of directions pathways points of entry and points of exit dark and light shadows. Moreover, a similar form of Nazi SS (satans subordinates), in an earlier form of Fascist Government attempted to gain momentum through the United States Confederacy during the United States Civil War of the 1860's. However, the Fascist Confederate Government Army was extinguished. Yet again, in full formation Nazi SS (satans subordinates), of Fascist Government made their dark impression of existence in Germany in the 1940's era. Also, more recent late 1979's era a similar rise to power rose up as a Fascist Baath Government party in Iraq with similar Nazi SS (satans subordinates) oppressive functions - as darkness bloomed a dark rose of thorns through the Middle East region. Moreover, yet another current era similar rise to power rose up as a Fascist North Korea Government party in North Korea with similar Nazi SS (satans subordinates) oppressive functions. However, all three forms of these type of Nazi SS (satans subordinates) Fascist Government apostasy's have since been extinguished including but not limited to, Fascist Confederate Government of America, Fascist German Government of Germany and Fascist Government of Iraq for the time being, but the fourth Fascist type of Government of North Korea remains predatory in their darkness of regime. Although, the other three similar Nazi SS (satans subordinates) Fascist Government Armies oppressive functions have been extinguished by the combined Christian Armies with the rise of Christendom the United States "Nation Under God". Long live the King of Kings Messiah Lord Christ.

The Priory of Sion

Fraternal Organization

Moreover the Prieuré de Sion ([pʁi.jœ.ʁe də sjɔ̃]), translated as Priory of Sion, is a fringe fraternal organization, founded and dissolved in France in 1956 by Pierre Plantard alleged as part of a hoax.

The Priory of Sion is a fascinating study in both history and conspiracy, especially in regard to its alleged connection to Jesus Christ, Mary Magdalene, the Medieval Knights Templar, and ultimately to Freemasonry courtesy of secret documents and various associations in history. In regard to the Priory, there is no lack of conspiracy theories which splinter in all directions from the eleventh century to the present.

Its origins as a secret organization are most definitely in dispute, some saying the group was founded in the 1950s, others claiming it dates back to the time of the crusades in 1099 A.D. Add to the mix a set of secret documents, connections to Frances's mystical Rennes le Chateau, and the alleged lineage of Mary Magdalene that became the Merovingian dynasty and one can see why the Priory is a subject rife with controversy.

The Prieure de Sion, or Priory of Sion, was founded in Annemasse, France, in 1956 by Prierre Plantard. With a membership of five men, the society claimed it was originated from the Ordere de Sion founded by Frenchman Godfroi de Bouillon in 1090. A leader during the Crusades, de Bouillon became the first ruler of the Kingdom of Jerusalem in 1099. It wasn't long after de Bouillon's death that the Knights Templar were officially recognized. Some experts have speculated that it was the Prieure de Sion who created the Knights Templar as their military and administrative order. The name Prieure de Sion was allegedly changed in 1188 to the Priory of Sion when its members and the Templars parted company.

The Priory of Sion was said to have been a secret society that during various eras was led by Grand Masters including Leoardo da Vinci, Isaac Newton, Victor Hugo, and Sandro Botticelli. The first Grand Master was Jean de Gisors, who served from 1188 to 1220. Plantard himself claimed he first served as secretary general before serving as Grand Master of the Priory from 1981 to 1984. If indeed the Priory existed, the list of previous Grand Masters includes aristocracy, occultists, alchemists, and Freemasons.

In 1975, a set of parchments was discovered in Paris's Bibliotheque Nationale, documents that came to be known as Les Dossiers Secrets. How the Dossiers came to the Paris library is unclear, but some speculate that it was through Plantard himself, in an effort to further his Priory's claim to antiquity. In order to understand the contents of the documents, which included genealogies and some type of Masonic charter, it's necessary to examine one of the legends associated with the discovery.

It is said that Plantard's Priory disbanded in 1957, but that he made an attempt to revive it several years later. In doing so he enlisted the help of French author Gerard de Sede and filmmaker and journalists Phiippe de Cherisey to create documents that would substantiate the Priory's claim to Godfroi's original Priory of Sion.

The documents are said to have originated at Rennes le Chateau in Languedoc, France a mysterious church that has long been an intriguing study of scholars and researchers for its alleged links to the Holy Grail, the Ark of the Covenant, Noah's Ark, and the hidden treasures of Solomon's Temple. The parish priests of the Chateau was Berenger Sauniere who allegedly discovered four parchments within a hollowed out Visigoth pillar.

The tale Plantard told his friend Gerard de Sede was that Jesus had in fact evaded death and lived in France with Mary Magdalene. Their lineage resulted in the Merovingian dynasty. The Holy Grail, as Plantard asserted, or San Greal in French, literally translates to "Holy Blood." The implication was, of course, that the blood of Christ flowed through the Merovingian lineage. When the dynasty eventually fell and the descendants went underground, the Priory of Sion were their protectors, along with their associates which included the Knights Templar and the Freemasons who among others were intimately involved with the Priory.

Whether or not Plantard's story is true or if he and his cohorts did or didn't create the documents of the Dossiere Secrets is a ongoing debate. As for another of Plantard's Masonic connections, there is an additional theory that links Plantard and the Dossier Secrets to the Swiss Grand Lodge Alpina. It is alleged that "Les descendants Merovingiens ou l'enigme du Razes Wisigoth," which was the first of the four documents, was published at the Swiss lodge. To date there is no proof of this claim, and the lodge itself has denied any involvement.

One theory suggests Plantard and his colleagues Gerard de Sede and Philippe de Cherisey eventually had a falling out and that Plantard made it known that two of Sede's published parchments were indeed fabricated by Cherisey. There are no firm answers to the mystery of the Priory of Sion, but many exceptional books have been written about the legendary organization's existence and possible connection to the Knights Templar, Freemasons, and other individuals, groups, and events in history.

Early Christianity

Early Christianity is the period of Christianity preceding the First Council of Nicaea in 325. It is typically divided into the Apostolic Age and the Ante-Nicene Period (from the Apostolic Age until Nicaea).

The first Christians, as described in the first chapters of the Acts of the Apostles, were all Jewish, either by birth, or conversion for which the biblical term proselyte is used and referred to by historians as the Jewish Christians.

The early Gospel message was spread orally, probably in Aramaic. The New Testaments Book of Acts and Epistle to the Galatians record that the first Christian community was centered in Jerusalem and its leaders included Peter, James, and John. Paul of Tarsus, after his conversion to Christianity, claimed the title of "Apostle to the Gentiles". Paul's influence on Christian thinking is said to be more significant than any other New Testament writer.

By the end of the 1st century, Christianity began to be recognized internally and externally as a separate religion from Rabbinic Judaism which itself was refined and developed further in the centuries after the destruction of the Second Jerusalem Temple. As shown by the numerous quotations in the New Testament books and other Christian writings of the 1st centuries, early Christians generally used and revered the Jewish Bible as Scripture, mostly in the Greek (Septuagint) or Aramaic (Targum) translations, much of which is written in narrative form where "in the biblical story God is the protagonist, Satan (or evil people/powers) are the antagonists, and Gods people are the agonists".

As the New Testament canon developed, the Letters of Paul, the Canonical Gospels and various other works were also recognized as scripture to be read in church. Paul's letters, especially Romans, established a theology based on Christ rather than on the Mosaic Law, but most Christian denominations today still consider the "moral prescriptions" of the Mosaic Law, such as the Ten Commandments, Great Commandment, and Golden Rule, to be relevant. Early Christians demonstrated a wide range of beliefs and practices, many of which were later rejected as heretical.

Narrative

It is no lesser than a phenomenon that is written from page to page in so many biblical, historical and theological studies performed by university professors, scientists and scholars. This study of phenomena, supernatural is of all creation the world, galaxy and universe. Focuses the most complex cognitive with critical thinkers. Epic artists geniuses of their times. The angelic miracles phenomena's both geological, meteorological, astronomic, celestial, and the power of the elements of God Creator of earth, wind, fire and water.

A visiting Pastor stood in front of our Church congregation in 1989 the same year I first concluded reading the entire Holy Bible, from the front pages to the farthest back pages indeed a most intriguing endeavor of pure clear truth. Reading the Holy Bible was one of my life goals I had completed reading the Holy Bible for the first time through the pages which have a total count of 1,281 pages consisting of 993 pages in the Old Testament and 288 pages in the New Testament. There are a total of 66 books in both Old and New Testaments, split into 1,189 chapters. I had completed this study journey of the Holy Ghost in a reading study time of 365 days one entire year. I have since restudied the Holy Bible in various versions of translations seven total times and am continuing to read the scriptures.

The Pastor stated, "God did not shortchange himself whatsoever when our God our Divine and Greater Being created Himself in the Body of our Lord Jesus Christ the Incarnation the Messiah conceived in His Mother the Virgin Mary."" He can be described as an NBA basketball player, 6'+ muscular build, the handsome chiseled features of a healthy Middle Eastern Man, brown eyes, brown thick long wavy well-groomed hair and thick well-groomed facial hair." "but I am still not finished, a psychic, telepath, clairvoyant, palm reading, future seeing and telling, the most epic ultimate sorcerer even supernatural superhuman, artist, genius, visionary, prophet, a healing hand, can give life and take life away, walk on water, and even levitation a rogue Rabbi with a linen white robe and sandals walking politely and kindly through 120+ degree deserts in a time before our time hostile to all men kind."

Perhaps we could view this Rabbi Jesus Christ as a Middle Eastern who walked out of India with a more than five-thousand-year-old Hindu or Muslim practice acculturated perfect with all the electromagnetic life existing in the entire universe, or a Buddhism practice of faith.

How should I describe this Rabbi Jesus Christ? He was it man the item. He was a visionary! Or should I say, He was a good man! Or should they say, He was a great man! Or again, should we say, The Rabbi Christ was a man with a plan. I can assure you this, Rabbi Jesus Christ Messiah is a genius artistic artist creative thinker with a plan! Rabbi Christ has a plan for you. If it is difficult to accept, again – Rabbi Jesus Christ Messiah has a plan for you! Rabbi Christ thinks about you. You are in His thoughts; He has a plan for you, and He is going to appear and tell you what His decision is.

Maybe I could describe this Jesus Christ written about within the Holy Bible scriptures as a long-haired bearded herb smoking wine drinking outspoken hippy protester two thousand plus years before His time.

We within the United States of America – Nation Under God, exist in a time which now has developed and enforced civil rights as of the 1950's and a Constituency established as of 1948 within the new Israel also consisting of civil rights. Perhaps if these laws existed at the time of Rabbi Jesus Christs' trial standing before the Pharisees, Rabbi Jesus Christ would not have been unjustly and falsely tried by a make shift trial in the middle of the night after 12:00 AM between witching hours of 04:00 AM before the first light of dawn, found guilty by the make shift at that era corrupt Judahite Court, flogged at first morning light by the pressured Roman Centurions, and unjustly crucified in accordance to biblical prophecy prophesied by the chosen Prophets of the Holy Bible.

Rabbi Jesus Christ Messiah taught in His indoctrination to the Apostles giving them their Epistles to deliver the "word" "love, forgiveness, and faith" the "gospel, holiness, and service" as a basic entry point for the uneducated or even egoistic highly educated scholars, wicked and sinful to transition into Godly good through the writings of the HOLY BIBLE, as this acronym means He Only Left You Basic Instructions Before Leaving Earth.

The absolute most artistic genius! God in the flesh of man the Incarnation! The covenant that will not - cannot be broken for it is not held in the sin of men kind but in the Incarnation of Jesus Christ Messiah. The Messiahs' one time Atonement Blood Sacrifice for all humanity to receive salvation His crucifixion. The Bread of Life His Body, The Chassell of His Blood, accept Him eat and drink of His Body the Lamb of Lambs who alone is the way to lifting our afflictions from us.

Truth came like a bolt of light and this bolt of light pierced my scull. At first, I bent to kneel to my knees my hands covering my face than I folded my hands before me with a single drop tearing down my cheek. The truth had come to me, the Trinity the Father the Son and the Holy Spirit. The battle between good and evil God and His Angles Satan, Gabrielle and Michelle. God so loved the world that He sent His Son and the most genius battle plan has been perfectly created by God to defeat Satan and all his workers.

God Creator of all was here on earth and Adam could not hold the covenant in Eden, So the Creator left putting the covenant in to Noah, God than placed the covenant with Abraham, than with Moses, and again with the Israelites at Sinai, again with Israel in Palestine, and again with David, than again placed the covenant in Jesus Christ the Messiah this time the covenant will not be broken, as well nor the future Covenant of Peace held by Him in Him for all who have faith and love for the Lord in abiding in His Greatest Commandment.

Nine Covenants of The Holy Bible

Old Testament, New Testament, and Future Testament of Peace

Note: additional writing of the covenant reference Topical Ties; Genesis 17:4 "As for me, behold, my covenant is with thee, and thou shalt be a father of many nations."

Covenant NIV Explained; Important in Genesis is Gods covenant. A covenant is an agreement between God and humans which God initiates and upholds. God made a covenant with Adam in the Garden of Eden, in which the condition was obedience, the promise was life, and the penalty was death. Yet when Adam and Eve sinned, He did not abandon them, but remained the faithful, covenant God.

God established a covenant with Noah before the flood and with all nature after the flood.

He entered into a special covenant with Abraham and confirmed it by the right of circumcision. In this covenant God promised to make of Abraham a great nation, to give him the land of

Canaan, and to bless all peoples of the earth through Him; this last promise was fulfilled in Jesus Christ. God repeated the Abrahamic covenant promises to Isaac and Jacob, our covenantal God still pledges His love and faithfulness to us and calls us to believe in Him. To walk in obedience and to make Him our personal Lord.

Note: additional writing of the covenant reference Topical Ties; Genesis 17:7 "And I will establish my covenant between me and thee and thy seed after thee in their generations for an everlasting covenant, to be a God unto thee, and to thy seed after thee."

Covenant NIV Explained; the family was the central unit of Gods covenant in the Old Testament, and the primary influence in the development of the personality and character of children. The father as the head of the family supervised all religious observances and education, and, until the establishment of the tabernacle, offered the sacrifices.

The Old Testament covenant provided a special relationship between God and the family unit. Some Christians believe that the same thing is true in the New Testament with regard to household salvation, stressing that God continues to operate in and through the family.

Others see more emphasis placed on the individual and his or her personal belief, and less on the family. In any case, the New Testament has examples of both families and individuals coming to salvation in Christ and being baptized. Apostle Paul emphasized the necessity of a well-ordered family and established proper lines of responsibility.

Finally, God uses the concept of family to picture the church local and worldwide in the New Testament.

Note: additional writing of the covenant reference Topical Ties; Jeremiah 31:31 "Behold, the days come, saith the Lord, that I will make a new covenant with the house of Israel, and with the house of Judah:"

Covenant NIV Explained; A covenant is an agreement or contract that God initiates with humanity; some have conditions some do not.

For example, Gods covenant with Adam before the fall required obedience to His commands, with the prospect of either life or death; the covenant with Abraham contained no conditions, but only promises of blessing to him and his descendants. These promises pertain to us as well, since those who love the Lord are children of Abraham through faith in Christ.

Some see as many as nine separate covenants in the Bible: in Eden, with Adam, with Noah, with Abraham, with Moses and the Israelites at Sinai, with Israel in Palestine, with David, the new covenant in Christ, and the future covenant of peace.

Others, preferring to emphasize only the division of old and new covenant Old and New Testament, see the other covenants on the same theme.

Note: additional writing of the covenant reference Topical Ties; Romans 4:11 "And he received the sign of circumcision, a seal of the righteousness of the faith which he had yet being uncircumcised: that he might be the father of all them that believe, though they be not circumcised; that righteousness might be imputed unto them also:"

Covenant NIV Explained; Because God could not be seen, He often demonstrated His presence and power by visible signs, such as the miraculous signs done before the Israelites, Pharaoh, Gideon, Saul, Jeroboam, Ahaz, the crowds around Jesus and the crowds around the Apostles.

God used visible signs to remind His people of His covenant with them, the rainbow, the rite of circumcision, the blood of the Passover Lamb at the Exodus, the Sabbath at Sanai, and the alter of the twelve stones at the crossing of the Jordan River.

The New Testament uses the water of baptism and the bread and wine of the Lords Supper as signs of our relationship with Jesus. Signs strengthen faith and draw us closer to God.

Note: additional writing of the covenant reference Topical Ties; Hebrews 7:27 "Who needeth not daily, as those high priests, to offer up sacrifice, first for his own sins, and then for the peoples: for this He did once, when He offered up Himself."

Covenant NIV Explained; Christ came to fulfill the Old Testament, not so much in terms of specific prophecies, but as a better revealer of truth than what God employed in the Old Testament, Christ is better than the angels, Moses, Aaron and the Levitical priests. Christs sacrifice, as a once for all sacrifice, is better than sacrifices of the Old sanctuary, and the covenant begun in Christ is superior to the covenant made through Moses at Mount Sinai.

The blood of Jesus speaks a better word than the blood of Abel, for it guarantees forgiveness. Jesus, in other words, offers us a complete salvation for all eternity.

Narrative

So, God returned in the flesh (Incarnation) of mankind to hold the Covenant that cannot be broken for it is held by Him Rabbi Jesus Christ the Messiah.

If there could be one legion equivalent to one brigade sum six thousand five hundred soldiers that could hold the divine strength of Rabbi Jesus Christ, the Messiah. This single legion of soldiers could walk across each body of water over every single mountain and through each mass of desert defeating all evil washing away all sin and healing the entire world for the glory of our eternal God in the flesh of Man Jesus Christ Messiah and for the glory of His Majesty's eternal Crown as King!

The works of God through miracles are what is being imagined by this single legion of soldiers. The works of God through miracles happen before us all too often these miracles are denied and referred to as coincidences or good luck even merely karma.

I personally called by the word of God, blind yet called by the voice of the Holy Spirit to the gospel holiness and service. Spoken to by the Holy Spirit through the Soul and told tell no one you have heard Me speak until I command you to do so then speak My Name, I am your God.

Train to serve Me. I have plans for you, you will work for Me, employed by Me. In the future I will give you sight and vision adequate to fulfill your assignments, your duties in severing Me. I am your God.

And it was so that I was blind and only the sight to see either the light or the dark. And the Lords voice was there guiding to the light. And by choosing the light I do have sight as the Lord said it would be.

However, before this sight this vision, I needed to train as the Lord had commanded. So, it was then, the Cancer approached and taught how to walk on waters of the oceans blind.

Then the Capricorn approached and taught how to fly through the air of the atmosphere blind.

And then the Leo approached and taught of the forests, the heights of the mountains the levels of the deserts, and the waters that flow through to the seas, and of the travel through the sharp learning curves of paths and roads lesser traveled.

Again, the Lord Holy Spirit spoke through the Soul, before you is this steel horse with the power of hundreds of horses breathing fire through its nostrils and bellowing flames and smoke. Ride this horse into the four winds greatly sin so you gain understanding in serving Me, no matter what happens always keep your thoughts on Me. I am your divine God.

Demons with wrinkled faces and crystal eyes consumed many who were in association with me. The drink could not quench thirst, the smoke could not smoke enough, the demon women witches could not satisfy the sin the lust. The fight the blood could not satisfy need for blood. Yet, angles were prevalent of witness, and supernatural entities and things were also prevalent – 98,984.7 miles of living sin, - that equates to 520,263,583.2 five hundred and twenty million two hundred and sixty-three thousand and five hundred and eighty-three point two feet of treading sin. However, nothing could cause harm no matter what accrued I was protected by the sword of the Lord provided I listened to the Lord when the Lord commanded me. I rode the steal horse powered by hundreds of horses breathing fire and belching smoke through sin as the Lord had commanded first through the East Wind and the demons hissed and drooled their wrinkle faces with their demonist crystal eyes gathering pursuing in their multitudes in the wake of the steal horse breathing fire belching smoke I rode faster and faster carrying the sword of the Lord. The Lord had now commanded the second command. Turn the steal horse South and ride through the South Wind. Turning a long high-speed turn from East gone South, the steal horse breathing fire belching smoke I rode faster, and faster demons hissed and drooled their wrinkle faces with their demonist crystal eyes gathering pursuing in their multitudes by their multitude in the wake of the steal horse breathing fire belching smoke into the South Wind I rode this steal horse. With demons gathered in their multitudes the Lord commanded me turn the steal horse into the West Wind. As commanded by the Lord I commanded the steal horse turning a long high-speed turn from South Wind gone West into the West Wind I rode the steal horse given to me by the Lord the steal horse breathing fire belching smoke, I rode faster, and faster demons hissed and drooled their wrinkle faces with their demonist crystal eyes gathering pursuing in their multitudes by their multitudes and their multitudes multiplying by numbers in the wake of the steal horse breathing fire belching smoke into the West Wind I rode this steal horse carrying the sword of the Lord. The Lord commanded me again, turn the steal horse into the North Wind. I commanded the steal horse turning a long high-speed turn from West Wind gone North into the North Wind I rode the steal horse given to me by the Lord the steal horse breathing fire belching smoke, I rode faster, and faster demons hissing and drooling their wrinkle faces with their demonist crystal eyes gathering pursuing in their multiplied multitudes by their multitudes and their multitudes multiplying by numbers in the wake of the steal horse breathing fire belching smoke into the North Wind I rode this steal horse carrying the sword of the Lord. The Lord now commanded me, turn the steal horse round about ride the steal horse South. The pursuing hordes of demons hissing and drooling their wrinkle faces with their demonist crystal eyes gathering pursuing in their multiplied multitudes. As the Lord had commanded, I commanded the steal horse turning a round about head on with the hordes of pursuing demons I rode this steal horse carrying the sword of the Lord. With the dust of the screaming winds rising by the hordes of violent approaching demons drooling their wrinkle faces with their demonist crystal eyes gathering pursuing, the Lord then commanded me again. Stop the steal horse. I stopped the steal horse, the steal horse whinnying to a full stop breathing fire belching smoke as commanded I stopped before these violent demons approaching in the rising dust cloud. Surrounded in sin of this fallen world the Lord then commanded me again, dismount the steal horse. I followed the Lord as command dismounting the steal horse, before this dust cloud of screaming wind hissing violent approaching demons. The Lord now commanded me again, draw your sword from its sheath, I command you this kneel, place the sword point to the earth with both your hands holding atop the handle of the sword upright. (the sword of the Lord is the cross of the Christ when held in this position) The Lord now commanded me place your thoughts on Me only. Glorify Me I am your God. I followed command as the Lord had commanded. By the sword of the Lord all of the demons by their multiplied multitudes dissipated. Glory be unto the Almighty Lord King Christ. As the Lord had said, train and learn to serve Me I am your God. And I the Lord will then give you sight and vision. As the Lord said it would be, I can now see.

Psalm 23 A Psalm of David

"The Lord is my shepherd; I shall not want. He maketh me to lie down in green pastures: he leadeth me beside the still waters. He restoreth my soul: he leadeth me in the paths of righteousness for his name's sake. Yea, though I walk through the valley of the shadow of death, I will fear no evil: for thou art with me; thy rod and thy staff they comfort me. Thou preparest a table before me in the presence of mine enemies: thou anointest my head with oil; my cup runneth over. Surely goodness and mercy shall follow me all the days of my life: and I will dwell in the house of the Lord forever."

Narrative

At twenty-seven years of passing earth time the Lord than again, commanded me to use in the service of Father both my sight and vision being adequate to serve the Lord. There after I was approached by a being not made of demon nor of angel with the gifts of the Father to fly within the atmosphere in serving the Lords Church. Along with this being not made of demon nor of angel gifted by the Father with ability to fly in service of the church, theretofore also, I by the command of the Lord was given the gift of the ability to fly to serve the Father in flight in the service to the church. When ordered by the Lord to take to flight, I followed the Lords order taking to flight in the illumination of the night. As well, during life altering experiences while in flight the Holy Spirits face appeared and with the sight and vision guided flight through phenomena. This occurred, I tell you by the miracles of the Lord, again and again and over again and then sum… while in flight serving the church of the Lord in the illumination of the night.

Biblically and historically our Christ is truly amazing. During His crucifixion the Romans, Pharisees, Apostles, Angels - Gabriel, Michael, Satan and the crowds of persons gathered and stood observing the phenomena's that accrued at His crucifixion and resurrection.

These witnessed testimonies are incredibly interesting studies etc. During the past two years preceding December 2015 and through 2016 and continued - these studies in Christian Athletics the practice of which includes the transformation of the human soul from the flesh into the spiritual body and even ascension. I have been in attending persistent extensive Biblical and Historical Studies and continue currently in these studies.

One of the Pastors became ill with cancer. The Pastor was healed completely through the power of Christian scripture and modern medicine combined. As well, one of our lead Biblical Study persons also became effected by a type of cancer that is terminal for most persons. This individual who is abounding in faith was cured from the illness of cancer through both the power of scripture and modern medicine.

During these Biblical Studies I have also been entirely healed from numerous extensive main frame fractures and neurologic damages through the power of faith and Christian scripture. Although I have extensive internal scaring, returning to an active healthy life again I am truly thankful the Lord is good to us.

The Lord keeps His Holy Hand on us to protect us all. If the Lord did not have His hand on us could you imagine the desolation and empty darkness! For it is the Lord that gives us the light and the breath that we breath.

And this current year 2016 one of our leading bible study friends passed away. And it is so amazing this person's faith was so consistent with a well-versed relationship established with the Lord, this fine individual was glowing in light as they passed, also passed away easier with lesser issues even smiling with comfort and joy.

Perhaps a reason why the Romans were so incredible is they were there at Christ's crucifixion with the Apostles and were of witness of Rabbi Jesus Christ the Messiah and His resurrection. This was the beginning of the Apostolic Age. The seed of the Church had been planted by Rabbi Christ the Messiah.

This is why the Apostles took the word of the Christ where they were able to walk and deliver their indoctrination of Christs Epistles, where they were able to walk in deliverance of love forgiveness and faith, the gospel holiness and service.

Chapter 7

Gods Divine Strategy

Throughout the Book of Acts, the Spirit of God is portrayed as actively leading Gods people. The apostles, for example, were led by the Spirit in dramatic and dynamic ways. There was a human side to the planning, planting, and development of the early church, but the leading of the Spirit was decisive for them. (Refer Acts 16:6-10)

I. Paul and Silas Were Forbidden by The Spirit to Speak The Word in Asia

Paul and Silas were traveling westward through territory known in the Bible as Asia. The places they visited are now in the country of modern Turkey. In verse 6, Luke says, "They passed through the Phrygian and Galatian region, having been forbidden by the Holy Spirit to speak the word in Asia." Here, we see the Holy Spirit at work in changing the plans of Paul and Silas.

When Luke says that the Spirit had forbidden Paul to speak the Word in Asia, he implies that Paul wanted to do so. No doubt, at some point, Paul had made his desire known to his missionary team. Although Luke does not mention Ephesus, the chief city of Asia, it seems likely that Paul wanted to proclaim the gospel there. Ephesus was a great commercial, religious, and cultural center. However, the Holy Spirit postponed Paul's preaching there. In Gods time he went to Ephesus for ministry. He went there near the end of his second missionary journey and returned on his third journey. (Acts 18:19-21)

II. The Spirit of Jesus Did Not Permit Them to go to Bithynia

After Paul and Silas arrived in Mysia, in the northwest of modern Turkey, they wanted to turn north into the northern province of Bithynia. Apparently, they had a strategy they wanted to implement. The northern part of Bithynia was on the southern coast of the Black Sea. A key city in this Northern Province was Nicea. This would be a great place to take the gospel.

Now, for a second time, the Holy Spirit intervened. The "Spirit of Jesus" did not permit the missionary team to go to Bithynia. This was an historic moment in the history of the church. The Spirit turned the attention of Paul and his team to Europe instead of to Bithynia. Throughout the Book of Acts, the pivotal moments are described as coming from the Spirit. God's strategy for world evangelism was Europe before Asia.

The title "Spirit of Jesus" is used for the Holy Spirit. This is the only time this title is used in the Bible. However, we have the "Spirit of Christ" in Romans 8:9, the "Spirit of Jesus Christ" in Philippians 1:19, and the "Spirit of His Son" in Galatians 4:6. All four titles express the close relationship there is between Christ and the Spirit. Christ and the Spirit are One and yet different; they are different, yet one. In communion The Father, The Son, And The Holy Spirit.

III. Bithynia Would be Reached in Gods Time

Within fifteen years, Peter took the gospel to that area, according to the salutation of his first epistle (I Pet. 1:1). By the beginning of the next century, Christianity was flourishing there, as we discover in a fascinating letter from Pliny, the Roman governor of Bithynia, to the Emperor Trajan. Pliny, who was not a Christian, described the worship services of the Christians in his province and their oath to abstain from all criminal acts and breaches of trust, and how their "contagious superstition" only spread further as he sought to bring individuals to trial. Nicaea became the birthplace of the Nicene Creed. The original version was adopted at the Council of Nicaea in 325 A.D.

When the Holy Spirit leads, we know we are acting in Gods time and with His purpose. Very often, we may wish to do very good things, but it is not Gods time. He alone is the Master of all things. He alone knows when to act. He alone knows the circumstances that prevail at any given time. Because of this, we can have full confidence in the guidance of the Spirit.

IV. Through a Vision, The Man From Macedonia Calls Paul to Macedonia

God speaks to us and leads in a variety of ways. Sometimes God reveals His will through a vision. God spoke to Ananias (Acts 9:10-12) in a vision about Paul and his ministry. The Lord spoke to Cornelius (Acts 10:3) and Peter (Acts 10:17-19 and 11:5) in visions. These visions led to the breakthrough of the gospel among the Gentiles.

At Troas, on the northwestern coast of modern Turkey, the Lord spoke to Paul through a vision (verse 9). In the vision a man from Macedonia was standing and appealing to Paul to come to Macedonia. This was a powerful and persuasive way for Paul to be called. God not only prevented Paul from preaching in Asia and going to Bithynia, but also gave them positive direction on what to do. He called them to Macedonia, which is a part of Europe.

The missionary team did not hesitate to respond to the call. Luke (verse 10) says, "immediately we sought to go into Macedonia, concluding that God had called us to preach the gospel to them." Luke says "we" sought and thereby includes himself. This is the first of his "we" passages. Apparently, Luke joined Paul's team at Troas.

We can conclude through Acts Paul and his team were supernaturally led by the Spirit. Then, Paul had his vision of the man from Macedonia. All this kept Paul in harmony with Gods plan to keep going through Asia and on to Europe. We can sum all this up with one of my favorite Bible verses, (Proverbs 16:9). "The mind of man plans his way, But the Lord directs his steps." As we commit ourselves to the Lord, we know that He will lead us day by day. God's strategy will prevail.

Chapter 8

Narrative

God's strategy will prevail. Indeed, most certainly, this is why the Romans with all the problems their early Republic and / or Democracy had endured decided in their choosing a direction of the Holy Roman Apostolic Catholic Christian Church and took the indoctrinated word of the Christ in deliverance where the Apostles could not.

The Romans took the word of the gospel holiness and service with their shields, chest plats, shin plates, helmets, gladius's, javelin's into Europe and Asia. As the seven Churches of Asia were formed this was done no matter how many Romans died clashing with armies far larger than their own, they had been sent on this mission of fulfilling this duty of expanding the Christian Church of King Christ where the Apostles Epistles could not so easily be accepted.

Summary

The imperial Roman army was the standing force deployed by the Roman Empire during the Principate era (30 B.C. – A.D. 284). Under the founder emperor Augustus (ruled 30 B.C. – A.D. 14), the legions, which were formations numbering about 5,000 heavy infantries recruited from the ranks of Roman citizens only, were transformed from mixed conscript and volunteer corps soldiers serving an average of 10 years, to all-volunteer units of long-term professionals serving a standard 25-year term. (Conscription was only decreed in emergencies.) In the later 1st century, the size of a legions First Cohort was doubled, increasing the strength of a legion to about 5,500.

To complement the legions, Augustus established the auxilia, a regular corps with numbers similar to those of the legions but recruited from the peregrini or non-citizen inhabitants of the empire. Peregrini constituted approximately 90 percent of the Empires population in the 1st century. In addition to large numbers of heavy infantry equipped in a similar manner to legionaries, the auxilia provided virtually all the army's cavalry, light infantry, archers and other specialists. The auxilia were organized in units about 500 strong. These units were termed cohorts if they consisted of infantry, alae if they consisted of cavalry and cohorts equitatae if they were composed of infantry with a cavalry contingent attached.

Until about A.D. 68, the auxilia were recruited by a mix of conscription and voluntary enlistment. After that time, the auxilia also became largely a volunteer corps, with conscription resorted to only in emergencies. Auxiliaries were required to serve a minimum of 25 years, although many served for longer periods. On completion of their minimum term, auxiliaries were awarded Roman citizenship, which carried important legal, fiscal and social advantages. Around A.D. 80, a minority of auxiliary regiments were doubled in size.

Alongside the regular forces, the army of the Principate employed allied native units (called numeri) from outside the Empire on a mercenary basis. These were led by their own aristocrats and equipped in traditional fashion. Numbers fluctuated according to circumstances and are largely unknown.

As all-citizen formations, and symbolic protectors of the dominance of the Italian "master-nation", legions enjoyed greater social prestige than the auxilia for much of the Principate. This was reflected in better pay and benefits. In addition, legionaries were equipped with more expensive and protective armour than auxiliaries, notably the lorica segmentata, or laminated strip armour. However, in 212, the Emperor Caracalla granted Roman citizenship to nearly all the Empires freeborn inhabitants. At this point, the distinction between legions and auxilia became moot, the latter becoming all-citizen units also. The change was reflected in the disappearance, during the 3rd century, of legionaries' special equipment, and the progressive break-up of legions into cohort-sized units like the auxilia.

By the end of Augustus' reign, the imperial army numbered some 250,000 men, equally split between 25 legions and 250 units of auxiliaries. The numbers grew to a peak of about 450,000 by 211, in 33 legions and about 400 auxiliary units. By then, auxiliaries outnumbered legionaries substantially. From this peak, numbers probably underwent a steep decline by 270 due to plague and losses during multiple major barbarian invasions. Numbers were restored to their early 2nd-century level of c. 400,000 (but probably not to their 211 peak) under Diocletian (r. 284-305). After the Empires borders became settled (on the Rhine-Danube line in Europe) by A.D. 68, virtually all military units (except the Praetorian Guard) were stationed on or near the borders, in roughly 17 of the 42 provinces of the empire in the reign of Hadrian (r. 117–138).

Soldiers, mostly drawn from polytheistic societies, enjoyed wide freedom of worship in the polytheistic Roman system. Only a few cults were banned by the Roman authorities, as being incompatible with the official Roman religion or being politically subversive, notably Druidism and Christianity. The later Principate saw the rise in popularity among the military of Eastern mystery cults, generally centered on one deity, and involving secret rituals divulged only to initiates. By far the most popular cult in the army was Mithraism, an apparently syncretism cult which mainly originated in Asia Minor

Roman Empire Invasion of The Barbarian Paganist Clans of Europe

Between 6 B.C. and A.D. 4, Roman legions established bases on the Lippe and Weser rivers, roughly 2,000 years ago.

One of the pivotal events in European history took place here, in A.D. 9, three crack legions of Rome's army were caught in an ambush and annihilated.

Ongoing finds ranging from simple nails to fragments of armor and the remains of fortifications have verified the innovative guerrilla tactics that according to accounts from the period, neutralized the Romans' superior weaponry and discipline.

It was a defeat so catastrophic that it threatened the survival of Rome itself and halted the empires conquest of Germany. This was a battle that changed the course of history.

It was one of the most devastating defeats ever suffered by the Roman Army, and its consequences were the most far-reaching. The battle led to the creation of a militarized frontier in the middle of Europe that endured for 400 years, and it created a boundary between Germanic and Latin cultures that lasted 2,000 years.

Had Rome not been defeated a very different Europe would have emerged. Almost all of modern Germany as well as much of the present-day Czech Republic would have come under Roman rule. All Europe west of the Elbe might well have remained Roman Catholic, Germans would be speaking a Romance language, the Thirty Years' War might never have occurred, and the long, bitter conflict between the French and the Germans might never have taken place.

Founded (at least according to legend) in 753 B.C., Rome spent its formative decades as little more than an overgrown village. But within a few hundred years, Rome had conquered much of the Italian peninsula, and by 146 B.C., had leapt into the ranks of major powers by defeating Carthage, which controlled much of the Western Mediterranean. By the beginning of the Christian Era, Rome's sway extended from Spain to Asia Minor, and from the North Sea to the Sahara. The imperial navy had turned the Mediterranean into a Roman lake, and everywhere around the rim of the empire, Rome's defeated enemies feared her legions or so it seemed to optimistic Romans. "Germania" (the name referred originally to a particular tribe along the Rhine), meanwhile, did not exist as a nation at all. Various Teutonic tribes lay scattered across a vast wilderness that reached from present-day Holland to Poland. The Romans knew little of this densely forested territory governed by fiercely independent chieftains. They would pay dearly for their ignorance.

Narrative

The United States of America "Nation Under God" serves much in comparison as the Roman Empire in the fulfilment of Gods Divine Strategy. Theretofore, it is greatly important to stand as One Church of King Jesus Christ appropriately armed as well, biblically versed. This can be obtained through the reading of scripture, also the understanding of the embedded biblical verses within the United States of America Declaration of Independence, Constitution, and Bill of Rights as they were originally written by the founders of our Nation Under God to better guide American peoples as a Sovereignty Republic functioning in Democracy with Liberty. As well, the USA "Nation Under God" can have identity as Christendom wherein supporting the Holy Land of God's chosen Israel in preparation for the future Covenant of Peace with Lord King Jesus Christ return all will be administrated by the Monarchy of King Christ as written in scripture within the Holy Bible.

Ancient Historians

There are many reasons, according to ancient historians, that the imperial Roman legate Publius Quinctilius Varus set out so confidently that September in A.D. 9. He led an estimated 15,000 seasoned legionnaires from their summer quarters on the Weser River, in what is now Northwestern Germany, West toward permanent bases near the Rhine. They were planning to investigate reports of an uprising among local clans. Varus, 55, was linked by marriage to the imperial family and had served as Emperor Augustus' representative in the province of Syria which included modern Lebanon and Israel, where he had quelled ethnic disturbances. To Augustus, he must have seemed just the man to bring Roman civilization to the barbarous tribes of Germany.

Like his patrons in Rome, Varus thought occupying Germany would be easy. Varus was a very good administrator, but he was not a soldier. To send him out into an unconquered land and tell him to make a province of it was a huge blunder on Augustus' part.

Rome's imperial future was by no means foreordained. At age 35, Augustus, the first emperor, still styled himself "first citizen" in deference to lingering democratic sensibilities of the fallen

Roman Republic, whose demise after the assassination of Caesar had brought him to power in 27 B.C., following a century of bloody civil wars. During Augustus' rule, Rome had grown into the largest city in the world, with a population that may have approached one million.

The German frontier held a deep allure for Augustus, who regarded the warring tribal clans east of the Rhine as little more than rock throwing blue painted long haired long hairy faced naked paganist savages ripe for conquest. Between 6 B.C. and A.D. 4, Roman legions had mounted repeated incursions into the tribal lands, eventually establishing a chain of bases on the Lippe and Weser rivers. In time, despite growing resentment of the Roman presence, the tribes exchanged iron, cattle, slaves and foodstuffs for Roman gold and silver coins and luxury goods. Some tribes even pledged allegiance to Rome; German mercenaries served with Roman armies as far away as the present-day Czech Republic.

One such German soldier of fortune, a 25-year-old prince of the Cherusci clan, was known to the Romans as Arminius. His tribal name has been lost to history. He spoke Latin and was familiar with Roman tactics, the kind of man the Romans relied on to help their armies penetrate the lands of the barbarians. For his valor on the field of battle, he had been awarded the rank of knight and the honor of Roman citizenship. On that September day, he and his mounted auxiliaries were deputized to march ahead and rally some of his own tribesmen to help in putting down the rebellion.

Arminius' motives are obscure, but most historians believe he had long harbored dreams of becoming king of his clan. To achieve his goal, he concocted a brilliant deception: he would report a fictitious "uprising" in territory unfamiliar to the Romans, then lead them into a deadly trap. A rival chieftain, Segestes, repeatedly warned Varus that Arminius was a traitor, but Varus ignored him. The Romans thought they were invincible.

Arminius had instructed the Romans to make what he had described as a short detour, a one- or two-day march, into the territory of the rebels. The legionnaires followed along rudimentary trails that meandered among the Germans' farmsteads, scattered fields, pastures, bogs and oak forests. As they progressed, the line of Roman troops already seven or eight miles long, including local auxiliaries, camp followers and a train of baggage carts pulled by mules became dangerously extended. The legionnaires were having a hard time of it, felling trees, building roads, and bridging places that required it. Meanwhile, a violent rain and wind came up that separated them still further, while the ground, that had become slippery around the roots and logs, made walking very treacherous for them, and the tops of the trees kept breaking off and falling down, causing much confusion. While the Romans were in such difficulties, the barbarians suddenly surrounded them on all sides at once. At first, they hurled their volleys from a distance; then, as no one defended himself and many were wounded, they approached closer to them. Somehow, the command to attack had gone out to the German tribes. This is pure conjecture, but Arminius must have delivered a message that the Germans should begin their assault.

The nearest Roman base lay at Haltern, 60 miles to the Southwest. So, Varus, on the second day, pressed on doggedly in that direction. On the third day, he and his troops were entering a passage between a hill and a huge swamp known as the Great Bog that, in places, was no more than 60 feet wide. As the increasingly chaotic and panicky mass of legionnaires, cavalrymen, mules and carts inched forward, Germans appeared from behind trees and sand mound barriers, cutting off all possibility of retreat. In open country, the superbly drilled and disciplined Romans would surely have prevailed. But here, with no room to maneuver, exhausted after days of hit and run attacks, unnerved, they were at a crippling disadvantage.

Varus understood that there was no escape. Rather than face certain torture at the hands of the Germans, he chose suicide, falling on his sword as Roman tradition prescribed. Most of his commanders followed suit, leaving their troops leaderless in what had become a killing field. An army unexcelled in bravery, the first of Roman armies in discipline, in energy, and in experience in the field, through the negligence of its general, the perfidy of the enemy, and the unkindness of fortune was exterminated to a man by the very enemy whom it has always slaughtered like cattle, according to the A.D. 30 account of Velleius Paterculus, a retired military officer who may have known both Varus and Arminius.

Only a handful of survivors managed somehow to escape into the forest and make their way to safety. The news they brought home so shocked the Romans that many ascribed it to supernatural causes, claiming a statue of the goddess Victory had ominously reversed direction. The historian Suetonius, writing a century after the battle, asserted that the defeat nearly wrecked the empire. Roman writers were baffled by the disaster. Though they blamed the hapless Varus, or the treachery of Arminius, or the wild landscape, in reality, the local societies were much more complex than the Romans thought. They were an informed, dynamic, rapidly changing people, who practiced complex farming, fought in organized military units, and communicated with each other across very great distances.

More than 10 percent of the entire imperial army had been wiped out the myth of its invincibility shattered. In the wake of the debacle, Roman bases in Germany were hastily abandoned. Augustus, dreading that Arminius would march on Rome, expelled all Germans and Gaul's from the city and put security forces on alert against insurrections.

Six years would pass before a Roman army would return to the battle site. The scene the soldiers found was horrific. Heaped across the field at Kalkriese lay the whitening bones of dead men and animals, amid fragments of their shattered weapons. In nearby groves they found barbarous altars upon which the Germans had sacrificed the legionnaires who surrendered. Human heads were nailed everywhere to trees. In grief and anger, the aptly named Germanicus, the Roman general leading the expedition, ordered his men to bury the remains, in the words of Tacitus, "not a soldier knowing whether he was interring the relics of a relative or a stranger, but looking on all as kinsfolk and of their own blood, while their wrath rose higher than ever against the foe."

Germanicus, ordered to campaign against the Cherusci, clan still under the command of Arminius, pursued the tribe deep into Germany. But the wily chieftain retreated into the forests, until, after a series of bloody but indecisive clashes, Germanicus fell back to the Rhine, defeated. Arminius was the liberator of Germany, Tacitus wrote, a man who, threw down the challenge to the Roman nation.

For a time, clans flocked to join Arminius' growing coalition. But as his power grew, jealous rivals began to defect from his cause. He fell by the treachery of his relatives, Tacitus records, in A.D. 21.

With the abdication of the Romans from Germany, the Kalkriese battlefield was gradually forgotten. Even the Roman histories that recorded the debacle were lost, sometime after the fifth century, during the collapse of the empire under the onslaught of barbarian invasions. But in the 1400s, humanist scholars in Germany rediscovered the works of Tacitus, including his account of Varus' defeat. As a consequence, Arminius was hailed as the first national hero of Germany. The myth of Arminius helped give Germans their first sense that there had been a German people that transcended the hundreds of small duchies that filled the political landscape of the time. By 1530, even Martin Luther praised the ancient German chieftain as a war leader and updated his name to "Hermann". Three centuries later, Heinrich von Kleist's 1809 play, Hermann's Battle, invoked the hero's exploits to encourage his countrymen to fight Napoleon and his invading armies. By 1875, as German militarism surged, Hermann had been embraced as the nation's paramount historical symbol, a titanic copper statue of the ancient warrior, crowned with a winged helmet and brandishing his sword menacingly toward France, was erected on a mountaintop 20 miles South of Kalkriese, near Detmold, where many scholars then believed the battle took place. At 87 feet high, and mounted on an 88-foot stone base, it was the largest statue in the world until the Statue of Liberty was dedicated in 1886. Not surprisingly, the monument became a popular destination for Nazi pilgrimages during the 1930s. But the actual location of the battle remained a mystery. More than 700 sites, ranging from the Netherlands to eastern Germany, were proposed.

Narrative

It is with the epic expansion of the Roman Empire and the missionary works of the Apostles Epistles the early Middle East, Africa, Europe and Asia receive the building of Christianity. The One Church of our Holy Supernatural Messianic Lord King Jesus Christ. Christ is our King ruling His Throne. His Majesties Administration are the leaders of the One Church of Christ formed of many reformations branches the body of the Church. Certainly, this has been achieved through the application of the Gospel, Holiness, and Service. From all of this missionary works, the first Cathedral of Europe is achieved.

The High Cathedral of Saint Peter in Trier

(German: Hohe Domkirche St. Peter zu Trier), or Cathedral of Trier (German: Trierer Dom), is a Roman Catholic Church in Trier, Rhineland-Palatinate, Germany. It is the oldest cathedral in the country. The edifice is notable for its extremely long-life span under multiple different eras each contributing some elements to its design, including the center of the main chapel being made of Roman brick laid under the direction of Saint Helen, resulting in a cathedral added onto gradually rather than rebuilt in different eras. Its dimensions, 112.5 m length by 41 m width, make it the largest church structure in Trier. In 1986 it was listed as part of the Roman Monuments, Cathedral of St. Peter and Church of Our Lady in Trier.

The structure is raised upon the foundations of Roman buildings of Augusta Treverorum. Following the conversion of the Emperor Constantine the Bishop Maximin of Trier (329-346) coordinated the construction of the grandest ensemble of ecclesiastical structures in the West outside Rome: on a ground plan four times the area of the present cathedral no less than four basilicas, a baptistery and outbuildings were constructed; the four piers of the crossing formed the nucleus of the present structure.

The fourth-century structure was left in ruins by the Franks and rebuilt. Normans destroyed the structure again in 882. Under Archbishop Egbert (d. 993) it was restored once more.

German Tribes Exerted Pressure on The Roman Frontier

In the 4th century A.D. most Germanic peoples in Europe were living East of the Rhine and North of the Danube. To the East, North of the Black Sea, were the East Goths (Ostrogoth's) and the West Goths (Visigoths). To the West of these clans and extending over a large area of the Rhine were the Vandals, Lombard's, Alemanni, Burgundians, and Franks. In and near present day Denmark lived the Jutes, Angles, and Saxons.

These groups were seminomadic, herding their flocks and tilling the soil. Large and vigorous, the people prized strength and courage in battle. They worshiped many gods, including Tiw, the god of war, Wotan, the chief of the gods, Thor, the god of thunder, and Freya, the goddess of fertility. (The names of these deities are preserved in the English words Tuesday, Wednesday, Thursday, and Friday.)

The German tribal assemblies were made up of voting freeman, and their laws were based on long-established customs of the tribe. These political practices were to have a strong influence in medieval England, where they laid a foundation for the rise of parliamentary government and English common law. The Roman historian Tacitus (55 to 117 A.D.), in his famous treatise (GERMANIA), gave a graphic account of how the Germans lived and wistfully compared these robust people with the weak, pleasure-loving Roman aristocracy.

The Germans were proud of being Goths, Burgundians, Franks, and Vandals. They wore German costumes and followed German customs. They had reddish or blond hair, blue eyes, great stature, and generally powerful physiques. Fonder of war than of work, they consumed quantities of a kind of beer in prolonged contests. Besides drinking, gambling was a favorite amusement. The men were primarily fighters who scorned labor and relegated all agricultural and household tasks to women and slaves. German family life was commonly a model of simplicity and virtue. In general, German society was tribal, that is, it emphasized the relation and loyalties of kinship rather than of citizenship. An injury to his kin must be avenged by them unless they were compensated by a graded system of penalties, known as Wergeld. Some tribes however, had coalesced into groups, which for lack of a better term, might be called "nations". Over such nations ruled kings, at first hardly more than war leaders elected by the freemen and subject to their wishes. But by the time they entered the Empire there was already a tendency to choose rulers from the same family, thus paving the way for hereditary succession.

For hundreds of years the Germans had exerted pressure on the frontiers of the empire. In 105 B.C. German warriors inflicted a terrible defeat on a Roman army, but four years later, a capable Roman leader, Marius, became a national hero when he outmaneuvered the Germans and defeated them. Again, in Julius Caesar's time, German invaders tried to conquer part of Gaul but were defeated. During the reign of Augustus, the Romans launched a drive against the restless German tribes between the Rhine and the Elbe rivers, but in 9 A.D. the Roman legions suffered a crushing defeat in the Battle of Teutoburg Forest. Three legions were completely wiped out. From then on, the Romans were content to hold the frontier on the Rhine-Danube line, and quite continued for a long period. Again, in the reign of Marcus Aurelius, from 161 to 180 A.D., and for 120 years afterward, the Romans had difficulty holding the Germans at the Frontier. But after 300 A.D. peace was maintained for some seventy-five years.

During tranquil interludes, the Romans and Germanic peoples had many opportunities for peaceful association. Some Germans were permitted to enter the Roman Empire to settle on vacant lands. Others, captured in war, became slaves on Roman estates, and still others accepted service in the legions. If intermingling had been allowed to continue, the Germans might have been gradually assimilated into the empire. However, pressure from the German tribes suddenly turned the gradual infiltration into a rushing invasion.

German Tribes Forced Their Way into All Parts of The Western Roman Empire

In Asia, during the 4th century, restless nomads called Huns were on the march from the East. Mounted on swift horses, they attacked with lightning ferocity all tribes in their path. Crossing the Volga River, they conquered the Ostrogoth's in Eastern Europe. Fearing that the Huns would attack them also, the Visigoths implored Roman authorities for sanctuary in the empire. The Roman officials agreed, promising them lands for settlement provided they came unarmed.

Neither side lived up to the agreement, however, and the Visigoths, without land and facing starvation, began to sack Roman settlements. When the Roman emperor Valens led a great army against the Visigoths, to the astonishment of Romans and Germans alike, the imperial force was scattered, and the emperor slain. This battle on the field of Adrianople in 378 A.D. is considered one of the decisive battles in world history because it rendered the Roman Empire defenseless. German tribes outside the frontiers began to round up their cattle, mobilize their fighting men, and move toward the Roman borders.

Marching Southwestward under their leader Alaric, the Visigoths reached Rome in 410 A.D. and looted the city. By that time other German clans--the Franks, Vandals, and Burgundians--were moving into the empire. And about 450 A.D., Germans from Northwest Europe--the Angles, Saxons, and Jutes--sailed to Britain, where they killed or enslaved the Britons whom they encountered and forced others to retreat into Wales and Scotland.

To add to the tumult, the Huns, led by Attila, had also invaded the empire, and were threatening to enslave or destroy both Romans and Germans. So, forgetting their own differences for a while, the Romans and Germans united against a common enemy. They fought together in Gaul and defeated Attila, the "Scourge of God," at the Battle of Chalon's in 451 A.D. Shortly afterward Attila died, and his savage cavalry drifted apart.

Chapter 9

The Western Empire Collapsed

Meanwhile, the power of the emperors in Rome had fallen to a point where they had become merely puppets of the legionaries, many of whom were of German birth. In the 476 A.D., Odoacer, a commander of the Roman armies, deposed the last of the Roman emperors and became the first German ruler of Rome. This date--476 A.D.--is often cited as the date for the "fall" of Rome. In a strict sense, there was no "fall." The decline of Roman imperial power was a gradual and complex process marked by weakling emperors, corrupt bureaucrats, and the gradual admission of German soldiers into the legions.

Since the early decades of the 4th century, emperors at Rome had sensed the growing weakness of the empire in the West. In the year 330 A.D. Emperor Constantine had moved his capital to the city of Byzantium, in the eastern part of the empire, changing its name to Constantinople. By the end of that century, the Roman Empire had become permanently divided, with one emperor ruling the West and another in the East. Although separated, the two sections of the empire continued to be thought of as one.

But the Western part of the empire was breaking up. By the year 476 A.D., when Odoacer ascended the throne, German kingdoms had been established in England by Anglo-Saxon invaders; the Visigoths had moved into Spain; the Vandals had built up a kingdom in North Africa and by 486 A.D., the Franks had gained control of Gaul. The Italian peninsula was to become the scene of conflict and strife, and near the end of the 5th century, it was to fall under the rule of the Ostrogoth's.

The Ostrogoth's had become free from the Huns after the death of Attila in 453 A.D. and they had built a settlement within the Roman Empire South and West of the Danube. In 471 A.D. they elected Theodoric their king, and soon afterward he led a march toward the Eastern part of the empire. To prevent the Ostrogoth's from encroaching on his lands, the emperor in the East encouraged Theodoric to invade Italy instead and to overthrow Odoacer who had ruled there since 476 A.D. Theodoric did so, and by 493 A.D. he was not only king of the Goths but of Italy also, with his capital established at Ravenna. His rule brought prosperity and peace to Italy, but at his death in 526 A.D. civil strife began again. In the middle of the 6th century a strong emperor at Constantinople, Justinian, won back Italy for a few years.

The Lombard's Invade Italy (Middle English Called Lumbarde)

Events of great importance were taking place during this period. It was while Clovis was establishing the Frankish kingdom in Gaul that Theodoric, the great Ostrogothic king, carved out for his people a kingdom in Italy, and while the sons of Clovis were conquering the remainder of Gaul, Justinian (483-565 A.D.) Byzantine emperor from 527 to 565 A.D. was making Italy once more a province under imperial rule. Within three years after the death of Justinian, another great change took place. A new nation of barbarian invaders, the Lombard's, swept down into Italy and opened a new chapter in its history.

The Lombard's were one of the East German nations. Their original home was on the banks of the Elbe River in Northern Germany. From there they migrated South and East to the Danube River, where they were converted to the Arian form of Christianity. In 568 A.D. they followed the track of earlier Germanic invaders from the Balkans down into Northern Italy, and a small group went off in a different direction to the Eastern parts of Dalmatia. Meeting with little opposition, for the country had been ravaged by war and plague, they occupied the great plain between the Alps and the Apennines, ever since called Lombardy. It was a thorough conquest. They made no pretense of alliance with the empire, as the Ostrogoth's had done, nor did they leave the conquered Italians in possession of their estates. The continuity of Roman civilization, which had survived so many invasions, was at last broken, or at least severely strained. About 575 A.D., marauding bands of Lombard's began to push farther South, and within a decade had occupied the center of Italy almost to the Southern end of the peninsula. The emperors made some attempt to check the Lombard's, but in vain. In 605 A.D. a truce was arranged between them. By that time, the Lombard's had conquered all of Italy except the territories around Ravenna, Rome, Naples, and to the extreme South. These were still ruled by representatives of the emperor, nominally under the Exarch of Ravenna, thought Rome and the other imperial possessions were so cut off from the exarchate as to be left practically independent. The unity of Italy was completely destroyed, to be recovered only after thirteen centuries has passed. The Lombard Kingdom itself was not strongly united. The Lombard dukes were always half independent and often rebellious, especially in the two great duchies of Spoleto and Benevento in the center and South, which were never firmly attached to the kingdom and where the Lombard's remained in the minority.

Out of the chaos of this last barbarian invasion, one Italian power, the Roman Papacy, rose with greater authority than ever before. The popes had lost much of their prestige since the days of Leo the Great, though they had gained much in wealth from estates bequeathed to them in all parts of Italy. The restoration of imperial rule in Italy had been a serious blow to their authority, for Justinian had introduced that domination of the Church by the state which had long been recognized in the Eastern Empire but had never been enforced in the West. Moreover, the pope's authority outside of Italy had suffered. The bishops of Gaul were controlled by the Frankish kings, and Spain under the Visigoths was Arian almost to the end of the sixth century. But the Lombard conquests broke the power of the emperor over the pope, and in 590 A.D. the Roman Church found in Pope Gregory the Great a leader who was to set the papacy back again on the road to independence and spiritual domination in the West.

Lombard's And Middle English Called Lumbarde

The term Middle Ages was given to the period of Western European history that extended from the decline of Rome to the discovery of America. The Western Europeans who lived just after the Middle Ages named it that because they thought it was a period of darkness between the splendor of Rome and the splendor of the civilization they were creating. They believed that nothing of importance happened for them. Today, however, we know that the Middle Ages was an important period in itself in Western Europe. Many of our cherished institutions started during that period of about a thousand years.

The Middle Ages are often divided into the Early Middle Ages, from the fall of Rome to about 1000 A.D., and the Late Middle Ages from 1000 A.D. to the discovery of America. These two periods differed in their character. The first was a period in which civilization was at a low ebb.

For about five hundred years there was almost no education, no city life, trade, or good government. The Latin literature was unread, and no new literature was produced. Small chieftains could not understand the Roman laws and issued their own decrees. Cities dwindled in size. Each family depended largely on itself for the necessities of life since there was not much commerce. Neighborhood wars were common. It was an age of invasion, robbery, and violence, as group after group of cruel people swept into neighboring countries looking for riches. There was very little physical security for anyone. Other groups of people seemed more interested in preparing for the next life than improving conditions in the world in which they lived. Their religion placed great stress on ceremony.

Beginning the eleventh century and increasing in the latter part of the Late Middle Ages, life in Western Europe took on a more rapid pace and became more colorful. Education changed and developed, towns grew, beautiful churches and strong castles were built, trade increased, nations developed, and parliaments came into existence. The institutions that came into being at that time form the basis upon which later peoples built.

While these conditions prevailed in Western Europe, the Eastern Roman Empire continued to exist. Its borders were constantly being clipped, however, by invaders from Asia. It continued until 1453.

Although the Western Europeans did not know it until late in the Middle Ages, all this time between 300 and 1500 A.D. civilizations were flourishing in India, China, Japan, and in the Western Hemisphere.

Lombard's in 15th and 16th century have called ME (Middle English) Lumbarde, Latin Longobardus, and French Longobardo. A member of a Teutonic people invading Italy in 568 A.D. settling in the Po valley and establishing a kingdom.

Migration of the Slavic tribes, Croats and Serbs from the Black Sea down to Greece and their occupation of the Balkan Peninsula.

Justinian's reign marked the culmination of Latin influence in Byzantine civilization. Thereafter, while certain Roman ideas continued to determine the course of Byzantine history--the emperors never ceasing to regard themselves as the legitimate successors of Augustus--Greek and Oriental influences prevailed. Greek became the official language of the administration and of the law, as it had been of the Church in the East.

Besides, the loss of the Western provinces rendered contact of the East with Rome and Italy more difficult. It is true that southern Italy, Rome, and Ravenna were not taken by the Lombard's, but continued as nominal possessions of the Emperor. Yet imperial power in Italy was tenuous in the extreme. More and more, people there turned for guidance, even in temporal matters, to the pope rather than to the exarch. The unity of Eastern and Western Christianity was also endangered by this loss of contact between the Latin--and, in the Byzantine view, barbarian--West and the Greek East. Finally, Justinian's successors were forced to deal with pressing Eastern problems which he had neglected. Foremost among these was the defense of the frontiers.

During Justinian's reign from 527 to 565 A.D., communities of Southern Slavs had been established along the Northern Byzantine frontier. The Slavs were an Indo-European people who migrated in various directions from the region of the Pripet marshes. The South Slavs (or Yugoslavs) had settled in some numbers North of the Black Sea by the fifth and sixth centuries. Although they had frequently suffered at the hands of Germans and also of Asiatic nomads, they were tenacious and prolific and maintained their identity. Unlike the nomads, they had reached an agricultural stage of civilization.

In the sixth century, much as the Goths had previously been driven on by the savage nomadic Huns, large numbers of South Slavs were pushed by the Avars, another Hunnic people, into the Balkan Peninsula. Sometimes in conjunction with the Avars, but finally on their own initiative, they advanced into imperial territory. By the end of the century a great many had settled in Thrace and Greece. And in 620 A.D. the Emperor Heraclius officially recognized a number of them as allies against the Avars. Somewhat later, as Avar raids continued, these Yugoslavs, ancestors of the modern Serbs and Croats, moved into the Illyrian provinces of Panonia, Bosnia, Dalmatia, and Serbia about 595 A.D.

Thus, it was that the Roman Empire of the East was forced in its turn to permit barbarian immigration. And although it was many years before the Yugoslavs were able to form stable kingdoms, the ethnic character of the Balkan Peninsula was permanently changed.

Meanwhile the Avars remained a formidable military menace. In 591, in 619, and again in 626 A.D., together with Slavs, they appeared before Constantinople. But the redoubtable fortifications of the city frustrated all their attacks. Thereafter, the Avars ceased to trouble the Byzantine Empire seriously, and the Slavs settled down within its frontiers.

Defense of Constantinople was complicated by an even more serious menace to the Eastern frontier. This resulted from a remarkable resurgence of Persian power. Under their King Chosroes, the Persians passed through Armenia and Syria and advanced into Palestine. Capturing Jerusalem, they carried away part of the relic of the Holy Cross, the Cross upon which Christ had been crucified. That the Emperor Heraclius (610-641 A.D.) was able to cope with this situation is a tribute to his skill and courage as well as to the inherent strength of the Empire. The Avars were temporarily appeased, and between 622 and 627 A.D. a series of brilliant campaigns not only drove the Persians from Syria and Palestine but carried the Emperor to a signal victory near the ruins of Nineveh on the Tigris River. In the following year Chosroes successor sued for peace. Meanwhile Constantinople had successfully withstood Avar assaults by sea and land. In 629 A.D. Heraclius returned in triumph to Constantinople bearing with him the relic of the True Cross. He was a savior of the Empire.

But except in name, it was no longer a Roman Empire. The Balkans were henceforth predominantly Slavic, for the Yugoslavs profiting from the exploits of the destructive Avars, were now firmly settled in the Balkan Peninsula. And though they were presently converted to Christianity and nominally incorporated in the Empire, they retained their own Slavic speech and ignored both Latin and Greek. Moreover, the long Byzantine war with Persia exhausted both countries and left them a prey to the Arabs, who, even before Heraclius's death, had invaded Egypt, Syria, Palestine, and Mesopotamia.

Thus, the Empire of the early eighth century consisted only of Constantinople, a portion of the Balkan Peninsula, Asia Minor, and a few areas in Italy and Sicily. But even in its reduced state-- and more losses were to follow--the Byzantine Empire was to remain for centuries a rampart of Graeco-Roman and Christian civilization in the Eastern Mediterranean.

Slavic Tribes Occupy Dalmatian Archipelago

Around 640 A.D., after occupying the Dalmatian islands they found a group of Lombard's--who had previously split from the major Lombard tribes who were on their way to Northern Italy--in the town of Lumbarde on the island of Corcyra (Korcula). Slavic tribes, from previous difficulty with German tribes, had animosity toward the German settlements in Lumbarde. Not long afterward the German tribes disappeared from Lumbarde and joined their tribes in Italy. Since that time, the Slavic people have called that town Lumbarde-a.

Chapter 10

Narrative

The Roman invasion of Europe was not only epic, but it is also the expansion of Christianity on behalf of the missionary works of the Apostles Epistles indoctrination by the supernatural Messiah King Jesus Christ Throne. Whereunto, a key to the United States existence, and title "Nation Under God" a sole purpose in our Gods Devine Strategy beneath the Canopy of Heaven.

Up Unto The Lord

Legio Nona Hispana ("Spanish Ninth Legion"), also Legio VIIII Hispana or Legio IX Hispana, was a legion of the Imperial Roman army which existed from the 1st century B.C. until at least A.D. 120. The legion fought in various provinces of the late Roman Republic and early Roman Empire but was then stationed in Britain following the Roman invasion in 43 A.D. The legion disappears from surviving Roman records after C.A. A.D. 120 and there is no extant account of what happened to it.

The unknown fate of the legion has been the subject of considerable research and speculation. One theory (Theodor Mommsen) was that the legion was wiped out in action in Northern Britain soon after 108, the date of the latest datable inscription of the Ninth found in Britain, perhaps during a rising of Northern tribes and / or clans. This view was popularized by the 1954 novel The Eagle of the Ninth in which the legion is said to have marched into Caledonia (Scotland), after which it was "never heard of again".

Narrative

The focus is the biblical prophecies historically and the continuing growth rate, as well, global expansion of the indoctrination of Christianity, beginning with the Christ His crucifixion and resurrection the Apostles their Epistles the continuing expansion and growth of a single person Jesus Christs indoctrinated teachings which only lasted during His life for one to three years of His Ministry. No other king, nor emperor divine nor other individual person has ever caused such impression globally. And His indoctrination and Throne expansion is continuing with an increasing rate. There is no other explanation, He is "The Anointed One" The Messiah our Supernatural King Jesus Christ.

Missionary Works

The Roman Ninth Legion was assigned a mission of which they had invaded Europe. What they were carrying with them was the Roman Gold Eagle the mark of their legion it has never been recovered which is much like the United States Eagle that is placed upon the top the stars and stripes banner. However, it is evident they were also carrying other things that cannot be denied nor can anyone prove this to be untrue. This has to do directly with the Nation Under God. The Book of Mormon was written on gold plates in Egyptian much as the ancient writing of the Holy Bible.

The Roman invasion of Europe with the Ninth Legion took place 43 A.D. the Ninth Legion disappeared 120 A.D., In or about the year A.D. 421, Moroni, the last of the Nephite prophet-historians, sealed the sacred record and hid it up unto the Lord, to be brought forth in the latter days, as predicted by the voice of God through His ancient prophets.

The Vikings found America earlier than around A.D. 1000 As well, the European Anglo Saxons clans or tribesmen converted from Pagans to Christians, drove the Empire of Rome out of Europe invading the Middle East for the Holy Land the First Crusades A.D. 1096.

Metal Plates Engraved by Prophets

The Book of Mormon is a sacred record of peoples in ancient America and was engraved upon metal plates. Sources from which this record was compiled include the following:

The Plates of Nephi, which were of two kinds: the small plates and the large plates. The former were more particularly devoted to spiritual matters and the ministry and teachings of the prophets, while the latter were occupied mostly by a secular history of the peoples concerned

(1 Nephi 9:2–4). From the time of Mosiah, however, the large plates also included items of major spiritual importance.

The Plates of Mormon, which consist of an abridgment by Mormon from the large plates of Nephi, with many commentaries. These plates also contained a continuation of the history by Mormon and additions by his son Moroni.

The Plates of Ether, which present a history of the Jadeite's. This record was abridged by Moroni, who inserted comments of his own and incorporated the record with the general history under the title "Book of Ether."

The Plates of Brass brought by the people of Lehi from Jerusalem in 600 B.C. These contained "the five books of Moses, … and also a record of the Jews from the beginning, … down to the commencement of the reign of Zedekiah, king of Judah: and also, the prophecies of the holy prophets" (1 Nephi 5:11–13). Many quotations from these plates, citing Isaiah and other biblical and nonbiblical prophets, appear in the Book of Mormon.

The Book of Mormon comprises fifteen main parts or divisions, known, with one exception, as books, usually designated by the name of their principal author. The first portion (the first six books, ending with Omni) is a translation from the small plates of Nephi. Between the books of Omni and Mosiah is an insert called the Words of Mormon. This insert connects the record engraved on the small plates with Mormons abridgment of the large plates.

The longest portion, from Mosiah through Mormon chapter 7, is a translation of Mormons abridgment of the large plates of Nephi. The concluding portion, from Mormon chapter 8 to the end of the volume, was engraved by Mormons son Moroni, who, after finishing the record of his father's life, made an abridgment of the Jaredite record (as the book of Ether) and later added the parts known as the book of Moroni.

In or about the year A.D. 421, Moroni, the last of the Nephite prophet-historians, sealed the sacred record and hid it up unto the Lord, to be brought forth in the latter days, as predicted by the voice of God through His ancient prophets. In A.D. 1823, this same Moroni, then a resurrected personage, visited the Prophet Joseph Smith and subsequently delivered the engraved plates to him.

About this edition: The original title page, immediately preceding the contents page, is taken from the plates and is part of the sacred text. Introductions in a non-italic typeface, such as in 1 Nephi and immediately preceding Mosiah chapter 9, are also part of the sacred text. Introductions in italics, such as in chapter headings, are not original to the text but are study helps included for convenience in reading.

Some minor errors in the text have been perpetuated in past editions of the Book of Mormon. This edition contains corrections that seem appropriate to bring the material into conformity with prepublication manuscripts and early editions edited by the Prophet Joseph Smith.

Gods Navigation by The Word of Faith

Nearly 500 years before the birth of Christopher Columbus, a band of European sailors left their homeland behind in search of a new world. Their high-prowled Viking ship sliced through the cobalt waters of the Atlantic Ocean as winds billowed the boats enormous single sail. After traversing unfamiliar waters, the Norsemen aboard the wooden ship spied a new land, dropped anchor and went ashore. Half a millennium before Columbus "discovered" America, those Viking feet may have been the first European ones to ever have touched North American soil.

Exploration was a family business for the expedition's leader, Leif Eriksson (variations of his last name include Erickson, Ericson, Erikson, Ericsson and Eiriksson). His father, Erik the Red, founded the first European settlement of Greenland after being expelled from Iceland around A.D. 985 for killing a neighbor. (Erik the Reds father, himself, had been banished from Norway for committing manslaughter.) Eriksson, who is believed to have been born in Iceland around A.D. 970, spent his formative years in desolate Greenland. Around A.D. 1000, Eriksson sailed east to his ancestral homeland of Norway. There, King Olaf I Tryggvason converted him to Christianity and charged him with proselytizing the religion to the pagan settlers of Greenland. Eriksson converted his mother, who built Greenland's first Christian Church, but not his outlaw father.

Icelandic legends called sagas recounted Eriksson's exploits in the New World around A.D. 1000. These Norse stories were spread by word of mouth before becoming recorded in the 12th and 13th centuries. Two sagas give differing accounts as to how Eriksson arrived in North America. According to the "Saga of Erik the Red," Eriksson crossed the Atlantic by accident after sailing off course on his return voyage from Norway after his conversion to Christianity. The "Saga of the Greenlanders," however, recounts that Eriksson's voyage to North America was no fluke. Instead, the Viking explorer had heard of a strange land to the West from Icelandic trader Bjarni Herjolfsson, who more than a decade earlier had overshot Greenland and sailed by the shores of North America without setting foot upon it. Eriksson bought the traders ship, raised a crew of 35 men and retraced the route in reverse.

After crossing the Atlantic, the Vikings encountered a rocky, barren land in present-day Canada. Eriksson bestowed upon the land a name as boring as the surroundings—Helluland, Norwegian for "Stone Slab Land." Researchers believe this location could possibly have been Baffin Island. The Norsemen then voyaged South to a timber-rich location they called Markland (Forestland), most likely in present-day Labrador, before finally setting up a base camp likely on the Northern tip of the island of Newfoundland.

The Vikings spent an entire winter there and benefitted from the milder weather compared to their homeland. They explored the surrounding region abounding with lush meadows, rivers teeming with salmon, and wild grapes so suitable for wine that Eriksson called the region Vinland (Wineland).

After spending the winter in Vinland, Eriksson and his crew sailed home to windswept Greenland with badly needed timber and plentiful portions of grapes. Eriksson, who would succeed Erik the Red as chief of the Greenland settlement after his father's death, never returned to North America, but other Vikings continued to sail West to Vinland for at least the ensuing decade. In spite of North Americas more bountiful resources, the Viking settlers remained in desolate Greenland. This was perhaps due to the violent encounters—including the slaying of Eriksson's brother Thorwald–they had with the indigenous population of North America.

Archaeologists have unearthed evidence that supports the sagas' stories of the Norse expeditions to America. In 1960, Norwegian explorer Helge Ingstad scoured the coasts of Labrador and Newfoundland for signs of a possible settlement, and he found it on the Northern most tip of Newfoundland at L'Anse aux Meadows. An international team of archaeologists that included Ingstad's wife, Anne, excavated artifacts of Viking origin dating from around A.D. 1000, and the remains of the Norse village are now part of a UNESCO World Heritage site.

While Columbus is honored with a federal holiday, the man considered to be the leader of the first European expedition to North America has not been totally forgotten on the calendar. In 1964, President Lyndon Johnson signed a proclamation that declared October 9 to be Leif Eriksson Day in honor of the Viking explorer, his crew and the country's Nordic-American heritage. The proximity of the days honoring Eriksson and Columbus is coincidence. October 9 was chosen because it is the anniversary of the 1825 arrival in New York of the ship Restoration, which carried the first organized band of Norwegian immigrants to the United States.

Chapter 11

Yahweh Gods Eloquent Artistic Architecture With Creation of Infrastructure

Narrative

Jesus previously entered the Holy City of Jerusalem on a donkey, this was the Passover Sabbath Sunday. His resurrection was according to prophesy. In Revelations the Apocalypse: Furthers, in the Book Revelation; Christ will be riding back into the Holy City of Jerusalem on a horse upon His return. This is a battle horse. After reading the Holy Bible and gaining insightful perceptions to understand the scripture writings, it is the breath of Yahweh God who speaks through this amazing supernatural book. It has become perceived, that for the Second Advent to accrue present must be Jesus Christ Lord and King personal appearance. This is listed in the Holy Bible "I will appear" or "where two or more are gathered in my name there I will appear in the midst of them." For the Second Coming to be there are certain events listed in the Holy Bible that have already accrued and other events that are already in the formation of accruing. These things include but are not limited to; Israel must be established as it is written in scripture, nation must rise against nation, war must be across the lands thereunto Jesus Christ future Covenant of Peace ruling from Israel will be well placed at His Throne ruling in His Monarchy as Lord and King. Christendom "Nation Under God" must not be within the Holy Land of Israel but well placed in support of the Will of God as this is currently, the Church lovingly in obedient service to Christ who lovingly serves His Church. Furtherance, the Euphrates River must be dried that the armies of the Middle East may cross uninhibited and attack the Holy Land of Israel. Thereunto, Israel defended by the Will of God as it is so written in scripture. For this to accrue, we as Christian's part of Christ beloved Church must comply to the Will of God. Reading scripture is our means in becoming educated, well-armed, and appropriately versed to the Holy Bible that is the Will of God. Amen

First Crusade

The First Crusade (1096–1099) started as a widespread pilgrimage (France and Germany) and ended as a military expedition by Roman Catholic Europe to regain the Holy Lands taken in the Muslim conquests of the Levant (632–661), ultimately resulting in the recapture of Jerusalem in 1099. It was launched on 27 November 1095 by Pope Urban II with the primary goal of responding to an appeal from Byzantine Emperor Alexios I Komnenos, who requested that Western volunteers come to his aid and help to repel the invading Seljuq Turks from Anatolia. An additional goal soon became the principal objective—the Christian reconquest of the sacred city of Jerusalem and the Holy Land and the freeing of the Eastern Christians from Islamic rule.

During the crusade, knights and peasants from many nations of Western Europe travelled over land and by sea, first to Constantinople and then on towards Jerusalem. The Crusaders arrived at Jerusalem, launched an assault on the city, and captured it in July 1099, massacring many of the city's Muslim, Christian, and Jewish inhabitants. They also established the crusader states of the Kingdom of Jerusalem, the County of Tripoli, the Principality of Antioch, and the County of Edessa.

Because the First Crusade was largely concerned with Jerusalem, a city which had not been under Christian dominion for 461 years, and the crusader army refused to return the land to the control of the Byzantine Empire, the status of the First Crusade as defensive or as aggressive in nature remains controversial.

The First Crusade was part of the Christian response to the Muslim conquests and was followed by the Second to the Ninth Crusades, but the gains made lasted for less than 200 years. It was also the first major step towards reopening international trade in the West since the fall of the Western Roman Empire.

After the First Crusade recaptured Jerusalem in 1099, many Christian pilgrims travelled to visit what they referred to as the Holy Places. However, though the city of Jerusalem was under relatively secure control, the rest of Outremer was not. Bandits abounded, and pilgrims were routinely slaughtered, sometimes by the hundreds, as they attempted to make the journey from the coastline at Jaffa into the Holy Land.

In 1120, the French knight Hugues de Payens approached King Baldwin II of Jerusalem and Warmund, Patriarch of Jerusalem and proposed creating a monastic order for the protection of these pilgrims. King Baldwin and Patriarch Warmund agreed to the request, probably at the Council of Nablus in January 1120, and the king granted the Templars a headquarters in a wing of the royal palace on the Temple Mount in the captured Al-Aqsa

Mosque. The Temple Mount had a mystique because it was above what was believed to be the ruins of the Temple of Solomon.

The Crusaders therefore referred to the Al Aqsa Mosque as Solomon's Temple, and it was from this location that the new Order took the name of Poor Knights of Christ and the Temple of Solomon, or "Templar" knights. The Order, with about nine knights including Godfrey de Saint-Omer and André de Montbard, had few financial resources and relied on donations to survive. Their emblem was of two knights riding on a single horse, emphasizing the Orders poverty.

The Templars' impoverished status did not last long. They had a powerful advocate in Saint Bernard of Clairvaux, a leading Church figure and a nephew of André de Montbard, one of the founding knights. Bernard put his weight behind them and wrote persuasively on their behalf in the letter 'In Praise of the New Knighthood' and, in 1129, at the Council of Troyes he led a group of leading churchmen to officially approve and endorse the Order on behalf of the Church. With this formal blessing, the Templars became a favored charity throughout Christendom, receiving money, land, businesses, and noble-born sons from families who were eager to help with the fight in the Holy Land.

Another major benefit came in 1139, when Pope Innocent IIs papal bull Omne Datum Optimum exempted the Order from obedience to local laws. This ruling meant that the Templars could pass freely through all borders, were not required to pay any taxes, and were exempt from all authority except that of the pope.

With its clear mission and ample resources, the Order grew rapidly. Templars were often the advance force in key battles of the Crusades, as the heavily armoured knights on their warhorses would set out to charge at the enemy, in an attempt to break opposition lines. One of their most famous victories was in 1177 during the Battle of Montgisard, where some 500 Templar knights helped several thousand infantries to defeat Saladin's army of more than 26,000 soldiers.

Although the primary mission of the Order was military, relatively few members were combatants. The others acted in support positions to assist the knights and to manage the financial infrastructure. The Templar Order, though its members were sworn to individual poverty, was given control of wealth beyond direct donations. A nobleman who was interested in participating in the Crusades might place all his assets under Templar management while he was away. Accumulating wealth in this manner throughout Christendom and the Outremer, the Order in 1150 began generating letters of credit for pilgrims journeying to the Holy Land, pilgrims deposited their valuables with a local Templar preceptory before embarking, received a document indicating the value of their deposit, then used that document upon arrival in the Holy Land to retrieve their funds. This innovative arrangement was an early form of banking and may have been the first formal system to support the use of cheques; it improved the safety of pilgrims by making them less attractive targets for thieves, and also contributed to the Templar coffers.

Based on this mix of donations and business dealing, the Templars established financial networks across the whole of Christendom. They acquired large tracts of land, both in Europe and the Middle East; they bought and managed farms and vineyards; they built churches and castles; they were involved in manufacturing, import and export; they had their own fleet of ships; and at one point they even owned the entire island of Cyprus. The Order of the Knights Templar arguably qualifies as the world's first multinational corporation.

"A Templar Knight is truly a fearless knight, and secure on every side, for his soul is protected by the armour of faith, just as his body is protected by the armour of steel. He is thus doubly armed and need fear neither demons nor men."

Bernard de Clairvaux, c. 1135,
De Laude Novae Militae—In Praise of the New Knighthood.

Knights Templar

The Poor Fellow-Soldiers of Christ and of the Temple of Solomon (Latin: Pauperes commilitones Christi Templique Salomonici), commonly known as the Knights Templar, the Order of the Temple (French: Ordre du Temple or Templiers) or simply as Templars, were among the most wealthy and powerful of the Western Christian military orders and were among the most prominent actors of the Christian finance. The organization existed for nearly two centuries during the Middle Ages. Officially endorsed by the Catholic Church around 1129, the Order became a favored charity throughout Christendom and grew rapidly in membership and power. Templar knights, in their distinctive white mantles with a red cross, were among the most skilled fighting units of the Crusades. Non-combatant members of the Order managed a large economic infrastructure throughout Christendom, innovating financial techniques that were an early form of banking, and building fortifications across Europe and the Holy Land.

The Templars' existence was tied closely to the Crusades; when the Holy Land was lost, support for the Order faded. Rumors about the Templars' secret initiation ceremony created mistrust and King Philip IV of France, deeply in debt to the Order, took advantage of the situation. In 1307, many of the Orders members in France were arrested, tortured into giving false confessions, and then burned at the stake. Under pressure from King Philip, Pope Clement V disbanded the Order in 1312. The abrupt disappearance of a major part of the European infrastructure gave rise to speculation and legends, which have kept the "Templar" name alive into the modern day.

The Knights Templar is an international philanthropic chivalric order affiliated with Freemasonry. Unlike the initial degrees conferred in a Masonic Lodge, which only require a belief in a Supreme Being regardless of religious affiliation, the Knights Templar is one of several additional Masonic Orders in which membership is open only to Freemasons who profess a belief in the Christian religion. The full title of this Order is The United Religious, Military and Masonic Orders of the Temple and of St John of Jerusalem, Palestine, Rhodes and Malta.

The word "United" in this title indicates that more than one historical tradition and more than one actual Order are jointly controlled within this system. The individual Orders 'united' within this system are principally the Knights of the Temple (Knights Templar), the Knights of Malta, the Knights of St Paul, and only within the York Rite, the Knights of the Red Cross. The Order derives its name from the historical Knights Templar but does not claim any direct lineal descent from the original Templar order.

The earliest documented link between Freemasonry and the Crusades is the 1737 oration of the Chevalier Ramsay. This claimed that European Freemasonry came about from an interaction between crusader masons and the Knights Hospitaller. This is repeated in the earliest known "Moderns" ritual, the Berne manuscript, written in French between 1740 and 1744.

In 1751 Baron Karl Gotthelf von Hund und Altengrotkau began the Order of Strict Observance, which ritual he claimed to have received from the reconstituted Templar Order in 1743 in Paris. He also claimed to have met two of the "unknown superiors" who directed all of masonry, one of whom was Prince Charles Edward Stuart. The order went into decline when he failed to produce any evidence to support his claims and was wound up shortly after his death.

In 1779 the High Knights Templar of Ireland Lodge, Kilwinning, obtained a charter from Lodge Mother Kilwinning in Scotland. This lodge now began to grant dispensations to other lodges to confer the Knights Templar Degree. Sometime around 1790 the Early Grand Encampment of Ireland was formed, which began to warrant Templar Lodges, and evolved into the Supreme Grand Encampment in 1836.

The Early Grand Encampment chartered several Scottish "encampments" one of which, having been chartered in 1805 as the "Edinburgh Encampment No. 31", then became the" Grand Assembly of Knights Templar in Edinburgh". Who then sought a charter from the Duke of Kent, Grand Master of the Order in England. It seems that the Templar degree had filtered into the lodges of the Ancient's from Ireland about 1780 and was recorded at York about the same time. In the five-degree system developed by the York Masons, the Knights Templar degree sat between the Master Mason and the Sublime Degree of Royal Arch.

Templar masonry in England entered a new era in 1791, with the formation of its first Grand Conclave, with Thomas Dunckerley as Grand Master. At that time, there were eight known Templar encampments in England, the most senior being the Encampment of Redemption at York, and the Baldwyn encampment at Bristol, at whose request Dunckerley began his mission. Under his leadership, the number of encampments steadily grew until his death in 1795. Stasis then followed, until in 1805 their Royal Patron, Duke of Kent, became Grand Master himself, re-energizing the society and launching it into an era of growth and development. Dunckerley laid the foundation for this not only by promoting the order, but by standardizing the ritual and insisting on proper record keeping.

Chapter 12

Narrative

Difficult to accept is to view our civilization as war torn between evil and good. When viewing the timeline of wars there is no war during the time of Rabbi Jesus Christs Messiah three years of

Ministry teachings. In the Scripture of the Holy Bible, we can read of verses with parables in description of Yahweh God and / or Jehovah being the one and only true God of this universe, and there is no other God. Being the author of this research study of the supernatural Jesus Christ the Messiah, there is truth by testimony found through the scripture of this to be indeed evident. Wars have existed in power struggles since before Christ (BC). However, in the research study there is filtering of the greater of the evils of man's fall deeper into the abyss of sin in each institution moreover primitive faithless paganisms. In addition, there is reflection of filtering the lesser of the two evils or the lesser of the two goods from sin of mankind through wars after Rabbi Christ Ministry following His trial, crucifixion, and resurrection and ascension to the Throne of Heaven as King of Kings. Again, we can reflect the horrors of war there is no true right. Yet again, through the study of who the supernatural Jesus Christ is! It is here that can be perceived through the passion of this Lord King and Savior Jesus Christ of the small province of Nazareth, can clearly expand a Holy Thone of sovereignty, liberty, freedom and justice by the Law of God. Through this following timeline of wars, it is evident that global wars increase in their intensity beginning after the crucifixion of Jesus Christ and following His Majesty Lord King Christs resurrection in early AD. As well, seldom do we find in the pages of history after Rabbi Jesus Christ resurrection any lasting paganists nations. Liberating wars continue and sovereignty of nations with the word of God rise following most of these Wars with a better understanding of the Passion of the Christ. Indeed, the Lords hand will have victory by the lesser of the two evils or the better of the two goods. As the Holy Ghost is reaching to mankind in creation of connection and better balance. Long live His Holy Royal Majesty by His Crown and Throne of Heaven and of Earth King of Kings Lord of Lords Jesus Christ the Messiah.

Escalation of Liberating Wars (AD) Resurrection of Jesus Christ Lord King and Savior

Timeline of Wars Before 1 B.C.

1274 BC	Battle of Kadesh
1046 BC	Shang-Zhou War in China.
580 BC - 265 BC	Greek Punic Wars
499 BC - 448 BC	Persian Wars
431 BC - 404 BC	Peloponnesian War
395 BC - 387 BC	Corinthian War
343 BC - 290 BC	Samnite Wars between Rome and Samnium
334 BC - 323 BC	Wars of Alexander the Great
274 BC - 200 BC	Syrian Wars
264 BC - 146 BC	Punic Wars between Rome and Carthage
215 BC - 168 BC	Macedonian Wars
205 BC - 201 BC	Cretan War
191 BC - 188 BC	Roman-Syrian War
135 BC - 71 BC	Roman Servile Wars
89 BC - 63 BC	Mithridatic Wars
58 BC - 50 BC	Julius Caesars Gallic Wars
55 BC - 54 BC	Julius Caesars Roman invasion of Britain
53 BC - 51 BC	Parthian War of Marcus Licinius Crassus

49 BC - 45 BC	Caesar's civil war
44 BC - 30 BC	Roman Civil War
34 BC-22 BC	Chinese War

Timeline of Wars A.D. 1 – 999

3 - 96	Roman conquest of Britain
60 - 61	Boudicas Uprising
184 - 205	Yellow Turban Rebellion
533 - 534	Vandal War
772 - 804	Saxon Wars

Timeline of Wars A.D. 1 – 1199

1066 - 1088	Norman conquest of England
1096 - 1099	First Crusade
1145 - 1149	Second Crusade
1189 - 1192	Third Crusade

Timeline of Wars A.D. 1200 – 1299

1202 - 1204	Fourth Crusade
1206 - 1324	Mongol wars and conquests
1213 - 1221	Fifth Crusade
1215 - 1217	First Barons' War (England)
1248 - 1254	Seventh Crusade
1270 - 1270	Eighth Crusade
1271 - 1272	Ninth Crusade
1296 - 1328	First War of Scottish Independence

Timeline of Wars A.D. 1300 - 1399

1323 - 1328	Peasant revolt in Flanders
1326 - 1332	Polishâ "Teutonic War
1337 - 1453	Hundred Years' War

Timeline of Wars A.D. 1400 – 1499

1419 - 1434	Hussite Wars
1425 - 1454	Wars in Lombardy
1454 - 1466	Thirteen Years' War
1455 - 1485	Wars of the Roses

Timeline of Wars A.D. 1500 - 1599

1509 - 1512	Ottoman Civil War
1519 - 1521	Spanish conquest of the Aztec Empire
1529 - 1532	Inca Civil War
1531 - 1572	Spanish conquest of the Inca Empire
1537 - 1548	Conquistador Civil War in Peru
1554 - 1557	Russo-Swedish War
1563 - 1564	Burmeseâ "Siamese War
1568 - 1648	Eighty Years' War
1570 - 1573	Ottomanâ "Venetian War
1571 - 1571	Russo-Crimean War

Timeline of Wars A.D. 1600 - 1699

1600 - 1611	Polishâ "Swedish War
1602 - 1661	Dutchâ "Portuguese War
1618 - 1648	Thirty Years' War
1634 - 1638	Pequot War
1635 - 1659	Franco-Spanish War
1640 - 1701	Beaver Wars (Iroquois)
1642 - 1646	First English Civil War
1648 - 1649	Second English Civil War
1649 - 1651	Third English Civil War
1652 - 1654	First Anglo-Dutch War
1654 - 1660	Anglo-Spanish War
1655 - 1655	Peach Tree War (Susquehannock)
1675 - 1676	King Philip's War
1683 - 1699	Great Turkish War
1688 – 1697	Nine Years' War including King William's War
1689 - 1692	Jacobean Rising in Scotland

Timeline of Wars A.D. 1700 – 1799

1700 - 1721	Great Northern War
1711 - 1715	Tuscarora War
1712 - 1716	First Fox War
1715 - 1717	Yamasee War
1721 - 1763	Chickasaw Wars
1728 - 1733	Second Fox War
1739 - 1748	War of Jenkins' Ear
1744 - 1748	King George's War

1754 - 1763	French and Indian War (Part of the Seven Years' War)
1756 - 1763	
1758 - 1761	Seven Years' War
1763 - 1766	Anglo-Cherokee War
1775 - 1783	Pontiac's War
1776 - 1794	American Revolutionary War
1779 - 1783	Chickamauga Wars
1785 - 1795	Anglo-Spanish War
1789 - 1799	Northwest Indian War
1791 - 1804	The French Revolution
	Haitian Revolution

Timeline of Wars A.D. 1800 - 1899

1803 - 1815	Napoleonic Wars
1804 - 1813	Russo-Persian War
1808 - 1810	Rum Rebellion
1808 - 1833	Spanish American wars of independence
1810 - 1821	Mexican War of Independence
1812 - 1815	War of 1812
1813 - 1814	Creek War
1817 - 1858	Seminole Wars
1818 - 1828	Zulu Wars of Conquest
1820 - 1875	Texasâ "Indian wars
1821 - 1832	Greek War of Independence
1821 - 1848	Comancheâ "Mexico War
1825 - 1830	Java War
1827 - 1827	Winnebago War
1832 - 1832	Black Hawk War
1835 - 1836	Texas Revolution
1839 - 1842	First Opium War
1846 - 1864	Navajo Wars
1846 - 1848	Mexican-American War
1849 - 1924	Apache Wars
1850 - 1865	California Indian Wars
1853 - 1856	Crimean War
1861 - 1865	American Civil War
1864 - 1868	Snake War
1866 - 1868	Red Cloud's War
1867 - 1875	Comanche Campaign
1876 - 1877	Great Sioux War (Black Hills War)
1877 - 1877	Nez Perce War
1878 - 1879	Cheyenne War
1879 - 1879	Sheepeater Indian War
1879 - 1880	Victorio's War

| 1899 - 1901 | Boxer Rebellion |
| 1899 - 1902 | Second Boer War |

Timeline of Wars A.D. 1900 – 1999

1905	Russian Revolution
1910 - 1921	Mexican Revolution
1914 - 1918	World War I
1917 - 1923	Russian Civil War
1919 - 1923	Turkish War of Independence
1919 - 1921	Irish War of Independence
1927 - 1949	Chinese Civil War
1936 - 1939	Spanish Civil War
1939 - 1945	World War II
1946 - 1949	Greek Civil War
1948 - 1949	1948 Arabâ "Israeli War
1950 - 1953	Korean War
1952 - 1960	Mau Mau Uprising
1953 - 1959	Cuban Revolution
1954 - 1962	Algerian War
1955 - 1975	Vietnam War
1961 - 1961	Bay of Pigs Invasion
1979 - 1989	Soviet war in Afghanistan
1980 - 1988	Iranâ "Iraq War
1982 - 1982	Falklands War
1990 - 1991	Gulf War
1991 - 1995	Croatian War of Independence
1992 - 1995	Bosnian War
1998 - 1999	Kosovo War

Timeline of Wars A.D. 2000 Hereunto Current Date

2001	War in Afghanistan
2003 - 2011	Iraq War
2006 - 2009	War in Somalia
2008 - 2009	Gaza War

Missionary Christian Crusades to Lord King Christ Kingdom Come

Narrative

His Majesty our Holy Messianic Christian King Jesus Christs Crown and Throne has no end Heaven and Earth as one. Unto the unveiling of Lord Christ Messiah's revelations of the Holy Bible, the embracement of His Majesties Holy Supernatural Royal Reign by His Throne of Heaven and beneath the Canopy of Heaven upon the earth and all that is beneath and above the surface of the earth, there is a filtering of the lesser of the evils rising in Him. This is King Jesus Christ beloved Church who art thou the Unleavened New lump risen in Him and He in them. So Mote it be. Amen

Major Achievements

I. King Jesus's twelve Apostles missionary works establishing the Christian Church
II. The United States of America Declaration of Independence adopted by the Continental Congress on July 4, 1776
III. The Constitution of the United States adopted on September 17, 1787
IV. The United States of America Bill of Rights adopted by the House of Representatives on August 21, 1789, formally proposed by joint resolution of Congress on September 25, 1789
V. The Israeli Declaration of Independence (Hebrew: הכרזת העצמאות, Hakhrazat HaAtzma'ut or Hebrew: מגילת העצמאות Megilat HaAtzma'ut), was made on 14 May 1948
VI. A work in progress; there is no Constitution of Israel. Instead of a formal written constitution and in accordance with the 1948 Harari Decision (החלטת הררי) adopted during the Israeli Constituent Assembly, the State of Israel has enacted several Basic Laws of Israel dealing with the government arrangements and human rights.
VII. North Atlantic Treaty Organization created in 1949 by the United States, Canada, and several Western European nations to provide collective security.
VIII. The War in Afghanistan (2001–present) refers to the intervention by NATO and allied forces in the Afghan political struggle, following the terrorist attacks of September 11, 2001, to dismantle the al-Qaeda terrorist organization and to remove from power the Taliban government.
IX. The retaking of Babylon
X. The Iraq War was an armed conflict in Iraq that consisted of two phases. The first was an invasion of Iraq starting on 20 March 2003 by an invasion force led by the United States. It was followed by a longer phase of fighting, in which an insurgency emerged to oppose the occupying forces and the newly formed Iraqi government.
XI. Again, the crusades continue on with the rise of the ISIL ISIS Caliphate Vs. The Christian Crusader Roman Catholic Peshmerga and other Christian branches included in the NATO alliance current date. (What is the Levant? The Islamic State of Iraq and the Levant (ISIL; Arabic: الدولة الإسلامية في العراق والشام), also known as the Islamic State of Iraq and Syria (ISIS, /ˈaɪsɨs/) or the Islamic State of Iraq and ash-Sham, Daesh (داعش, Arabic pronunciation: [ˈdaːʕiʃ]), or Islamic State (IS), is a Salafi jihadist extremist militant group.)

Narrative

There is record of the Caliphate and of the militant organization in a risen apocalyptic ideology every one-thousand years since before Christ existed, the groups acts have surely been global terror and certainly un-Godly evil unto humanities morality. This has been to empower their own dark faith, and the human blood of the Jihad is what is spent, which also re-empowers the black X of Islamabad and / or the Islamic black hex which requires human blood. The Roman Catholics have endured a brunt of criticism of the historical Apostolic Age and of the birth of the Holy Roman Apostolic Catholic Christian Church. However, I find the filtering process of the lesser of the evils marked through the events during the changes in historical times both biblical of the Holy Ghost and apocalyptic evolving hereunto the indoctrination of faith by the teachings of Lord King Jesus Christ into Christianity. The Romans have been repelling this oppressive Caliphate since B.C. and continue. By this Messiah Jesus Christ and His resurrection there is the Holy Roman Apostolic Catholic Christian Church now of the oldest branches of the one Church of Jesus Christ our Lord King and Savior.

Chapter 13

Mark of The Beast

Will you accept the mark of the beast? Without it, you will not be able to buy or sell. With it, you will suffer the plagues of Revelation. What should you do?

There has been much speculation about the mark of the beast mentioned in Revelation. What do you need to know about this mysterious mark?

It seems that no subject has intrigued, and baffled people more than this mysterious mark spoken of in the book of Revelation. Many books have been written and many sermons have been preached about this subject. Scholars and theologians have offered many different ideas about it. Some suggest it is a microchip implanted in one's forehead or an invisible mark or a visible mark. Some even think it could be one's credit card or debit card. But what does the Bible reveal about this puzzling mark?

The key passage reads: "He causes all, both small and great, rich and poor, free and slave, to receive a mark on their right hand or on their foreheads, and that no one may buy or sell except one who has the mark or the name of the beast, or the number of his name" (Revelation 13:16-17).

If one does not have this identifying sign, he or she will not be able to legally transact business. This person will find it difficult to earn a living, to hold a job or to run a business.

Beast of Revelation

John, the one God chose to write down the book of Revelation, saw a vision of the future. Here is what he wrote concerning this beast: "Then I stood on the sand of the sea. And I saw a beast rising up out of the sea, having seven heads and ten horns, and on his horns ten crowns, and on his heads a blasphemous name. Now the beast which I saw was like a leopard, his feet were like the feet of a bear, and his mouth like the mouth of a lion. The dragon gave him his power, his throne, and great authority" (Revelation 13:1).

To understand what this beast in the book of Revelation is, we need to begin in Daniel 7:1-8, where we find the imagery of four animals, representing the four great historical empires. These were a lion (Babylon), a bear (Persia), and a leopard (Greece) and a fourth beast (Rome).

It is this fourth beast described by Daniel and recorded by John that would have "ten horns" and receive a "deadly wound" before rising again before the end of this age (Daniel 7:7-8; Revelation 13:3). This empire is the "beast" of the book of Revelation. We should note that the human leader of this revived empire is also referred to as "the beast" (Revelation 19:20). The mark of the beast is the mark or identifying sign of this empire.

The book of Revelation explains that the dragon gives the beast its power and authority. This dragon is Satan the devil (Revelation 12:9; Revelation 20:2). Satan uses this beast to rule and deceive the world.

A Second Beast

Let's now turn our attention to the word "he" in Revelation 13:16. The passage says, "He causes all … to receive a mark." Who is "he"? Verse 11 says, "Then I saw another beast coming up out of the earth, and he had two horns like a lamb and spoke like a dragon."

These characteristics indicate a false religious leader who "causes the earth and those who dwell in it to worship the first beast" (verse 12). This second beast is called the "false prophet" (Revelation 19:20). This mark or sign represents a final revival of the Roman Empire at the time of the end. The religious leader that supports the beast "causes" people to accept it.

Mark of Disobedience to God

The mark of the beast will separate people into two groups. One group will accept the mark and the other group will reject it.

The apostle John writes, "Then a third angel followed them, saying with a loud voice, 'If anyone worships the beast and his image, and receives his mark on his forehead or on his hand, he himself shall also drink of the wine of the wrath of God, which is poured out full strength into the cup of His indignation. He shall be tormented with fire and brimstone in the presence of the holy angels and in the presence of the Lamb'" (Revelation 14:9-10).

This shows great suffering will come on those who receive this mark of the beast.

In verse 12 we see the group of people who do not receive this mark. "Here is the patience of the saints; here are those who keep the commandments of God and the faith of Jesus." This is speaking of the saints of God. In instructing the ancient Israelites how to observe the Days of Unleavened Bread, God said this act of obedience to His law would "be as a sign to you on your hand" (Exodus 13:9).

The mark of the beast thus represents disobedience to Gods commandments and rejection of the faith of Jesus. The book of Revelation says that those who receive the mark will be subject to the seven last plagues, while the obedient saints are described as having attained "victory over the beast" (Revelation 15:2). These faithful people will be given eternal life and reign with Christ at His second coming (Revelation 20:4).

Mark of The Beast

As we have already seen, this specific sign determines who may officially transact business. One who has this identifying sign will be able to "buy and sell." The Bible clearly explains the financial repercussions that will come based upon whether one has this mark or not.

We also note that there is one commandment of God that is often intricately connected to one's ability to do business and that identifies Gods people. Of Gods 10 Commandments, the Fourth Commandment is the one most likely to affect one's ability to work, earn a living and do business. The command says, "Remember the Sabbath day, to keep it holy. Six days you shall labor and do all your work, but the seventh day is the Sabbath of the Lord your God" (Exodus 20:8-10).

Most people think it does not make any difference what day one observes, but it does to God. In this age, it takes the "faith of Jesus" to avoid working on the Sabbath and to keep it holy.

A Mark in The Bible

The Greek word charagma in Revelation 14:9 means "a scratch or etching, that is, stamp (as a badge of servitude)" (Strong's Hebrew and Greek Dictionaries). A mark is thus a brand or sign of identification.

The Sabbath is called a "sign" between God and His people in the Bible (Exodus 31:13, 17; Ezekiel 20:12). It identifies Gods people as being sanctified or set apart by God. Jesus said, "The Sabbath was made for man, and not man for the Sabbath. Therefore, the Son of Man is also Lord of the Sabbath" (Mark 2:27-28). The Sabbath today is still a commandment and an identifying sign of Gods people.

Another occasion of marking or identifying people is found in the book of Ezekiel where God tells the prophet, "Go through the midst of the city, through the midst of Jerusalem, and put a mark on the foreheads of the men who sigh and cry over all the abominations that are done within it" (Ezekiel 9:4). This mark identified those who obeyed God and mourned over the sins of the city.

Location of The Mark

The account in Revelation says those who receive the mark of the beast will receive it "on their right hand or on their foreheads" (Revelation 13:16). Many people think it will be some kind of physical mark in or on one's skin, and this certainly could be. Yet because the book of Revelation employs many symbols, we must also consider the possibility that these references to the "right hand" and "forehead" are symbolic.

The right hand can represent our actions, works and labor. The forehead can symbolize the inner beliefs, the intellect and what is in the mind. The mark of the beast is thus related to what we believe in our mind and what we do with our hands. Compare this with Deuteronomy 6:8, where God commanded ancient Israel to bind the commandments "as a sign on your hand, and … as frontlets between your eyes."

The connection between our thoughts and our actions is a good explanation of faith. In the Bible the real "faith of Jesus" has two parts, belief and acting in faith on those beliefs.

God Our Own Free Will Decision

gives those who read the Bible and believe the Scriptures a clear choice. May we all hold to and practice the faith of Jesus and keep the commandments of God. This is the choice we must make in order to avoid the mark of the beast and to receive eternal life in the family of God.

Narrative

The Bible says the mark of the beast will be forced on an unsuspecting world before the return of Jesus Christ. This world will not realize it is following the teachings of a false religious system. From reading scripture there is a relevant truth even enchantment of the strength of Messiah Jesus Christ with unification by the Holy Ghost. By this understanding of the covenants of God explained in another part of this writing, the covenant held in the Passion of the Christ is held by Abba Father Yahweh God Jehovah. We can have faith in this covenant, this is held by Him this covenant will not be broken. The Church is lovingly loved by Rabbi Priest Savior Jesus Christ Messiah as the Unleavened New lump born again risen in Him. Thereunto, we shall not fear so greatly being we are held in the arms of Rabbi Jesus Christ Messiah. Amen

Armageddon

Armageddon (from Ancient Greek: Ἁρμαγεδών Harmagedōn, Late Latin: Armagedōn) will be, according to the Book of Revelation, the site of a battle during the end times, variously interpreted as either a literal or symbolic location. The term is also used in a generic sense to refer to any end of the world scenario.

The word "Armageddon" appears only once in the Greek New Testament, in Revelation 16:16. The word may come from Hebrew har məgiddô (הר מגידו), meaning "Mountain of Megiddo". "Mount" Megiddo is not actually a mountain, but a tell (a hill created by many generations of people living and rebuilding on the same spot) on which ancient forts were built to guard the Via Maris, an ancient trade route linking Egypt with the Northern Empires of Syria, Anatolia and Mesopotamia. Megiddo was the location of various ancient battles, including one in the 15th century B.C. and one in 609 B.C.

Modern Megiddo is a town approximately 25 miles (40 km) West-Southwest of the Southern tip of the Sea of Galilee in the Kishon River area.

According to one premillennial Christian interpretation, the Messiah will return to earth and defeat the Antichrist (the "beast") and Satan the Devil in the Battle of Armageddon.

Then Satan will be put into the "bottomless pit" or abyss for 1,000 years, known as the Millennium. After being released from the abyss, Satan will gather Gog and Magog (peoples of two specific nations) from the four corners of the earth. They will encamp surrounding the "Holy Ones" and the "Beloved City" (this refers to Jerusalem).

Fire will come down from God, out of Heaven and devour Gog and Magog after the Millennium. The Devil, death, hell, and those not found written in the Book of Life are then thrown into Gehenna (the lake of fire burning with brimstone).

Psalm 91 King James Version (KJV)

"He that dwelleth in the secret place of the most High shall abide under the shadow of the Almighty."

"I will say of the Lord, He is my refuge and my fortress: my God; in him will I trust."

"Surely he shall deliver thee from the snare of the fowler, and from the noisome pestilence."

"He shall cover thee with his feathers, and under his wings shalt thou trust: his truth shall be thy shield and buckler."

"Thou shalt not be afraid for the terror by night; nor for the arrow that flieth by day;"

"Nor for the pestilence that walketh in darkness; nor for the destruction that wasteth at noonday."

"A thousand shall fall at thy side, and ten thousand at thy right hand; but it shall not come nigh thee."

"Only with thine eyes shalt thou behold and see the reward of the wicked."

"Because thou hast made the Lord, which is my refuge, even the most High, thy habitation;"

"There shall no evil befall thee, neither shall any plague come nigh thy dwelling."

"For he shall give his angels charge over thee, to keep thee in all thy ways."

"They shall bear thee up in their hands, lest thou dash thy foot against a stone."

"Thou shalt tread upon the lion and adder: the young lion and the dragon shalt thou trample under feet."

"Because he hath set his love upon me, therefore will I deliver him: I will set him on high, because he hath known my name."

"He shall call upon me, and I will answer him: I will be with him in trouble; I will deliver him, and honour him."

"With long life will I satisfy him and shew him my salvation."

Plagues of The Bible Listed in Order

Natural explanations have been suggested for most of the phenomena

I.   Plague 1 — water turned into blood; fish died.
II.   Plague 2 — frogs.
III.   Plagues 3 and 4 — biting insects and wild animals.
IV.   Plagues 5 and 6 — livestock disease and boils.
V.   Plague 7 — fiery hail.
VI.   Plague 8 — locusts.
VII.   Plague 9 — darkness.

Revelation speaks of seven final plagues that will come upon the earth at the end of this present age. What are these plagues and why will God send them?

"And there were noises and thundering's and lightning's; and there was a great earthquake, such a mighty and great earthquake as had not occurred since men were on the earth" (Revelation 16:18).

In readings we have noted that seven seals, seven trumpets and seven last plagues outline end-time prophetic events recorded in the book of Revelation that will occur before and at the time of Christs return to earth. The first five seals depict consequences for mankind's sinful behaviors and Satan's wrath toward the people of God and mankind in general. The sixth seal announces the soon-to-come wrath of God. The seventh seal includes the wrath of God, which will be dispensed via seven trumpets and seven final plagues.

These seven plagues complete the wrath of God. As John wrote: "Then I saw another sign in heaven, great and marvelous: seven angels having the seven last plagues, for in them the wrath of God is complete" (Revelation 15:1, emphasis added throughout).

We should note that the concept of Gods wrath being "complete," as noted in this passage, applies to the judgment of humans who will live in the end time just before Christs return. It does not mean God cannot or will not punish people for disobedience in the future.

During the Millennium, for example, "Whichever of the families of the earth do not come up to Jerusalem to worship the King, the Lord of hosts, on them there will be no rain. If the family of Egypt will not come up and enter in, they shall have no rain; they shall receive the plague with which the Lord strikes the nations who do not come up to keep the Feast of Tabernacles" (Zechariah 14:17-18).

Bowls of Punishment

Revelation 15:7 describes these seven last plagues as "golden bowls full of the wrath of God" to be poured out upon the earth. Some translations of the Bible, such as the King James Version and Young's Literal Translation, use the word vial instead of bowl in this passage and in Revelation 16:1.

Albert Barnes in his Notes on the Bible states: "The word used here—φιάλη phialē—means properly, 'a bowl or goblet, having more breadth than depth' (Robinson, Lexicon). Our word vial, though derived from this, means rather a thin long bottle of glass, used particularly by apothecaries and druggists. The word would be better rendered by 'bowl' or 'goblet,' and probably the representation here was of such bowls as were used in the temple service. The allusion seems to be to a drinking cup or goblet filled with poison, and given to persons to drink—an allusion drawn from one of the methods of punishment in ancient times" (comments on Revelation 15:7).

Why More Punishment is Necessary

Before considering these seven last plagues, it is important for us to note mankind's response to the seals and trumpets that will precede these last bowls of punishment. In spite of the severity of the pain and suffering that will be inflicted upon earths inhabitants by the seals and trumpets, humanity will still refuse to repent of its sins (Revelation 9:20-21).

Reviewing what will have previously occurred during the seals and trumpets, we note that, in addition to grievous suffering, more than one-fourth of mankind is destined to die via the first four seals, which are also called the four horsemen of the apocalypse (Revelation 6:8). Many more will die during the third trumpet plague (Revelation 8:11), and then a third of the remaining population will die through the sixth trumpet (Revelation 9:15, 18).

Despite these truly apocalyptic horrors, mankind will continue to reject God. They will not worship or obey the Almighty, Eternal Sovereign. Deceived by Satan the devil (Revelation 12:9) through an end-time political and religious power called the "beast," humanity will continue to defy and blaspheme God even as the seven last plagues are poured out (Revelation 16:9, 11, 21).

As the first of the seven last plagues is poured out, we are told that it will come "upon the men who had the mark of the beast and those who worshiped his image" (Revelation 16:2). Note also that the fifth plague repeats that it will be poured out "on the throne of the beast, and his kingdom" (verse 10).

Being part of the end-time political and religious system called the beast will have serious consequences.

The Seven Last Plagues Listed

First plague: The contents of the first bowl will cause painful sores upon those "who had the mark of the beast and those who worshiped his image" (Revelation 16:2).

Second plague: When this bowl is poured out, the sea will become blood and cause all life in it to die (verse 3).

Third plague: After the third angel pours out its bowl, the rivers and springs of water will become blood (verse 4).

Fourth plague: The fourth bowl will cause the sun to become so hot as "to scorch men with fire" (verse 8).

Fifth plague: This punishment will bring darkness, pains and sores (verses 10-11).

Sixth plague: The bowl containing this plague will be poured out on the Euphrates River, causing it to dry up and make land travel easier for the armies of "the kings of the earth and of the whole world" to assemble at Armageddon (the area of Megiddo, which is approximately 18 miles or 30 kilometers southeast of the modern city of Haifa). From this location, the assembled armies will then advance toward Jerusalem for a final battle against Jesus Christ (verses 12-16).

Seventh plague: This final plague will consist of "noises and thundering's and lightning's" and "such a mighty and great earthquake as had not occurred since men were on the earth" (verse 18). Babylon, a powerful false religion, will fall (verse 19, compare Revelation 18:2) and there will be devastating hail, with hailstones weighing up to a "talent"—approximately 100 pounds (verse 21).

Parallels to These Plagues

There are two interesting historical parallels to the seven last plagues.

First, these seven last plagues are typed by some of the punishments God brought upon the nation of Egypt to free the ancient Israelites from slavery. In the 10 plagues preceding the Exodus, water was turned to blood (Exodus 7:17), people had painful "sores" (Exodus 9:9), and the Egyptians experienced darkness for three days (Exodus 10:21-23). There are obvious similarities to these punishments in the seven last plagues (note the first, second, third and fifth plagues above). And just as Pharaoh hardened his heart toward God and His plan, so will the people who experience the seven last plagues harden their hearts against God.

It is also interesting to note that in Revelation 15, which introduces the seven last plagues, we find Gods faithful people singing "the song of Moses" (verse 3), a song composed by Moses after God had brought 10 plagues upon the Egyptians and delivered Israel (Exodus 15:1-19).

Second, the seven last plagues of Revelation 15 and 16 have similarities to the seven trumpets, but with increased intensity. Note that the first four trumpets cause a third of the trees to be burned up, a third of the sea to become blood, a third of the creatures in the sea to die, a third of fresh water to become poisonous and the light of the sun, moon and stars to be diminished by a third (Revelation 8:7-12). The seven last plagues will cause all waters (both in the sea and fresh) to become blood, all life in the sea to die and more darkness (Revelation 16:3, 4, 10).

Why God Punishes People

Some people have the mistaken idea that God is harsh and cruel delighting in making people suffer. But this is most definitely not the reason God will bring these seven last plagues upon mankind.

As our loving Father, God always administers punishment to encourage us to turn from sinful conduct to obedience to His holy and beneficial laws so we can be blessed. Conveying this principle to ancient Israel, God told the prophet Ezekiel: "Say to them, 'As I live,' says the Lord GOD, 'I have no pleasure in the death of the wicked, but that the wicked turn from his way and live. Turn, turn from your evil ways! For why should you die, O house of Israel?'" (Ezekiel 33:11).

Chapter 14

Narrative

This principle that God explained to ancient Israel is true for all peoples, not just Israelites. God loves everyone (John 3:16) Jesus God in the flesh of man experience. And "desires all men to be saved and to come to the knowledge of the truth" (1 Timothy 2:4). This God breathed knowledge Yahweh God in the flesh of man Jesus Christ experience, Abba Father saves. Holy Ghost saves, Jesus saves, Immanuel, God is with us. His Majesty our Lord King Jesus Christ will not be as the world knew Him; our Messianic Christian King Jesus Christ will be in the Glory of His age. Amen

The Rapture of The Second Advent by His Holy Royal Majesty Our Messianic Christian King Jesus Christ Our Lord

In Christianity, the Second Coming of Christ, the Second Advent, sometimes called the Parousia, is the anticipated return of Jesus to Earth. The Second Coming belief is based on prophecies found in the canonical gospels and in most Christian eschatology's. Christians generally believe the anticipated event is predicted in Biblical Messianic Prophecies. Views about the nature of Jesus' Second Coming vary among Christian Denominations and sometimes among individual Christians.

Most English versions of the Nicene Creed in current use include the following beliefs about Jesus: " He ascended into Heaven and is Seated at the Right Hand of the Father. He will come again in glory to judge the living and the dead, and His Kingdom will have no end. We look for the resurrection of the dead, and the life of the world to come."

According to some bible scholars, prophetic scriptures seem to speak of two separate events— the Rapture and the Second Coming of Christ.

The Rapture will occur when Jesus Christ returns for his Church. This is when all True Believers in Christ will be taken from the earth by God into Heaven (1 Corinthians 15:51-52; 1Thessalonians 4:16-17).

The Second Coming is when Jesus Christ returns with the Church to defeat the antichrist, overthrow evil and then establish His thousand-year reign (Revelation19:11-16).

I.) Meeting in the air - versus - returning with Him

In the Rapture, Believers meet the Lord in the air.

> 1 Thessalonians 4:16-17

"For the Lord Himself will come down from heaven, with a loud command, with the voice of the archangel and with the trumpet call of God, and the dead in Christ will rise first. After that, we who are still alive and are left will be caught up together with them in the clouds to meet the Lord in the air. And so, we will be with the Lord forever." (NIV)

In the Second Coming, Believers return with the Lord.

> Revelation 19:14

"The Armies of Heaven were following Him, riding on white horses and dressed in fine linen, white and clean." (NIV)

II.) Before Tribulation - versus - after Tribulation

The Rapture will happen before the Tribulation.

> 1 Thessalonians 5:9
> Revelation 3:10

The Second Coming will happen at the end of the Tribulation.

> Revelation 6-19

III.) Deliverance - versus - judgment

In the Rapture believers are taken from the earth by God as an act of deliverance.

> 1 Thessalonians 4:13-17
> 1 Thessalonians 5:9

In the Second Coming unbelievers are removed from the earth by God as an act of judgment.

> Revelation 3:10
> Revelation 19:11-21

IV.) Hidden - versus - seen by all,

The Rapture, according to scripture, will be an instantaneous, hidden event.

> 1 Corinthians 15:50-54

The Second Coming, according to scripture, will be seen by everyone.

> Revelation 1:7

V.) At any moment - verses - only after certain events

The Rapture could happen at any moment.

> 1 Corinthians 15:50-54
> Titus 2:13
> 1 Thessalonians 4:14-18

The Second Coming will not happen until certain events take place.

- ➢ 2 Thessalonians 2:4
- ➢ Matthew 24:15-30
- ➢ Revelation 6-18

Narrative

Noting it is common in Christian theology that there are conflicting views regarding the Rapture and the Second Advent. One source of confusion over these two end times' events comes from the verses found in Matthew Chapter 24. While speaking of the end of the age, this chapter references both the Rapture and the Second Coming. Also, it is important for us as Believers to perform in the Will of God actively as Disciples who were of the first twelve, who have so well delivered their Epistles in the building of the Church of Jesus Christ Messiah Lord and Savior. In addition, it is important to be aware of the purpose of Rabbi Christ the Messiahs teaching for Believers to be watchful and live each day as though Rabbi Christ the Messiahs return is imminent. The message is clearly spoken, we must not tread through this final stretch unsober staggering as an apostasy in a Laodicean complacency. The signs and the symbols of the end of this age of a sinful world and the signs and symbols by prophecy of the Chosen Prophets of the Holy Bible unveiling truth of the second coming, this being His Age of the return of Rabbi Jesus Christ the Messiah. Listening to the Church ordained administrative staff is recommended, these are the persons current day chosen to serve Messiah Rabbi Jesus Christs' Administration.

The Three Pillars of The First Century Christian Church

"And when James, Peter, and John, who seemed to be pillars," (Galatians 2:9)

The Apostle Paul recognized that James, Peter and John were "pillars" in the church. The dictionary defines a pillar as a column of support in a building or a person of authority. While these men certainly were a supporting authority in the early church, they also represent the three pillars of foundational doctrine that are vital to the spiritual health of the believer.

It is a sad, Biblical fact that when the original anointed leadership of the church dies out the people begin to fall away. We see this happening shortly after Joshua's death (Judges 2) and the same was true of the early Christians. After the first century, the church slowly began the long descent into the prophesied apostasy, (II Timothy 4:3.) While there have been revivals and reformation along the way, they are always needed and God is always calling His remnant back to her foundation.

When the church falls away from the Word of God, it falls into apostasy. The Word of God is amazingly simple, and the Apostles were the expositors that were ordained by God to explain His message. John, Peter and James were the ones that were handpicked by God to be foundational pillars of the church. When we begin to place others above these first foundational leaders' apostasy is not very far behind.

What about the Apostle Paul? Paul was called directly by God and after a time in Arabia returned to the Apostles to receive confirmation that what he had received from the Lord was correct. Paul's doctrine is based on the original three pillars of doctrine and Paul is a similitude of the believer who is called and receives his confirmation directly from the Word of God and does not divert from its authority.

In the book of Ezekiel chapters forty through forty-two, is a detailed description of Ezekiel's vision of a temple. In chapter forty-three we are told this is Gods building. God tells Ezekiel that the people have placed the "setting of their threshold by My thresholds, and their posts by My posts," (verse eight). In this verse God tells Ezekiel that His people have defiled His work "by their abominations."

Gods work, His building in Ezekiel's vision is symbolic of God's Word, His pattern, His design which has been defiled by the addition of posts and thresholds of doctrine and practices that were never part of Gods original message to His people.

God brought great judgments upon Israel when they diverted from their purpose. It was vital that they remained holy and separated to their God, for they were the womb through which God would birth our Messiah, Jesus. It is also vital for the present-day church to remain separated and holy in order to bring a credible witness to the Gospel in these last days.

We fall into apostasy when we fail to cleave to the foundational pillars of the first century church and in order to hold on to them, we need to understand exactly what they are.

The pillars themselves are grounded firmly upon the foundation of our Lord Jesus, the Messiah. The first pillar represented by the Apostle, John, is the first to emerge from this foundation. John's doctrine emphasizes the Gospel of love. "For God so loved the world that He gave His only Son that whoever believes in Him should not perish but have everlasting life," (John 3:16.) It is the gospel of Gods forgiving grace and mercy.

The Gospel is the purpose of the church; without it we have no church and no reason to exist. The church or individual Christian that allows the Gospel to take second place to anything else is a church that has made the first step toward apostasy. The Gospel of the first century emphasized repentance and faith in the blood atonement through a thorough understanding of the Messiahs role as outlined in the Old Testament. The Apostles did not have yet the Gospels in writing when they first began to preach. They preached from seeing Jesus in the Old Testament and lived the fulfillment of it in the New. The plan of salvation was the same. We are saved by repentance and faith in blood atonement, for without the shedding of blood there can be no remission of sins (Leviticus 17:11.)

Salvation in the Old Testament was never achieved by legalistic works. The law was always accompanied by the provision for the forgiveness of sins through repentance and atonement as outlined in the plan of the Tabernacle that was given to Moses along with the Ten Commandments.

In the New Testament, The Old Testament sacrifices had been replaced and fulfilled in the onetime offering of the Lamb of God. Now in the fulfillment of the Divine Plan, God Himself is joined to the believer through the blood of Jesus by His Holy Spirit - Hereby we know that we dwell in Him, and He in us, because He has given us of His Spirit (I John 4:13) - and we have access to God the Father by One Spirit (Ephesians 2:18.) This union with God through His Son produces the fruit of a changed life, as we "Abide in the Vine," (John 15:4.)

When the Gospel is presented according to the pattern contained in the Scriptures, it produces within the true believer a conversion of heart, for without a genuine repentance, there cannot be a genuine change.

Out of this "conversion of heart" arises the second pillar represented by the Apostle Peter. Peters Epistles directs us to an understanding of the 'Divine Nature,' (II Peter 1:4) a God – breathed holiness, void of legalism, and a willing separation or cleaving to God.

A reformed life is the evidence of a genuine response to the Gospel. A church that does not emphasize a God produced holiness as the result of the Gospel is a church that is opening the door to the apostasy of compromise. It is a church that is not concerned with the inner reformation of the believer and cannot produce disciples or reproducers of the faith. A God breathed holiness produces people who adorn the Gospel of Christ with credibility. The testimony of their lives glorifies God and draws people to Jesus.

The third pillar arises naturally, because those who have been so transformed practice a living faith that serves others as the Holy Spirit will lead them to do. The Holy Spirit is the "leaven" in these souls that causes them to rise and be seen as living testimonies of the new life that is operating inside of them.

James' Epistle and this third pillar characterizes the fruit of a genuine response to the first two pillars. A genuine faith will serve or "work," because faith without works is a dead faith, (James 2:17.) A Christian in whom the living Christ abides will possess the compassion that naturally will reach out to serve those in need. In summary, the church that is not based on the three pillars of Christianity is a church in apostasy.

The three pillars are the Gospel, Holiness and Service. Each one must be well balanced and supported by the other. For example, if a church emphasizes holiness without an equal view of the Gospel of Grace, then we get a church whose service is tainted with legalism. If we serve without holiness, we breed hypocrisy and discredit our witness. If we diminish the Gospel of repentance, atonement, and holiness we end up with a liberal apostate church whose service will never bear fruit that can be pleasing to God.

If the Gospel that is being preached is not producing changed lives zealous to serve, it is not the gospel of the Bible. If the Gospel is preached without Biblical repentance, it will not produce changed lives. If the Gospel is preached without the Biblical pillar of holiness it will produce compromise. If the Gospel is preached without the Biblical pillar of a call to serve, it will produce the stupor of a Laodicean complacency. Without these fundamental pillars of doctrine, we will find that the church has fallen into the deception of preaching another Gospel that our founding Apostles did not preach.

The pillars of our faith were eyewitnesses and handled the word of Glory, Jesus, (II Peter 1:16.) It is wisdom to cling to the support these Apostles offer and if we do so we can be assured we will not fall away into apostasy and the work we are building for God will stand fully supported and secure for eternity.

Chapter 15

Building of The House of The Lord That There Will be no Breaches in The House of God

Narrative

Song of Solomon, (Love 1:2) The Song of Songs is a song about Love, marital love between a man and a woman. The two principal characters, the lover and the beloved, openly talk about all aspects of their love, especially the physical. Their love is exclusive, spontaneous, and unquenchable. Since both the Old and New Testament use marriage to depict Gods relationship with his people, the message of this book can help develop our relationship with God. As well, this message of love was reinforced in great emphases by Lord King Jesus Christ Messiah and Savior through His ministry in the building of His beloved Church formed of the faith of Believers in Him. Amen

Song of Songs

As it is written in scripture; We have a divine and loving God whom we are created in the image of; There is a someone somewhere that no matter how you are perceived by anybody else that one divine individual will view you as a (Song of Songs 1: 2) "Let Him kiss me with the kisses of His mouth – for your love is more delightful than wine."

Our Lord is the glowing light of divinity; ministry of His Holy Royal Majesty our Christian King Jesus Christ our Lord; (Jeremiah 29:11) "For I know the thoughts that I think toward you, saith Jehovah, thoughts of peace, and not of evil, to give you hope in your latter end".

Narrative

Building a relationship with the Lord is a process we are here to experience before we make our way into the heavenly realms. This relationship is achieved through the process of sanctification where we as faithful believers in Him Rabbi Christ Messiah must first give Him due acknowledgement with gratitude for the many blessings and grace Lord King Christ has given freely and lovingly onto us in the forming of the Church of Christ.

Acknowledgement With Gratitude in The Process of Sanctification

Gratitude unlocks the fullness of life. It turns what we have into enough, and more. It turns denial into acceptance, chaos to order, confusion to clarity. It can turn a meal into a feast, a house into a home, a stranger into a friend. Gratitude makes sense of our past, brings peace for today, and creates a vision for tomorrow.

I used to spend so much time reacting and responding to everyone else that my life had no direction. Other people's lives, problems, and wants set the course for my life. Once I realized it was okay for me to think about and identify what I wanted, remarkable things began to take place in my life.

Make New Year's goals. Dig within and discover what you would like to have happen in your life this year. This helps you do your part. It is an affirmation that you are interested in fully living life in the year to come.

Goals give us direction. They put a powerful force into play on a universal, conscious, and subconscious level. Goals give our life direction.

What would you like to have happen in your life this year? What would you like to do, to accomplish? What good would you like to attract into your life? What areas of growth would you like to have happen to you? What blocks, or character defects, would you like to have removed?

What would you like to attain? Little things and big things? Where would you like to go? What would you like to have happen in friendship and love? What would you like to have happen in your family life?

What problems would you like to see solved? What decisions would you like to make? What would you like to happen in your career?

The New Year stands before us, like a chapter in a book, waiting to be written. We can help write that story by setting goals.

The plan will happen in spite of us, not because of us.

Furthermore, worrying about people and problems does not help. It does not solve problems, it doesn't help other people, and it doesn't help us. It is wasted energy.

It is consciously perceived and so decided that sooner or later you had to learn to live without almost everybody, at least for a while. Even people you did not think you could live without. Love always found itself again, like it or not, I was already learning that in the worst and darkest time, I would find specks of light, moments of joy. What I did not want to learn was the other, harsher lesson - that in life's brightest moments there would also be unbearable pain.

You do not blast a heart open, you coax and nurture it open, like the sun does to a rose. The lesson I was learning involved the idea that I could feel compassion for people without acting on it. Codependents are reactionaries. They overreact. They under-react. But rarely do they act. They react to the problems, pains, lives, and behaviors of others. They react to their own problems, pains, and behaviors. I trust so much in the power of the heart and the soul; I know that the answer to what we need to do next is in our own hearts. All we must do is listen, then take that one step further and trust what we hear. (Isaiah 30:21) "Whether you turn to the right or to the left, your ears will hear a voice behind you, saying, "This is the way; walk in it".

We will be taught what we need to learn. I have been talked with while in briefings that I am reckless or even fly in where angels fear to tread. However, I learned who I am. And I know I am blessed. Further, the mission objective is fully completed. Or all one thousand five hundred forty-four flight missions were fully completed successfully. Therefore, I have chosen to witness of Him Lord and Savior Jesus Christ. Also, the gospel, holiness, and service to the Church in supporting His words scripture of the Holy Bible. As well, supporting the Bible is a true book. And how to effectively apply scripture. A true quote: "we made it somehow." This was the quote from a believer who understands the Christian Church is formed of each individual believer of each Christian denomination in hole forming the body of our Christian Church of Christ the Incarnation King Jesus Christ who has been resurrected and who is coming again. Of each denomination formed of believer's servers of the Holy King Christs personal divisions. Each individual Christian denomination by their faithful division too our Christian King Jesus Christ will be issued their individual orders from His Holy Royal Majesty our Christian King Lord Jesus Christ.

One perception I am certain of, a Divine and Greater Being. This Greater Divine Being is nothing lesser than a brilliant, artistic creator of genius innovations. This is simpler than it could sound for it is not a manmade theory such as pie times pie divided by pie equals pie. No! This pure and utter creative creativity from a Divine Creator who is the genius of creation, a creative genius who is an artist of both gifted artists who are a gifted genius.

Simply, because to be an artist you must be gifted, whether you are an artist of music, or crafts, or a teacher, and to be a genius you must be a gifted genius who is also an artist who has the gifted genius of artistic creation. It does sound as grooving with the Lord indeed!

Make a new goal to complete a mission assignment; evaluate, perceive, improvise, adjust, adapt, and overcome. Do all of this through God and Gods glory will shine through you.

We are in a circle of life designed by the most genius artist. A cathedral our world our universe artistically designed by the genius of all artistic creative genius for us to grow in, a work in progress and fully educate in, and one day graduate from. Graduate from, into the artistic creative genius of divinity itself, (the Image of our Divine God). It is when we progress or de-progress to the maximum level in color which is either dark or of light and nothing in-between (a Laodicean complacency) there is no grey, we will be evaluated as ready or never ready enough. At this point we will all graduate from this Cathedral. We will be either graduated with a pass of light Divinity of our Lord God. Or we will graduate with a pass of dark a total failure who did not reach too Divinity with gratitude to our Lord God. (Luke 11:35) "Take heed therefore that the light which is in thee be not darkness". To graduate by the passing of the light of God, practice of these four virtues will assist. Practice an act of faith in being humble, patient gracious.

To graduate with the pass of light achieving divinity there are many artistic genius creations within the cathedral. It is our own free will to choose which method with gratitude. (Matthew 17:20) "And Jesus said unto them, Because of your unbelief: for verily I say unto you, if ye have faith as a grain of mustard seed, ye shall say unto this mountain, remove hence to yonder place; and it shall remove; and nothing shall be impossible unto you".

A quote of the Special Forces; "Nothing ever remains the same, each moment we either allow ourselves to become worse, or each moment we strive to become better. It is only then when we strive to improve ourselves that we then become better." Although, you do not need to be in the Special Forces to reach with gratitude to the Divinity of our Divine Lord to become Divine in the Image of our Divine God.

Three primary teachings from the Ministry of Christ to the Apostles delivered in their Epistle: "love, forgiveness, and faith". The Incarnation of the Lord our Christ is our Divine Christian King. The only virgin our God ever needed our God appointed Immaculate Conception of The Virgin Mary Mother of Our Incarnation Messianic Christian King Jesus Christ Messiah.

The place we are in however putrid or great is only temporary here in this world of corruption, pollution, darkness of evil, sin, and imbalance of Gods balance in the beauty of creation. Here this corrupt world we reside in a war of the lesser of the evils filtering to the better of the good those who are of the eternal death or of the eternal living in Christ Jesus this is a war of people's souls' eternal placement the most serious on-going interview indeed epic even if I may so shrewdly proclaim. A war between our God and the fallen dark angel Satan. The battle ground earth. Our God is not looking for virgin recruits. Our God is looking for battle hardened Believers. Choose a method provided in the Cathedral and meet God, become better reaching too divinity with gratitude in becoming better. This is most highly recommended by this author of faith.

Testimony About God

(1 Corinthians 2)

"And so, it was with me, brothers and sisters. When I came to you, I did not come with eloquence or human wisdom as I proclaimed to you the testimony about God."" For I resolved to know nothing while I was with you except Jesus Christ and Him crucified." "I came to you in weakness with great fear and trembling." "My message and my preaching were not with wise and persuasive words, but with a demonstration of the Spirit's power," "so that your faith might not rest on human wisdom, but on God's power."

Gods Wisdom Revealed by The Spirit

"We do, however, speak a message of wisdom among the mature, but not the wisdom of this age or of the rulers of this age, who are coming to nothing." "No, we declare God's wisdom, a mystery that has been hidden and that God destined for our glory before time began." "None of the rulers of this age understood it, for if they had, they would not have crucified the Lord of glory." "However, as it is written: What no eye has seen, what no ear has heard, and what no human mind has conceived the things God has prepared for those who love Him." "These are the things God has revealed to us by his Spirit."

"The Spirit searches all things, even the deep things of God." "For who knows a person's thoughts except their own spirit within them? In the same way no one knows the thoughts of God except the Spirit of God." "What we have received is not the spirit of the world, but the Spirit who is from God, so that we may understand what God has freely given us." "This is what we speak, not in words taught us by human wisdom but in words taught by the Spirit, explaining spiritual realities with Spirit-taught words." "The person without the Spirit does not accept the things that come from the Spirit of God but considers them foolishness and cannot understand them because they are spiritually discerned." "The person with the Spirit makes judgments about all things, but such a person is not subject to any human judgments," "for, who has known the mind of the Lord that he may instruct Him? But we have the mind of Christ."

Lord And in His Mighty Power

The Armor of God

(Ephesians 6:10-18)

"Finally, be strong in the Lord and in his mighty power." "Put on the full armor of God, so that you can take your stand against the devil's schemes." "For our struggle is not against flesh and blood, but against the rulers, against the authorities, against the powers of this dark world and against the spiritual forces of evil in the heavenly realms." "Therefore, put on the full armor of God, so that when the day of evil comes, you may be able to stand your ground, and after you have done everything, to stand." "Stand firm then, with the belt of truth buckled around your waist, with the breastplate of righteousness in place," "and with your feet fitted with the readiness that comes from the gospel of peace." "In addition to all this, take up the shield of faith, with which you can extinguish all the flaming arrows of the evil one." "Take the helmet of salvation and the sword of the Spirit, which is the word of God."

"And pray in the Spirit on all occasions with all kinds of prayers and requests. With this in mind, be alert and always keep on praying for all the Lord's people."

Chapter 16

Three Supporting Factors: "The Holy Bible is a True Book,"

- ➢ The Ark is Located
- ➢ The Christian Church of Jesus Christ Lord King Savior Messiah is Built
- ➢ Usage of The Application of Scripture in Faith is Achieved

Summary Noah's Ark

The Ark of Noah is located and undergoing carful excavation. The Bible says that around 4,400 years ago God sent a world-wide flood upon the earth and had a man named Noah build a large boat (Ark) to save his family and the animals. God gave Noah the exact dimensions of the Ark for two reasons: I.) Obviously Noah could not know how large it must be to hold all of the animals (no doubt small, young specimens), and importantly for us the second reason II.) So that future generations who found the Ark could verify the measurements to know it is one and the same boat.

Many people believe that Noah's Ark should be up on Mt. Ararat in Eastern Turkey, and many have looked there over the years because they think the Bible says it is on that mountain. But does it really? Let us look at the Bible verse in question:

"The ark came to rest on the mountains of Ararat." (Genesis 8:4)

Ararat is the newer Armenian name of Urartu from the Hebrew Torah written by Moses (C. 1406-1446 B.C.) which only included the consonants "rrt". However, the translators of the Bible replaced the "rrt" with the later name, "Ararat" or "Armenia." The Assyrians wrote about battles against the Urartian tribes from the thirteenth century B.C. until the sixth century B.C. when Urartu was destroyed by the Medes. The name Urartu then vanished from history (until archaeologists re-discovered it in the 1800s) and was replaced by Ararat and Armenia in the vicinity as well as in English Bible translations, maps, etc. As history went on in the first and second millennia A.D., the mountain became known as Ararat and the region as Armenia. Many people believe that Mount Ararat is the place where Noah's Ark landed but the Bible does not state this. It simply says that the boat landed in the Urartian Mountains, of which there are hundreds, although Ararat is the highest and is the only one with a permanent ice cap, which is around 17 square miles in size. Since Mount Ararat is the highest location in Urartu, some people in recent history have jumped to the conclusion that it was the landing place and promoted that concept as a regional tradition. It is quite possible that at the time of the Arks landing, Mt. Ararat was still a baby volcano. So, there is no special reason to think it is on that mountain.

Historical Narrative Noah's Ark

In Flavius Josephus' time (1st-century A.D.) the Ark of Noah was well-known because he mentions in Antiquities of the Jews. The famous Jewish historian stated, "Its remains are shown there by the inhabitants to this day." He quotes Berosus the Chaldean, C. 290 B.C., who indicated tourists would take home pieces of the ark for making good-luck charms, "It is said there is still some part of this ship in Armenia, at the mountain of the Cordyaeans; and that some people carry off pieces of the bitumen, which they take away, and use chiefly as amulets for the averting of mischiefs." These comments tend to indicate its location would not be in an inaccessible area. At some point, the ark was covered by a mud and lava flow which caused future generations to lose its location.

Noah's Ark vs. The Great Flood

Noah's Ark was discovered in May of 1948 by a local Kurdish shepherd boy named Reshit Sarihan, who last known (Sep. 2000), to reside in the village of üzengili (previously called "Nasar" but changed to üzengili after the ark was discovered. One should take note that "Nisir" was the Babylonian name for Noah's city). Heavy rains in May of 1948, combined with three noteworthy earthquakes exposed the ark impression from the collapsing, expansive and loose mud that had entrapped it for nearly 2 thousand years revealing the ark impression standing up, out of the terrain.

It is believed the Ark landed higher up the mountain and has since slid down, probably more than once. Based on the evidence, and the shape of the mountain, precisely how the ark would have landed on Mt. Cudi pronounced "Judi" (the "mountain of the Kurds" "kHuD" meaning, in Hebrew, "the first." The slightly crescent shape of the island (mountain) keeps the ark from being washed around by fast currents. The Ark sits in a mud flow today. It originally came to rest higher on the mountain after the Flood. At some point in the first two thousand years of resting in the mountains of Ararat, the ark moved further down the mountain and became impaled on a rock outcropping where it rests today.

The ark rests on Cesnakidag Mountain, which is interpreted as "Doomsday" Mountain. The Flood would be considered a real "doomsday" since it destroyed the world. The mountain is made of sedimentary cretaceous water laid rock, which means it was formed by the Flood waters and is not a post Flood formation.

The Turkish government has double verified the discovery. The announcement appeared in Turkey's largest newspaper on June 21, 1987. The area was first designated a National Park, and then it was upgraded to the status of a National Treasure. The government has built a visitors' center overlooking the site and issued official tourist brochures so people of all races can come and see the ark!

God told Noah the exact size to make the Ark, obviously for two reasons: I.) Noah could not know how large it must be to hold all of the animals (no doubt younger, smaller specimens), and importantly for us the second reason II.) So that future generations who found the Ark could verify the measurements to know it is one and the same boat.

"Make a ship of gopher wood. You shall make rooms in the ship and shall seal it inside and outside with pitch. This is how you shall make it. The length of the ship will be three hundred cubits, its breadth fifty cubits, and its height thirty cubits. You shall make a roof in the ship, and you shall finish it to a cubit upward. You shall set the door of the ship in its side. You shall make it with lower, second, and third levels." (Genesis 6:14-16)

The length of the ark hulk is 515 ft., which is exactly 300 Egyptian cubits (20.6 inches). The sides have splayed outwards, as we would expect on a 4,500-year-old boat hulk. Moses was schooled in Egypt and was not familiar with the Hebrew cubit which was not even in existence when Moses wrote Genesis. So, the length exactly matches the Holy Bible. Of course, this is just what we should expect. The Holy Bible is true as it is written in scripture.

Sub-surface Radar scans show a regular pattern of timbers inside the ark formation, revealing keels, keelsons, gunnels, bulkheads, animal chambers, ramp system, door in right front, two large barrels in the front 14' x 24', and an open center area for air flow to all three levels.

12 Drogue Stones were discovered uphill in 1977. Some have 8 crosses and other depictions of the 8 people who were on the Ark. Many other supporting details exist including manmade iron brackets with rivets and hot struck indented pins all over the formation in the strengthening hull structure.

Best example of many metallic rivets found. Contains high tech metal alloy, as proven by separate lab analyses. Aluminum metal and titanium metal was found in the fittings which are manmade metals.

In addition, petrified coral found at 6,500 feet in elevation at the formation with a smooth flat backside that shows that it was attached to an object that was not natural.

Drogue stones were a feature of ancient ships and were the ancient equivalent of a storm anchor. They have been found in the Nile and elsewhere in the Mediterranean area, and like the stones found, they are heavy and flat with a hole for connecting a line at one end. Their purpose was to create drag in the water or along shallow sandy bottoms: the stone was attached to one end of a boat, and the drag produced would cause the bow or stern to face into the wind and the oncoming wind-blown waves. These anchor stones are found near the Ark site (a few kilometers), no doubt cut loose by Noah as he approached land.

Narrative Noah's Ark

I. It is in the shape of a boat, with a pointed bow and rounded stern.
II. Exact length as noted in biblical description, 515 feet or 300 Egyptian cubits. (Egyptian not Hebrew cubit would have been known to Moses who studied in Egypt then wrote Genesis.)
III. It rests on a mountain in Eastern Turkey, matching the biblical account, "The ark rested upon the mountains of Ararat" (Genesis 8:4). (Ararat being the name of the ancient country Urartu which covered this region.)
IV. Contains petrified wood, as proven by lab analysis.
V. Contains high-tech metal alloy fittings, as proven by separate lab analyses. Aluminum metal and titanium metal was found in the fittings which are man-made metals.
VI. Vertical rib timbers on its sides, comprising the skeletal superstructure of a boat. Regular patterns of horizontal and vertical deck support beams are also seen on the deck of the ark.
VII. Occupied ancient village at the ark site at 6,500 ft. elevation matching Flavius Josephus' statement "Its remains are shown there by the inhabitants to this day."
VIII. Archaeologist found an ancient pottery sherd within 20 yards of the ark which has a carving on it that depicts a bird, a fish, and a man with a hammer wearing a headdress that has the name "Noah" on it. In ancient times these items were created by the locals in the village to sell to visitors of the ark. The ark was a tourist attraction in ancient times and today.

IX. Recognized by Turkish Government as Noah's Ark National Park and a National Treasure. Official notice of its discovery appeared in the largest Turkish newspaper in 1987.

X. Visitors' center built by the government to accommodate tourists further confirms the importance of the site.

XI. Huge anchor stones were found near the ark and in the village Kazan, 15 miles away, which hung off the rear of the ark to steady its ride.

XII. The ark rests upon Cesnakidag (or Cudi Dagi) Mountain, which is translated as "Doomsday" Mountain.

XIII. Noah's Ark, the site is immediately below the mountain of Al Judi, named in the Qur'an as the resting place of the Ark. (Houd Sura 11:44)

XIV. Radar scans show a regular pattern of timbers inside the ark formation, revealing keels, keelsons, gunnels, bulkheads, animal chambers, ramp system, and door in right front, two large barrels in the front 14' x 24', and an open center area for air flow to all three levels.

Chapter 17

Narrative

This entire Holy Bible study is insightful of the works of Yahweh God Abba Father in Gods divine time of intervention written throughout the pages of the Holy Bible. As well, the extent of detail to the supernatural Jesus Christ Messiah as it is written in scripture. In addition, the supporting missionary works of the Apostles deliverance of their Epistles given them by Rabbi Jesus Christ during His Ministry to build the Church. The Church is formed of the body of believers explained in this demographic study of more than 200 countries.

Demographic Study of More Than Two Hundred Countries

A comprehensive demographic study of more than 200 countries finds that there are 2.18 billion Christians of all ages around the world, representing nearly a third of the estimated 2010 global population of 6.9 billion. Christians are also geographically widespread – so far-flung, in fact, that no single continent or region can indisputably claim to be the center of global Christianity.

A century ago, this was not the case. In 1910, about two-thirds of the world's Christians lived in Europe, where the bulk of Christians had been for a millennium, according to historical estimates by the Center for the Study of Global Christianity. Today, only about a quarter of all Christians live in Europe (26%). A plurality – more than a third – now are in the Americas (37%). About one in every four Christians lives in sub-Saharan Africa (24%), and about one-in-eight is found in Asia and the Pacific (13%).

The number of Christians around the world has nearly quadrupled in the last 100 years, from about 600 million in 1910 to more than 2 billion in 2010. But the worlds overall population also has risen rapidly, from an estimated 1.8 billion in 1910 to 6.9 billion in 2010. As a result,

Christians make up about the same portion of the world's population today (32%) as they did a century ago (35%).

This apparent stability, however, masks a momentous shift. Although Europe and the Americas still are home to most of the world's Christians (63%), that share is much lower than it was in 1910 (93%). And the proportion of Europeans and Americans who are Christian has dropped from 95% in 1910 to 76% in 2010 in Europe as a whole, and from 96% to 86% in the Americas as a whole.

At the same time, Christianity has grown enormously in sub-Saharan Africa and the Asia-Pacific region, where there were relatively few Christians at the beginning of the 20th century. The share of the population that is Christian in sub-Saharan Africa climbed from 9% in 1910 to 63% in 2010, while in the Asia-Pacific region it rose from 3% to 7%. Christianity today – unlike a century ago – is truly a global faith.

Narrative

The Church is built globally of many Denominations – Reformations in Faith, viewable in the super-structure of regional Chapels, Churches, Temples, and Cathedrals. These have served as the well architected artistic even powerful superstructures in honoring the Holy Ghosts divine works through the body of the living Yahweh God inhabiting Rabbi Jesus Christ Messiah mortal flesh of man experience the Incarnation Jesus Christ Rabbi Abba Father Priest Messiah Yahweh God works of the indoctrination of discipleship of His beloved Church of Global Universal Faith. Amen! All of which correlating the supernatural power of Jesus Christ Messiah Savior Lord and King in the establishment of His Throne and Rule in Heaven and beneath the Canopy of Heaven, beneath the surface of the earth, and above the surface, as well this Universe for there is no other God. Other than, this God of this Universe. We are not meant to stay here in this sinful world. We are meant to sanctify ourselves through the Light of God from the mustard seed of faith given us by the Messiah Jesus Christ Son of Yahweh God who will show the way. Amen

Chapter 18

Narrative

Usage of the application of scripture in faith is achieved as it is written in Prophecy by the Chosen Prophets within the scriptures of the Holy Bible. The word of Yahweh God delivered by the Messiah Rabbi Jesus Christ and there after missionaries works of the deliverance of the indoctrinated Apostles Epistles have translated the Holy Ghosts words into all languages and delivered this word of God to all regions. This word of the Holy Ghost is translated in all languages of tongue including and not limited to computer binary encoded and not stopping short of encoded sypher text. This global indoctrination of Jehovah's breathed words through Messiah Rabbi Jesus Christ have formed the church of this current time and remain the effective works of the Father Abba Son Jesus Christ and Holy Ghost trinity Incarnation for eternity. When King Christ the Messiah returns, we will be successfully ruled by His Monarchy as the Messiah is King of Kings Lord of Lords. Although, monarchies of the past have not been fully successful in excusing their authority over their peoples of lawless corruption in this sinful world, some have been documented as following well in the Law of God proving better establishment of order. However, again we can observe the truth of Rabbi Jesus Christ the Messiah and His Covenant held in Him that cannot be broken, unlike other covenants placed in other men. This covenant is held by the Messiah Lord King Jesus Christ theretofore, His covenant will not be broken. His Monarchy and Throne will be eternal as well without corruption. For it will be perfectly ruled by Him. By the Law of God in perfect balance.

We may indeed acknowledge the Holy Ghost through the many translations the word has been delivered through the Lord's Prayer. As these first five translations of the Holy Bible were well placed as follows, Arabic, Hebrew, Greek, Latin, and English bringing forward the standard Geneva translation most certainly impactive indeed.

The Lord's Prayer Listed in Order of Biblical Translations (KJV), (GNV)

Arabic

مائيو 6: 9-13
نسخة الملك جيمس

9 ليتقدس اسمك ، ابانا الذي في السماء: هكذا هكذا انتم صلوا هكذا.

10 لتكن مشيئتك كما في السماء على الارض. لتأت ملكوتك.

11 خبزنا كفافنا اعطنا اليوم.

12 واغفر لنا ذنوبنا كما نغفر نحن للمذنبين إلينا.

13 ولا تدخلنا في تجربة ، بل نجنا من الشر ، لأن لك الملك والقوة والمجد إلى الأبد. آمين.

Hebrew

מתיו 6: 9-13
גרסת קינג ג'יימס

9 עַל פִּי דרך זו התפללו אפוא: אבינו שבשמים, קדוש שמך.

10 בוא מלכותך, רצונך נעשה בארץ כמו בשמים.

11 תן לנו היום את הלחם היומיומי שלנו.

12 וסלח לנו את חובותינו כמו שאנחנו סולחים לחייבינו.

13 ואל תוביל אותנו לפיתוי אלא הצל אותנו מרע: כי המלכות שלך היא והכוח והתפארת לנצח. אָמֵן.

Greek

Ματθαίος 6: 9-13 (Έκδοση King James)

9 Με αυτόν τον τρόπο λοιπόν προσευχηθείτε: Πατέρα μας που είναι στον ουρανό, άγιο να είναι το όνομά σας.

10 Το βασίλειό σου έρχεται, Θα γίνει στη γη, όπως είναι στον ουρανό.

11 Δώστε μας αυτήν την ημέρα το καθημερινό μας ψωμί.

12 Και συγχωρέστε μας τα χρέη μας, καθώς συγχωρούμε τους οφειλέτες μας.

13 Και μην μας οδηγήσετε στον πειρασμό, αλλά ελευθερώστε μας από το κακό: Διότι είναι το βασίλειο, και η δύναμη και η δόξα, για πάντα. Αμήν.

Latin

VI Matth: 9-13 (King James Version)

IX Sic ergo vos orabitis: Pater noster, qui es in caelis, sanctificetur nomen tuum.

X adveniat regnum tuum, fiat voluntas tua in terris sicut est in caelis.

XI Da nobis hodie panem nostrum cotidie.

XII Et dimitte nobis debita nostra, sicut et nos dimittimus debitoribus nostris.

XIII Et ne nos inducas in tentationem, sed libera nos a malo: Quia tuum est regnum, et potestas, et gloria in saecula. Amen.

English

Matthew 6:9-13 1599 Geneva Bible (GNV)

9 After this manner therefore pray ye, Our father which art in heaven, hallowed be thy name.

10 Thy kingdom come. Thy will be done even in earth as it is in heaven.

11 Give us this day our daily bread.

12 And forgive us our debts, as we also forgive our debtors.

13 And lead us not into temptation but deliver us from evil: for thine is the kingdom, and the power, and the glory forever. Amen.

Narrative

Connection with the Father God Creator through prayer with Messiah Jesus Christ as Mediator for the connection as One with the Holy Ghost – Father Son Holy Ghost has been effectively achieved by persons of Credible Witness of Faith, for some of the purposes of love, forgiving, healing, redeeming and even just to have a good connecting talk with the Lord. These methods of prayer being descriptively written have effectively assisted the healing of persons of tragic injuries including assisting recovery of persons from a koma, also a paraplegic, and also, assisted a person through recovery of neurologic conditions caused by injury accidents. These methods of prayer have also assisted healing of sickness. How these payers work effectively is first have any amount of Faith even that of a mustard seed of Faith in Messiah Jesus Christ as the Mediator. (Me·di·a·tor /ˈMēdēˌādər/ Noun; a person who attempts to make people involved in a conflict come to an agreement; a go-between.) The Prayer for most effectiveness, must be respectfully with the Will of God Creator the Father Holy Ghost. Understand what God wants will help effectiveness in prayer. God Creator is an artist who has created good things in balance. God Creator wants the good things created with such marvel of creationism and fine balance as Gods artistic works as God Creator in Marvel of artistic balance created the creation to be, this means redeemed as God originally designed before Gods creation had become altered. Theretofore, God wants things to mend to return to how God created them to be in good balance. Ultimately, the purpose of prayer is to connect with God Creator. Demonstrating recognition of authority to Rabbi Jesus Christ the Messiah as the Mediator first with the given gratitude with acknowledgement of authority by title and by His purposed function which is love, forgiving, healing and redeeming in connection with the Holy Father God Creator. Yet, their all in one the Trinity of the Father Son and Holy Ghost. This proven effective method of connection is performed with one hand turned palm up purposing as a lightning rod of connectivity, and meaningfully connect with Jesus, in saying what Jesus does, Loving Jesus, Forgiving Jesus, Healing Jesus, Redeeming Jesus, Rabbi Christ connect with me, Messiah Jesus Christ connect with me. Pathway me through this Lord Jesus Christ my Savior, Savior Jesus Christ I welcome you Lord be my light, show me the way Lord connect with me. Amen

Prayer Effectively Applied Through Scripture

James 5:15 "And the Prayer of Faith shall save the sick, and the Lord shall raise him up; and if he have committed sins, they shall be forgiven him"

The only verse in Scripture that contains the phrase, "Prayer of Faith", is James 5:15. Though spoken of only once, the prayer title conveys an assurance of success in prayer. The conviction that life, if lived with Faith in God, rewards with an Eternity spent in God's presence, encourages us to believe that Faith accomplishes whatever it sets out to do. "For whatsoever is born of God overcometh the world: and this is the victory that overcometh the world, even our Faith" (1 John 5:4).

With the Promise of victory beforehand, prayer linked by Faith that is founded in God assures itself to be both rewarding and exciting in "exploits" for God. "The people that do know their God shall be strong and do exploits" (Daniel 11:32).

Many times, prayer does not yield the desired results we yearn for. "Hope deferred maketh the heart sick" (Proverbs 13:12). Hope precedes all prayer, but only when the answer comes do, we recognize the difference that Faith makes in praying. "But when the desire cometh, it is a Tree of Life" (13:12).

Picture lightning. When Gods will makes contact with our hope, Faith is established and grace races down the lightning rod of experience. Faith is the way you use God's grace. It's our part to exercise the Faith God authors, but it's Gods part to finish it.

Connecting With God in Prayer

    I.   The "Prayer of Faith" is prayer that always gets answered. If the "Prayer of Faith" is for the sick, "the lord shall raise" the sick up. If the "Prayer of Faith" is Godly repentance, then sins "shall be forgiven".

    II.   The reason that the "Prayer of Faith" always gets answered is because of the very nature of Faith. "Faith is the substance of things hoped for, the evidence of things not seen" (Hebrews 11:1).
"Faith is... substance" and "evidence". Faith cannot be held in the hand, or gazed upon with the eye, but Faith in God and His Character is more real than anything your bodily senses can physically verify. Faith based in the Word of God is as realistic as "substance" and "evidence" gets. Nothing in this world is more real. Therefore, Faith always produces fruit and the "Prayer of Faith" always gets answered. Faith is always substance!

    III.   Since the "Prayer of Faith" is always answered, it must always be according to gods will.
- ➢ Colossians 4:12 "Always labouring fervently for you in prayers, that ye may stand perfect and complete in all the will of God."
- ➢ Hebrews 10:36 "For ye have need of patience, that, after ye have done the will of God, ye might receive the Promise."
- ➢ Romans 8:27 "the Spirit... maketh intercession for the saints according to the will of God."

    IV.   Since the above points are absolutes, there are no exceptions to them. For the "Prayer of Faith" to be the "Prayer of Faith", these elements must be present.

The "Prayer of Faith":

- ➢ Always gets answered
- ➢ Is always substance

➤ Must always be according to gods will
➤ There are no exceptions

Prayer Hinges on The Covenant

"And I, behold, I establish My Covenant with you, and with your seed after you... Now therefore, if ye will obey My Voice indeed, and keep My Covenant, then ye shall be a peculiar treasure unto Me above all people: for all the Earth is Mine" (Genesis 9:9; Exodus 19:5).

Our first prayer to God, the prayer of repentance that brought us into the family circle of Heaven, was our beginning to build upon the foundation, which is Jesus Christ Messiah, for all our future prayers. "For other foundation can no man lay than that is laid, which is Jesus Christ" (1 Corinthians 3:11).

That first prayer was our promise (our affirmation of His Covenant) with God that we belonged to Him, and He to us. All prayer, therefore, is valid and honorable before God if we have kept our Covenant with Him. Our walk with God is a binding "all or nothing" agreement-- Covenant-- it is pass of dark or pass of light, Heaven or Hell. The Lord has given on the Cross, and continues to give, His infinite 100%. We give Him our finite 100%. "Be ye therefore perfect (your 100%), even as your Father which is in Heaven is perfect (His 100%)" (Matthew 5:48). "Jesus answered them, My Father worketh hitherto, and I work" (John 5:17).

He Gives His 100%

➤ Philippians 2:13 "For it is God which worketh in you both to will and to do of His good pleasure."
➤ Hebrews 13:20,21 "Now the God of peace...make you perfect in every good work to do His will, working in you that which is well pleasing in His sight, through Jesus Christ."

I. The Lord Covenants (promises) "all or nothing" forgiveness!
➤ 1 John 1:9 "If we confess our sins, He is Faithful and Just to forgive us our sins, and to cleanse us from all unrighteousness."
➤ Titus 2:14 "Who gave Himself for us, that He might redeem us from all iniquity, and purify unto Himself a peculiar people, zealous of good works."

II. The Lord Covenants (promises) "all or nothing" of His Spirit
➤ Acts 5:32 "The Holy Ghost, Whom God hath given to them that obey Him."
➤ 1 Thessalonians 5:19 "Quench (literally, extinguish) not the Spirit."
➤ Ephesians 1:13 "Ye were sealed with that Holy Spirit of Promise."

We Give Our 100%

- 1 Corinthians 15:10 "But by the grace of God I am what I am: and His grace which was bestowed upon me was not in vain; but I laboured more abundantly than they all: yet not I, but the grace of God which was with me."
- Titus 3:8 "This is a faithful saying, and these things I will that thou affirm constantly, that they which have believed in God might be careful to maintain good works. These things are good and profitable unto men."

I.   Our Covenant (promise) is "all or nothing" love.
- Matthew 22:37 "Jesus said unto him, thou shalt love the Lord thy God with all thy heart, and with all thy soul, and with all thy mind."
- 1 John 2:15 "If any man loves the world, the love of the Father is not in him."
- Matthew 6:24 "No man can serve two masters... Ye cannot serve God and mammon."

II.   Our Covenant (promise) is "all or nothing" obedience unto Lord and King Jesus Christ Messiah.
- James 2:10 "For whosoever shall keep the whole Law, and yet offend in one point, he is guilty of all."
- James 4:4 "Know ye not that the friendship of the world is enmity with God? Whosoever therefore will be a friend of the world is the enemy of God."
- Galatians 1:10 "For do I now persuade men, or God? Or do I seek to please men? For if I yet pleased men, I should not be the servant of Christ."

III.   Even so, in our walk with God, our Covenant (promise) is "all or nothing" Faith in Him for everything in this world, and in the next.
- 2 Timothy 1:12 "I know whom I have believed and am persuaded that He is able to keep that which I have committed unto Him against that day."
- Psalm 62:8 "Trust in Him at all times; ye people, pour out your heart before Him: God is a Refuge for us."
- 2 Chronicles 20:20 "Believe in the Lord your God, so shall ye be established."
- Psalm 37:3, 5 "Trust in the Lord, and do good; so shalt thou dwell in the land, and verily thou shalt be fed... Commit thy way unto the Lord; trust also in Him; and He shall bring it to pass."
- Isaiah 26:4 "Trust ye in the Lord forever: for in the Lord Jehovah is Everlasting Strength."

Truth in Jesus Christ Lord King Messiah by Prophesy of The Holy Bible

Only a cleansed through the blood of Jesus clean hearted believer, that is a repentant soul walking with the word of Christ without known sin may offer to God the true fulfilling sacrifice of prayer. We must seek reconciliation with sanctification through Christ. King Christ knows the way to Heaven and will shew us the way.

- Psalm 66:18-20 "If I regard iniquity in my heart, the Lord will not hear me: But verily God hath heard me; he hath attended to the voice of my prayer. Blessed be God, which hath not turned away my prayer, nor his mercy from me."
- Psalm 18:40-41 "Thou hast also given me the necks of mine enemies... they cried, but there was none to save them: even unto the Lord, but he answered them not."
- Proverbs 1:28-30 "Then shall they call upon me, but I will not answer; they shall seek me early, but they shall not find me: For that they hated knowledge and did not choose the fear of the Lord: They would none of my counsel: they despised all my reproof."
- Proverbs 28:9 "He that turneth away his ear from hearing the law, even his prayer shall be abomination."
- Isaiah 1:15-16 "And when ye spread forth your hands, I will hide mine eyes from you: yea, when ye make many prayers, I will not hear: your hands are full of blood. Wash you, make you clean; put away the evil of your doings from before mine eyes; cease to do evil."
- John 9:31 "Now we know that God heareth not sinners: but if any man be a worshipper of God, and doeth his will, him he heareth."
- James 4:3 "Ye ask, and receive not, because ye ask amiss, that ye may consume it upon your lusts."

Christianity is a Way of Life Also a Practice Consisting of Types of Prayer

The two kinds of prayer addressed here are basically the same but differ in results.

I.   The "Prayer of Faith" always secures the answer.
II. The Prayer That Demonstrates Faith by the mere act of asking yet does not secure the answer.
III. The Prayer That Demonstrates Faith must be in the general Will of God Abba Father, Son Lord King Messiah Savior Jesus Christ, Holy Ghost Holy Spirit, (Yahweh Incarnation) for He will definitely not answer anything we know to be unscriptural "Wherefore be ye not unwise but understanding what the Will of the Lord is" (Ephesians 5:17).

- The character of God reveals His Will. Galatians 1:3-4 "Our Lord Jesus Christ, who gave himself for our sins, that he might deliver us from this present evil world, according to the Will of God and our Father."
- The Word of God reveals His Will. Romans 12:2 "And be not conformed to this world: but be ye transformed by the renewing of your mind, that ye may prove what is that good, and acceptable, and perfect, Will of God."

Narrative

Looking unto Jesus the Author and finisher of our faith, who for the joy that was set before him endured the cross, despising the shame, and is set down at the right hand of the Throne of God. (Hebrews 12:2, KJV)

May I as author of lesser light listener of Jesus Author of greater Light that is not of this world, but what is an ever-Greater Light of God Eternal that we are whereunto beneath the Canopy Heaven speaketh and so also be heard. For Aloweth thy ears to hear, aloweth thy touch to feel, aloweth thy eyes to see, aloweth thy smell to be smeleth of thine Messiah Rabbi Jesus Christs' essence of rich soil beneath the Canopy of Heaven, and thine taste of the Blood of Messiah Jesus Christ Holy Vine, and thine taste of the Bread of Life thine Body of Messiah Rabbi Jesus Christ our Savior. Who alone is the way to lift afflictions of this sinful world. Amen

> The Spirit of God reveals His will. Colossians 1:9 "For this cause we also, since the day we heard it, do not cease to pray for you, and to desire that ye might be filled with the knowledge of His Will in all wisdom and Spiritual understanding."

But the "Prayer of Faith" must be His specific Will.

Only The Holy Spirit Authors The "Prayer of Faith"

Even after all your best intentions are prayerfully carried out, it is still only the Holy Spirit Who can make the difference between the Prayer That Demonstrates Faith in asking and the true "Prayer of Faith". The "Prayer of Faith" must be in the specific will of God. Only the Holy Spirit that can lead and inspire the direction that we are to take in fulfilling Gods specific will.

> Romans 8:26-27 "The Spirit also helpeth our infirmities: for we know not what we should pray for as we ought: but the Spirit (Himself) maketh intercession for us with groaning's which cannot be uttered. And He (the Father) that searcheth the hearts knoweth what is the mind of the Spirit, because He maketh intercession for the saints according to the will of God."

Persevering in prayer is essential to the "Prayer of Faith", or else the answer that surely would have come will not.

> Ephesians 6:18 "Praying always with all prayer and supplication in the Spirit and watching thereunto with all perseverance and supplication for all saints."
> Colossians 4:2 "Continue in prayer and watch in the same with thanksgiving."
> 1 Thessalonians 5:17 "Pray without ceasing."

If persevering in prayer proves impossible because the answer is a definite, "No", then there was no Securing Faith. The prayer was Prayer That Demonstrated Faith but wasn't ever inspired by the Spirit according to Gods specific Will. Therefore, He did not answer it. Understand that negative answers to prayer will never be given by the Lord. However, His Conditions need be met.

1 John 5:14-15 "And this is the confidence that we have in Him that, if we ask any thing according to His will, He heareth us: And if we know that He hear us, whatsoever we ask, we know that we have the petitions that we desired of Him."

Prayer Demonstrates Faith in Asking

When you pray you are petitioning God in either Faith or Hope. Prayer That Demonstrates Faith by the mere task of asking is praying in Hope. Hope yields anticipation but does not secure the answer. But even though this kind of prayer cannot bring forth the answer you seek, Prayer That Demonstrates Faith by the mere task of asking glorifies God because it seeks God as the Giver and is in obedience to the command.

Every prayer ought to be prayed in Faith. When we pray, we are commanded to believe God and to take Him at His Word. We have no right to doubt God. There is nothing that can be proven logical, scientific, nor astronomic, nor mathematical equation absolutely anyone who has tried to prove there is no God, can only prove there isn't anything other than a Devine and Greater Being does exist – who is our God. As well, we are an advanced people, China has a space station, Russia has a space station, and the United State has a space station. In addition, an international space station by joined nations that includes missions of deep space exploration. It states in the Holy Bible that God is the God of our Universe and there is no other God.

> John 15:16 "Ye have not chosen Me, but I have chosen you, and ordained you, that ye should go and bring forth fruit, and that your fruit should remain that whatsoever ye shall ask of the Father in My Name, He may give it you."
> John 16:24 "Hitherto have ye asked nothing in My Name: ask, and ye shall receive, that your joy may be full."
> Mark 11:22 "And Jesus answering saith unto them, Have Faith in God."
> Mark 11:24 "Therefore I say unto you, what things soever ye desire, when ye pray, believe that ye receive them, and ye shall have them."
> Matthew 7:7 "Ask, and it shall be given you; seek, and ye shall find; knock, and it shall be opened unto you."

We are to pray about all things, exercising our Faith in God and His Promises.

> Philippians 4:6 "Be careful for nothing; but in everything by prayer and supplication with thanksgiving let your requests be made known unto God."

But how can we know the prayer was prayed in Faith? You can "feel" you prayed in Faith, and you ought to believe you did. However, you will not know it by sight until the "substance" and "evidence" (Hebrews 11:1) of Faith, which isn't visible at first, becomes visible at the arriving of the answer.

Paul is an example of walking by Faith yet praying a prayer that was not in Faith.

> ➤ 2 Corinthians 12:7-9 "Lest I should be exalted above measure through the abundance of the revelations, there was given to me a thorn in the flesh, the messenger of Satan to buffet me, lest I should be exalted above measure. For this thing I besought the Lord thrice, that it might depart from me. And He said unto me, My grace is sufficient for thee: for My strength is made perfect in weakness. Most gladly therefore will I rather glory in my infirmities, that the power of Christ may rest upon me."

It was not the Lords specific will to remove Paul's "thorn in the flesh". It is always the Lords general Will to Heal. "Himself took our infirmities and bare our sicknesses and great multitudes came together to hear, and to be healed by Him of their infirmities" (Matthew 8:17; Luke 5:15).

Paul prayed as he ought to have. Paul believed as he ought to have. But since the Holy Spirit knew Gods specific will in this particular matter, He did not excite securing Faith in Paul. This is an excellent example of how a Faithful Servant could not pray the "Prayer of Faith", but instead prayed Prayer That Demonstrates Faith in the mere asking.

Quantity or Quality in Faith

How much "Faith" is needed to pray the "Prayer of Faith"? There can be a great deal of confusion on this point because we often think of Faith in terms of quantity, when instead we should think of quality. While it does take Faith to begin to pray at all, the "Prayer of Faith" needs a higher degree of quality to persevere until the answer comes. It takes a better grade of Faith to persevere in prayer than to just begin praying. "Do I have enough Faith to expect God to answer this prayer?"

Quantity can be seen in this lowly, smallest of small seeds, the mustard seed.

When responding to the Apostles' desire for more Faith, "Increase our Faith" (Luke 17:5), the Lord Jesus said that the smallest amount of Faith, even "as a grain of mustard seed… which indeed is the least of all seeds" (Luke 17:6; Matthew 13:32), was enough to do even the impossible, i.e., "ye might say unto this sycamine tree, Be thou plucked up by the root, and be thou planted in the sea; and it should obey you" (Luke 17:6). The smallest quantity of Faith is equivalent to the smallest of all seeds. The smallest of all seeds can accomplish the impossible. Therefore, as far as quantity is concerned, any Faith is enough Faith.

God is not unfair in His dealings with men. "God is no respecter of persons" (Acts 10:34). The Lord gives "The Measure of Faith" to all men, therefore, no one has a reason to boast because no one has an unfair advantage in their "walk by Faith" (2 Corinthians 5:7). "For I say... to every man that is among you, not to think of himself more highly than he ought to think; but to think soberly, according as God hath dealt to every man The Measure of Faith" (Romans 12:3). "The Measure of Faith" that is "dealt to every man" is even "as a grain of mustard seed", and is enough to do anything needed, even the impossible.

Any Quantity of Faith is enough Faith. There are no levels in amount or quantity. The Lord gives us "The Measure of Faith" (Romans 12:3). If you have Any "Measure of Faith", even if "The

Measure of Faith" is "as a grain of mustard seed", then you have enough "Measure" in life to accomplish anything even moving mountains.

Matthew 17:19-20 "Then came the disciples to Jesus apart, and said, why could not we cast him out? And Jesus said unto them, Because of your unbelief: for verily I say unto you, if ye have Faith as a grain of mustard seed, ye shall say unto this mountain, remove hence to yonder place; and it shall remove; and nothing shall be impossible unto you."

Quality can be seen in this lowly, smallest of small seeds, the mustard seed.

Quality of Faith is another matter. While there are no levels in the quantity of Faith possessed, there are levels of quality, i.e., "strong" versus "weak".

➢ Romans 4:19-21 "And being not weak in Faith, he (Abraham) considered not his own body now dead, when he was about an hundred years old, neither yet the deadness of Sarah's womb. He (Abraham) staggered not at the Promise of God through unbelief; but was strong in Faith, giving glory to God. And being fully persuaded that, what He had promised, He was able also to perform."

➢ Note Abrahams Reward: (4:22) "Therefore it was imputed to him for Righteousness."

➢ 1 Corinthians 16:13 "Watch ye, stand fast in the Faith, quit you like men, be strong."

You build strength in Faith the same way you build strength in muscle, by exercise. The way you use Faith, the areas of life in which you apply Faith, the advantage you take in the opportunities the Lord lays before you these are the means by which Faith grows strong. Do you seek reliance upon God only, and trust Him even when the situation gives you other options? This not only pleases Him, for "without Faith it is impossible to please Him" (Hebrews 11:6), but this exercise of Faith causes you to trust God more.

Faith is like a mustard seed. It grows in strength and might, in glory and perfection. "The Kingdom of Heaven is like to a grain of mustard seed…which indeed is the least of all seeds: but when it is grown, it is the greatest among herbs, and becometh a tree, so that the birds of the air come and lodge in the branches thereof" (Matthew 13:31-32). To be one of these "birds of the air" that "come and lodge in the branches" of "The Kingdom of Heaven" is to have "The Mighty One" declare, "all flesh shall know that I the Lord am thy Saviour and thy Redeemer, The Mighty One of Jacob" (Isaiah 49:26). This is quality of Faith grown to its "greatest", most glorious potential.

➢ 1 Peter 1:7 "That the trial of your Faith, being much more precious than of gold that perisheth, though it be tried with fire, might be found unto praise and honour and glory at the appearing of Jesus Christ."

The Use of The Phrase "Little Faith"

There are five times in Scripture where the phrase "little Faith" is used:

I. Matthew 6:30 "Wherefore, if God so clothe the grass of the field, which today is, and tomorrow is cast into the oven, shall He not much more clothe you, O ye of little Faith?"

II. Luke 12:28 "If then God so clothe the grass, which is today in the field, and tomorrow is cast into the oven; how much more will He clothe you, O ye of little Faith?"

III. Matthew 8:26 "And He saith unto them, why are ye fearful, O ye of little Faith? Then He arose and rebuked the winds and the sea; and there was a great calm."

IV. Matthew 16:8 "Which when Jesus perceived, He said unto them, O ye of little Faith, why reason ye among yourselves, because ye have brought no bread?"

V. Matthew 14:31 "And immediately Jesus stretched forth His hand, and caught him, and said unto him, O thou of little Faith, wherefore didst thou doubt?"

We find "little Faith" as meaning "trusting too little", i.e., "Faith"-- singular in quality (not plural, as in quantity):

Of Little Faith, Trusting too Little

"Little" can mean "of number: multitude, quantity, or size"; but it can also mean "of degree or intensity: light, slight", i.e., quality.

I. Little, small, few
II. Of number: multitude, quantity, or size
III. Of time: short
IV. Of degree or intensity: light, slight

Therefore, to rightly divide the Spirits meaning of "little Faith", and determine if Faith could be in quantity, as opposed to just quality, we must study the context.

The first two references of "little Faith" in Matthew 6:30 and Luke 12:28 are parallel passages.

Matthew 6:24-33 "No man can serve two masters: for either he will hate the One and love the other; or else he will hold to the One and despise the other. Ye cannot serve God and mammon." (In other words, choose the single master you will love and hold to - God or the world.) "Therefore, I say unto you, take no thought (or don't worry) for your life, what ye shall eat, or what ye shall drink; nor yet for your body, what ye shall put on. Is not the life more than meat, and the body than raiment?" "Behold the fowls of the air: for they sow not, neither do they reap, nor gather into barns; yet your Heavenly Father feedeth them. Are ye not much better than they?" "Which of you by taking thought (or, worrying) can add one cubit unto his stature?" "And why take ye thought for raiment? Consider the lilies of the field, how they grow; they toil not, neither do they spin:" "And yet I say unto you, that even Solomon in all his glory was not arrayed like one of these." "Wherefore, if God so clothe the grass of the field, which today is, and tomorrow is cast into the oven, shall He not much more clothe you, O ye of little Faith?" "Therefore, take no thought, saying, what shall we eat? Or what shall we drink? Or Wherewithal shall we be clothed?" "(For after all these things do the Gentiles seek:) for your

Heavenly Father knoweth that ye have need of all these things." "But seek ye first the Kingdom of God, and His Righteousness; and all these things shall be added unto you."

If our Heavenly Father completely meets the need of all life in the natural world, "Are ye not much better than they?" Which master deserves your trust? Hasn't the Father earned perfect Faith, of the highest quality and degree of intensity? To fall short of that is to trust "too little" or have "little Faith".

The Third Passage of "Little Faith" is in Matthew:

Matthew 8:23-27 "And when He was entered into a ship, His disciples followed Him." "And behold, there arose a great tempest in the sea, insomuch that the ship was covered with the waves: but He was asleep." "And His disciples came to Him, and awoke Him, saying, Lord, save us: we perish." "And He saith unto them, why are ye fearful, O ye of little Faith? Then He arose and rebuked the winds and the sea; and there was a great calm." "But the men marveled, saying, what manner of man is this, that even the winds and the sea obey Him!"

Again, we find that "little Faith" means to fall short in quality of trust, or to trust "too little", which can dangerously lead to fear. "Why are ye fearful, O ye of little Faith?" And when fear isn't handled properly, i.e., "What time I am afraid, I will trust in Thee" (Psalm 56:3), it leads to sin, i.e., "But the fearful, and unbelieving... shall have their part in the lake which burneth with fire and brimstone: which is the second death" (Revelation 21:8). High quality Faith "will trust in Thee".

The Fourth Passage of "Little Faith":

Matthew 16:5-12 "And when His disciples were come to the other side, they had forgotten to take bread." "Then Jesus said unto them, take heed and beware of the leaven of the Pharisees and of the Sadducees." "And they reasoned among themselves, saying, it is because we have taken no bread." "Which when Jesus perceived, He said unto them, O ye of little Faith, why reason ye among yourselves, because ye have brought no bread?" "Do ye not yet understand, neither remember the five loaves of the five thousand, and how many baskets ye took up?" "Neither the seven loaves of the four thousand, and how many baskets ye took up?" "How is it that ye do not understand that I spake it not to you concerning bread, that ye should beware of the leaven of the Pharisees and of the Sadducees?" "Then understood they how that He bade them not beware of the leaven of bread, but of the doctrine of the Pharisees and of the Sadducees."

Jesus was trying to warn His disciples about "the leaven of the Pharisees and of the Sadducees" by using "leaven" as an illustration of Truth. But instead of seeing the broader picture of Faith, the disciples, in their "little Faith" could only misunderstand Him. They forgot His past demonstrations of miraculous supply. "Do ye not yet understand, neither remember... How is it that ye do not understand that I spake it not to you concerning bread, that ye should beware of the leaven of the Pharisees and of the Sadducees?" It was only after the reproof that "then understood they how that He bade them not beware of the leaven of bread, but of the doctrine of the Pharisees and of the Sadducees." If the disciples had a zealous quality of Faith, if they had trusted Jesus more for the supply, He had previously shown them, then they wouldn't have tripped over His lesson.

The Last Passage, Still in The Book of Matthew:

Matthew 14:25-31 "And in the fourth watch of the night Jesus went unto them, walking on the sea." "And when the disciples saw Him walking on the sea, they were troubled, saying, it is a spirit; and they cried out for fear." "But straightway Jesus spake unto them, saying, be of good cheer; it is I; be not afraid." "And Peter answered Him and said, Lord, if it be, Thou, bid me come unto Thee on the water." "And He said, Come. And when Peter was come down out of the ship, he walked on the water, to go to Jesus." "But when he saw the wind boisterous, he was afraid; and beginning to sink, he cried, saying, Lord, save me." "And immediately Jesus stretched forth His hand, and caught him, and said unto him, O thou of little Faith, wherefore didst thou doubt?"

The disciples thought they saw a ghost walking on the water. Jesus calmed their fears by identifying Himself. Peter was beginning to demonstrate Faith in this identifying process by saying, "Lord, if it be, Thou, bid me come unto Thee on the water." But Peters Faith was low quality. He trusted "too little", and his "Little Faith" turned into "doubt" as he took his eyes off the Author of Faith (Hebrews 12:2) and placed them instead on the object of defeat. Peter wavered from Faith, changing his ultimate purpose, "he was afraid"(Matthew 14:30) but, quickly returned to his condition of "Little Faith", when he cried, "Lord, save me" (14:30).

"Little Faith" is still Faith. But remember, "Little Faith" means to fall short in quality of trust, or to trust "too little", which can dangerously lead to sin.

Faith Versus Doubt

When a Christian, who is to "walk by Faith" (2 Corinthians 5:7), finds himself about to do something morally questionable, and proceeds against his conscience, without clearing the matter by determining, "what saith the Scripture?" (Romans 4:3), this person is clearly in doubt.

> Romans 14:23 "And he that doubteth is damned if he eats, because he eateth not of Faith: for whatsoever is not of Faith is sin."

Faith Secures All Doubt Receives Nothing

> James 1:6-8 "Let him ask in Faith, nothing wavering. For he that wavereth is like a wave of the sea driven with the wind and tossed. For let not that man think that he shall receive any thing of the Lord. A double minded man is unstable in all his ways."

If you know "beyond a shadow of doubt" that Gods will for you is to curse a fig tree, or move a mountain, and you refuse to believe Him for it, then you drop from one, who trusts God to use you to do the impossible, to one who doubts God. "And he that doubteth is damned."

- Matthew 21:21 "Jesus answered and said unto them, Verily I say unto you, if ye have Faith, and doubt not, ye shall not only do this which is done to the fig tree, but also if ye shall say unto this mountain, be thou removed, and be thou cast into the sea; it shall be done."
- Mark 11:23 "For verily I say unto you, that whosoever shall say unto this mountain, be thou removed, and be thou cast into the sea; and shall not doubt in his heart but shall believe that those things which he saith shall come to pass; he shall have whatsoever he saith."
- Galatians 4:19-21 "My little children, of whom I travail in birth again until Christ be formed in you, I desire to be present with you now, and to change my voice; for I stand in doubt of you. Tell me, ye that desire to be under the law, do ye not hear the law?"
- John 10:23-26 "And Jesus walked in the temple in Solomon's porch. Then came the Jews round about Him, and said unto Him, how long dost Thou make us to doubt? If Thou be the Christ, tell us plainly. Jesus answered them, I told you, and ye believed not: the works that I do in My Father's Name, they bear witness of Me. But ye believe not, because ye are not of My sheep, as I said unto you.

One Faith Different Areas of Application

When the Lord is allowed by you to prove Himself Faithful, the accumulated experience will strengthen your boldness and cause you to exercise Faith in even more areas.

- "We glory in tribulations also: knowing that tribulation worketh patience; And patience, experience; and experience, hope: And hope maketh not ashamed" (Romans 5:3-5).

As we continue on the Path of Light (Proverbs 4:18) that is Life to the Christian, "be ready always to give an answer to every man that asketh you a reason of the hope that is in you" (1 Peter 3:15). "Jesus answering saith unto them, Have Faith in God" (Mark 11:22). Pray the "Prayer of Faith" for others. The one time "Prayer of Faith" is declared in Scripture is in intercession for others. "And the Prayer of Faith shall save the sick, and the Lord shall raise him up" (James 5:15).

- Acts 3:16 "And His Name through Faith in His Name hath made this man strong, whom ye see and know yea, the Faith which is by Him hath given him this perfect soundness in the presence of you all."
- Acts 11:24 "For he was a good man, and full of the Holy Ghost and of Faith: and much people was added unto the Lord."

Application of Faith (As Demonstrated in The Book of Hebrews, Chapter 11)

Faith in Action

"Now faith is confidence in what we hope for and assurance about what we do not see. This is what the ancients were commended for."

"By faith we understand that the universe was formed at God's command, so that what is seen was not made out of what was visible."

"By faith Abel brought God a better offering than Cain did. By faith he was commended as righteous, when God spoke well of his offerings. And by faith Abel still speaks, even though he is dead."

"By faith Enoch was taken from this life, so that he did not experience death: He could not be found, because God had taken him away. For before he was taken, he was commended as one who pleased God. And without faith it is impossible to please God, because anyone who comes to him must believe that he exists and that he rewards those who earnestly seek him."

"By faith Noah, when warned about things not yet seen, in holy fear built an ark to save his family. By his faith he condemned the world and became heir of the righteousness that is in keeping with faith."

"By faith Abraham, when called to go to a place he would later receive as his inheritance, obeyed and went, even though he did not know where he was going. By faith he made his home in the promised land like a stranger in a foreign country; he lived in tents, as did Isaac and Jacob, who were heirs with him of the same promise. For he was looking forward to the city with foundations, whose architect and builder is God. And by faith even Sarah, who was past childbearing age, was enabled to bear children because she considered him faithful who had made the promise. And so, from this one man, and he as good as dead, came descendants as numerous as the stars in the sky and as countless as the sand on the seashore."

"All these people were still living by faith when they died. They did not receive the things promised; they only saw them and welcomed them from a distance, admitting that they were foreigners and strangers on earth. People who say such things show that they are looking for a country of their own. If they had been thinking of the country they had left, they would have had opportunity to return. Instead, they were longing for a better country a heavenly one. Therefore, God is not ashamed to be called their God, for he has prepared a city for them."

"By faith Abraham, when God tested him, offered Isaac as a sacrifice. He who had embraced the promises was about to sacrifice his one and only son, even though God had said to him, "It is through Isaac that your offspring will be reckoned." Abraham reasoned that God could even raise the dead, and so in a manner of speaking he did receive Isaac back from death."

"By faith Isaac blessed Jacob and Esau in regard to their future."

"By faith Jacob, when he was dying, blessed each of Joseph's sons, and worshiped as he leaned on the top of his staff."

"By faith Joseph, when his end was near, spoke about the exodus of the Israelites from Egypt and gave instructions concerning the burial of his bones."

"By faith Moses' parents hid him for three months after he was born, because they saw he was no ordinary child, and they were not afraid of the king's edict."

"By faith Moses, when he had grown up, refused to be known as the son of Pharaoh's daughter. He chose to be mistreated along with the people of God rather than to enjoy the fleeting pleasures of sin. He regarded disgrace for the sake of Christ as of greater value than the treasures of Egypt, because he was looking ahead to his reward. By faith he left Egypt, not fearing the king's anger; he persevered because he saw him who is invisible. By faith he kept the Passover and the application of blood, so that the destroyer of the firstborn would not touch the firstborn of Israel."

"By faith the people passed through the Red Sea as on dry land; but when the Egyptians tried to do so, they were drowned."

"By faith the walls of Jericho fell, after the army had marched around them for seven days."

"By faith the prostitute Rahab, because she welcomed the spies, was not killed with those who were disobedient."

"And what more shall I say? I do not have time to tell about Gideon, Barak, Samson and Jephthah, about David and Samuel and the prophets, who through faith conquered kingdoms, administered justice, and gained what was promised; who shut the mouths of lions, quenched the fury of the flames, and escaped the edge of the sword; whose weakness was turned to strength; and who became powerful in battle and routed foreign armies. Women received back their dead, raised to life again. There were others who were tortured, refusing to be released so that they might gain an even better resurrection. Some faced jeers and flogging, and even chains and imprisonment. They were put to death by stoning; they were sawed in two; they were killed by the sword. They went about in sheepskins and goatskins, destitute, persecuted and mistreated, the world was not worthy of them. They wandered in deserts and mountains, living in caves and in holes in the ground."

"These were all commended for their faith, yet none of them received what had been promised, since God had planned something better for us so that only together with us would they be made perfect."

"Blessed be the Lord for Evermore. Amen, and Amen" (Psalm 89:52).

Chapter 19

Authors Closing

We are in the time of millennium in revelations somewhere just preceding the tribulation, an age of our Messianic Christian King Jesus Christs apocalypse; An apocalypse (Ancient Greek: ἀποκάλυψις apokálypsis, from ἀπό and καλύπτω meaning "uncovering"), translated literally from Greek, is a disclosure of knowledge, i.e., a lifting of the veil or revelation. In religious contexts it is usually a disclosure of something hidden.

In the Book of Revelation (Greek: Ἀποκάλυψις Ἰωάννου, Apokalypsis Ioannou – literally, Johns Revelation), the last book of the New Testament, the revelation which John receives is that of the ultimate victory of good over evil and the end of the present age.

We need to prepare ourselves in how we are going to present ourselves in receiving our Messianic Christian King Christ.

It could be an idea to practice what our church leaders are teaching in the gospel holiness and service. These teachings do not fall short in how to present ourselves to His Holiness in Royalty of His eternal age. I do say simply kneel indeed, bow our heads, and pronounce His name with appropriate Title in welcoming His Messianic Christian Holiness King Jesus Christ our Savior.

Ecclesiastes 12: 13 - 14

"Let us hear the conclusion of the whole matter: Fear God and keep his commandments: for this is the whole duty of man. For God shall bring every work into judgment, with every secret thing, whether it be good, or whether it be evil."

Isaiah 45: 22 - 25

"Look unto me, and be ye saved, all the ends of the earth: for I am God, and there is none else. I have sworn by myself; the word is gone out of my mouth in righteousness, and shall not return, that unto me every knee shall bow, every tongue shall swear. Surely, shall one say, in the Lord have I righteousness and strength: even to him shall men come; and all that are incensed against him shall be ashamed. In the Lord shall all the seed of Israel be justified and shall glory."

Romans 14: 11

"For it is written, as I live, saith the Lord, every knee shall bow to me, and every tongue shall confess to God."

Philippians 2: 11

"And that every tongue should confess that Jesus Christ is Lord, to the glory of God the Father."

Epilogue

I cannot trust a man to control others who cannot control himself.

It is well that war is so terrible – otherwise we would grow too fond of it.

A true man of honor feels humbled himself when he cannot help humbling others.

Obedience to lawful authority is the foundation of manly character.

Never do a wrong thing to make a friend or to keep one.

I like whiskey. I always did, and that is why I never drink it.

I have been up to see the Congress and they do not seem to be able to do anything except to eat peanuts and chew tobacco, while my army is starving.

In all my perplexities and distresses, the Bible has never failed to give me light and strength.

We failed, but in the good providence of God apparent failure often proves a blessing.

The devil's name is dullness.

(By The Religious General Robert E. Lee)

Authors Concluding

Author 1969 Baptized by Holy Water - Saint Cyril of Jerusalem Roman Catholic Christian Church, continuing Born Again Christian practice, again Baptized Born Again 2013 by Saltwater Pacific Ocean – Evangelic Calvary Chapel.

Son of a Roman Catholic Born Again Christian Eucharistic Minister of more than 20 years of ministry service to Saint Cyril of Jerusalem Roman Catholic Christian Church.

The Holy Bible is more than awesome to read. Victories of God vs. Satan are proclaimed, victories through the faithful too God-though greatly outnumbered. Biblical witness to battles and victories for God are imminent and are current. While reading the Holy Bible I found the most epic indeed, Luke 7 where Jesus Christ performs many miracles in several provinces in a single day the Lord was on a walk while performing acts of glory. As well epic indeed, the book of James the Apostle who was Jesus Christs brother, I have brothers this brought me to the sensation of what it must have been like for James the brother of the Messiah. And 1 Thessalonians 5 indeed a letter everyone should read.

(A quotation of authors own Father veteran survivor of World War II D Day, Battle of The Bulge Arden Forest, Crossing of the Rhine River, Fall of Nazi Germany, Accordionist Musician and Roman Catholic Christian Eucharistic Minister Raymond Vincent Klein 1919-1996; "keep your faith, where there is faith there is a will, where there is a will there is a way.")

Recommended Screen Viewings by Author

Authors recommended movies in this order of viewing for the earliest crusades spreading of Christianity; "SON OF GOD" "THE PASSION OF THE CHRIST" A film detailing the final hours and crucifixion of Jesus Christ. And "THE EAGLE" A fictional story based on true historical and archeological findings of the Roman Empire early age Roman Catholic Christian invasion of pagan Europe. Better known as "THE LOST LEGION." In the year 140 AD, 20 years after the Ninth Legion disappeared in the north of Britain, Marcus Flavius Aquila, a young Roman centurion, arrives in Britain to serve at his first post as a garrison commander. Shortly afterward, only Marcus's alertness and decisiveness save the garrison from being overrun by pagan Celtic Clans and / or tribesmen.

Recommended Readings

"The New International Reader's Version: What, Who, and Why". International Society of Bible Collectors. Retrieved 2014-09-14.

"New International Version: Official Site". Retrieved 2014-09-14.

"Biblegateway About The NIV, Version Information". Retrieved 2014-09-14.

"August 2009 CBA Best Sellers" (PDF). Christian Business Association. Retrieved 2014-09-14. New International Version #1 in dollar and unit sales

The Bible in American Life

Ronald F. Youngblood; Glen G. Scorgie; Mark L. Strauss; Steven M. Voth, eds. (2003). The Challenge of Bible Translation: Communicating God's Word to the World. Zondervan. pp. 236–245. ISBN 0310246857. Retrieved 2014-09-13.

"Nueva Versión Internacional - Version Information - BibleGateway.com".

"Update of popular 'NIV' Bible due in 2011". USA TODAY. 2009-09-01. Retrieved 2011-09-20.

Smietana, Bob. "New Bible drops gender-neutral language of '05 version". About USATODAY.com. USA TODAY, a division of Gannett Co. Inc. Retrieved 2015-07-30. But they also made changes — like going back to using words like "mankind" and "man" instead of "human beings" and "people" — in order to appease critics.

"Updated NIV Text Available for Online Viewing November 1". Zondervan. Retrieved 2011-02-09.

World's most popular Bible to be revised, MSN.com, 1 September 2009, retrieved 2011-02-19

Irwin, Ben (2002). History of the English Bible. Zondervan. p. 61.

Barker, Kenneth L. (1991). The NIV The Making of a Contemporary Translation. International Bible Society. p. 54.

"About the NIV".

"History of the New International Version". About.com. Retrieved 2011-02-09.

Irwin, Ben (2002). History of the English Bible. Zondervan. p. 60.

"Bible Translation Chart" (PDF). Retrieved 2011-02-09.

Adams, David Phineas; Thacher, Samuel Cooper; Emerson, William (1811). The Monthly Anthology, and Boston Review. Munroe and Francis.

Bois, John; Allen, Ward; Walker, Anthony (1969). Translating for King James; being a true copy of the only notes made by a translator of King James's Bible, the Authorized Version, as the

Final Committee of Review revised the translation of Romans through Revelation at Stationers' Hall in London in 1610–1611. Taken by John Bois ... these notes were for three centuries lost, and only now are come to light, through a copy made by the hand of William Fulman. Here translated and edited by Ward Allen. Nashville: Vanderbilt University Press. OCLC 607818272.

Anon (1783). A call to the Jews. J. Johnson.

Anon (1801). The Anti-Jacobin Review and Magazine. J. Whittle.

Anon (1814). Missionary Register. Seeley, Jackson, & Halliday for the Church Missionary Society.

Anon (1856). The Original Secession Magazine. vol. ii. Edinburgh: Moodie and Lothian.

Anon (1996). The Elizabeth Perkins Prothro Bible Collection: A Checklist. Bridwell Library. ISBN 978-0-941881-19-7.

Barber, Charles Laurence (1997). Early modern English (second ed.). Edinburgh: Edinburgh University Press. ISBN 0-7486-0835-4.

Bobrick, Benson (2001). Wide as the waters: the story of the English Bible and the revolution it inspired. New York: Simon & Schuster. ISBN 0-684-84747-7.

Browne, George (1859). History of the British and Foreign Bible Society.

Bruce, Frederick Fyvie (2002). History of the Bible in English. Cambridge: Lutterworth Press. ISBN 0-7188-9032-9.

Butler, Charles (1807). Horae Biblicae. Vol 1 (fourth ed.). London: J. White. OCLC 64048851.

Chadwick, Owen (1970). The Victorian Church Part II. Edinburgh: A&C Black. ISBN 0-334-02410-2.

Chapman, James L. (1856). Americanism versus Romanism: or the cis-Atlantic battle between Sam and the pope. Nashville, TN: the author. OCLC 1848388.

Cloud, David (2006). "Isn't the King James Bible too Antiquated and Difficult to Understand?". Way of Life Literature. Retrieved 1 August 2009.

Daiches, David (1968). The King James Version of the English Bible: An Account of the Development and Sources of the English Bible of 1611 with Special Reference to the Hebrew Tradition. Hamden, Conn: Archon Books. ISBN 0-208-00493-9.

Daniell, David (2003). The Bible in English: its history and influence. New Haven, Conn: Yale University Press. ISBN 0-300-09930-4.

DeCoursey, Matthew (2003). Edward A. Malone, ed. British Rhetoricians and Logicians, 1500-1660: Second series. Gale Group. ISBN 978-0-7876-6025-3.

Dore, John Read (1888). Old Bibles: An Account of the Early Versions of the English Bible. 2nd edition. Eyre and Spottiswoode.

Douglas, James Dixon, ed. (1974). New International Dictionary of the Christian Church. Zondervan.

Melton, J. Gordon (2005). Encyclopedia of Protestantism. Infobase Publishing. ISBN 978-0-8160-6983-5.

Hacket, John (1715). Bishop Hacket's Memoirs of the Life of Archbishop Williams ... Abridg'd: With the Most Remarkable Occurrences and Transactions in Church and State. Sam. Briscoe.

Hague, Dyson (1948). Through the Prayer Book. Church Book Room Press.

"Raymond Edward Brown." Encyclopædia Britannica. 2009. Encyclopædia Britannica Online. 23 Dec. 2009

Pope Pius XII, Divino Afflante Spiritu, 30 September 1943

A Wayward Turn in Biblical Theory - Msgr. George A. Kelly - Catholic Dossier - Jan/Feb 2000

Felix Corley (August 19, 1998). "Obituary: The Rev Raymond E. Brown". The Independent. Retrieved January 29, 2010.

Gustav Niebuhr, "Raymond E. Brown, 70, Dies; A Leading Biblical Scholar, New York Times, August 11, 1998.

Henry V. King, Traditional Catholic Scholars Long Opposed Fr. Brown's Theories

Felix Corley, "Obituary: The Rev Raymond E. Brown", The Independent, London, 19 August 1998

R. Kendall Soulen, Handbook of Biblical Criticism, Westminster John Knox Press (2001), page 49

William James O'Brian, Riding Time Like a River: The Catholic Moral Tradition Since Vatican II, Georgetown University Press, 1993, page 76.

Dei verbum, 11.

Raymond Brown, The Critical Meaning of the Bible, Paulist Press (1981), page 18.

Most Reverend Terrence T. Prendergast, 'The Church's Great Challenge: Proclaiming God's Word in the New Millennium', in John R Donahue, ed, Life in Abundance: Studies of John's Gospel in Tribute to Raymond E. Brown, Liturgical Press, 2005, p4

"Does the New Testament call Jesus God?" in Theological Studies, 26, (1965) p. 545-73

An Introduction to New Testament Christology, p. 189

It takes a while, hundreds of years, before this son of God becomes the one "begotten" and only God of Christianity by the power struggles and democratic votes of the early Church.
See: Voting About God in Early Church Councils by Ramsay MacMullen, Yale University Press, 2006[original research?]

Francis J Moloney, 'The Legacy of Raymond E Brown and Beyond', in John R Donahue, ed, Life in Abundance: Studies of John's Gospel in Tribute to Raymond E. Brown, Liturgical Press, 2005, p19.

Most Reverend Terrence T. Prendergast, 'The Church's Great Challenge: Proclaiming God's Word in the New Millennium', in John R Donahue, ed, Life in Abundance: Studies of John's Gospel in Tribute to Raymond E. Brown, Liturgical Press, 2005, p3-4

James T. Bretzke, Consecrated Phrases: A Latin Theological Dictionary, Liturgical Press (1998), page 90.

The New Jerome Biblical Commentary. Ed. Raymond E. Brown, Joseph A. Fitzmyer, and Roland E. Murphy. Englewood Cliffs, NJ: Prentice-Hall, 1990.

Pope Benedict XVI, Jesus of Nazareth (Bloomsbury, 2007) chapter 8.

Francis J Moloney, 'The Legacy of Raymond E Brown and Beyond', in John R Donahue, ed, Life in Abundance: Studies of John's Gospel in Tribute to Raymond E. Brown, Liturgical Press, 2005, p251, footnote quoting Origins, 17/35, (February 11, 1988), p.595.

Frank Kermode, New York Review of Books, 29 June 1978, p39-42.

Geza Vermes, The Nativity: History and Legend, London, Penguin, 2006, p21

Dunn, James DG (2003). "Jesus Remembered". Eerdmans Publishing: 324.; D. A. Carson, Douglas J. Moo and Leon Morris. An Introduction to the New Testament. Grand Rapids, MI: Zondervan Publishing House, 1992, 54, 56; Michael Grant, Jesus: An Historian's Review of the Gospels, Scribner's, 1977, p. 71.; Ben Witherington III, "Primary Sources," Christian History 17 (1998) No. 3:12–20.

Eerdmans Dictionary of the Bible 2000 Amsterdam University Press ISBN 90-5356-503-5 page 249

The Bible Knowledge Background Commentary: Matthew-Luke, Volume 1 by Craig A. Evans 2003 ISBN 0-7814-3868-3 pages 67-69

Paul L. Maier "The Date of the Nativity and Chronology of Jesus" in Chronos, kairos, Christos: nativity and chronological studies by Jerry Vardaman, Edwin M. Yamauchi 1989 ISBN 0-931464-50-1 pages 113-129

Craig Evans, 2006 "Josephus on John the Baptist" in The Historical Jesus in Context edited by Amy-Jill Levine et al. Princeton Univ Press ISBN 978-0-691-00992-6pages 55-58

Herodias: at home in that fox's den by Florence Morgan Gillman 2003 ISBN 0-8146-5108-9 pages 25-30

International Standard Bible Encyclopedia: E-J by Geoffrey W. Bromiley 1982 ISBN 0-8028-3782-4 pages 694-695

The Riddles of the Fourth Gospel: An Introduction to John by Paul N. Anderson 2011 ISBN 0-8006-0427-X pages 200

Herod the Great by Jerry Knoblet 2005 ISBN 0-7618-3087-1 page 183-184

J. Dwight Pentecost, The Words and Works of Jesus Christ: A Study of the Life of Christ (Zondervan, 1981) pages 577-578.

Funk, Robert W.; Jesus Seminar (1998). The acts of Jesus: the search for the authentic deeds of Jesus. San Francisco: Harper.

The Word in this world by Paul William Meyer, John T. Carroll 2004 ISBN 0-664-22701-5page 112

Jesus & the Rise of Early Christianity: A History of New Testament Times by Paul Barnett 2002 ISBN 0-8308-2699-8 pages 19-21

The Cradle, the Cross, and the Crown: An Introduction to the New Testament by Andreas J. Köstenberger, L. Scott Kellum 2009 ISBN 978-0-8054-4365-3 pages 77-79

Paul's early period: chronology, mission strategy, theology by Rainer Riesner 1997 ISBN 978-0-8028-4166-7 page 19-27 (page 27 has a table of various scholarly estimates)

The Cradle, the Cross, and the Crown: An Introduction to the New Testament by Andreas J. Köstenberger, L. Scott Kellum 2009 ISBN 978-0-8054-4365-3 page 114

Sanders (1993). "The Historical Figure of Jesus": 11, 249.

Colin J. Humphreys and W. G. Waddington, The Date of the Crucifixion Journal of the American Scientific Affiliation 37 (March 1985)

Jesus in history, thought, and culture: an encyclopedia, Volume 1 by James Leslie Houlden 2003 ISBN 1-57607-856-6 pages 508-509

Brown, Raymond E. (1994). The Death of the Messiah: from Gethsemane to the Grave: A Commentary on the Passion Narratives in the Four Gospels. New York: Doubleday, Anchor Bible Reference Library. p. 964. ISBN 978-0-385-19397-9.

Christology: A Biblical, Historical, and Systematic Study of Jesus by Gerald O'Collins2009 ISBN 0-19-955787-X pages 1-3

Jesus as a Figure in History: How Modern Historians View the Man from Galilee by Mark Allan Powell 1998 ISBN 0-664-25703-8 pages 168-173

Encyclopedia of theology: a concise Sacramentum mundi by Karl Rahner 2004 ISBN 0-86012-006-6 pages 730-731

Interpreting Gospel Narratives: Scenes, People, and Theology by Timothy Wiarda 2010 ISBN 0-8054-4843-8 pages 75-78

Paula Fredriksen, 1999, Jesus of Nazareth, King of the Jews, Alfred A. Knopf Publishers, pages=6–7, 105–10, 232–34, 266

Matthew by David L. Turner 2008 ISBN 0-8010-2684-9 page 613

Sanders, EP (1995). "The Historical Figure of Jesus". London: Penguin Books: 3.

Jesus and the Gospels: An Introduction and Survey by Craig L. Blomberg 2009 ISBN 0-8054-4482-3 pages 431-436

In a 2011 review of the state of modern scholarship, Bart Ehrman wrote: "He certainly existed, as virtually every competent scholar of antiquity, Christian or non-Christian, agrees" B. Ehrman, 2011 Forged: writing in the name of God ISBN 978-0-06-207863-6. page 285

 Ramm, Bernard L (1993). "An Evangelical Christology: Ecumenic and Historic". Regent College Publishing: 19. There is almost universal agreement that Jesus lived

Borg, Marcus (1999). "The Meaning of Jesus: Two Visions (Ch. 16, A Vision of the Christian Life)". HarperCollins: 236. some judgements are so probable as to be certain; for example, Jesus really existed

New Testament History by Richard L. Niswonger 1992 ISBN 0-310-31201-9 pages 121-124

Encyclopedia of theology: a concise Sacramentum mundi by Karl Rahner 2004 ISBN 0-86012-006-6 page 731

Nikos Kokkinos, 1998, in Chronos, kairos, Christos 2 by Ray Summers, Jerry Vardaman ISBN 0-86554-582-0 pages 121-126

Murray, Alexander, "Medieval Christmas", History Today, December 1986, 36 (12), pp. 31 – 39.

The Cradle, the Cross, and the Crown: An Introduction to the New Testament by Andreas J. Köstenberger, L. Scott Kellum 2009 ISBN 978-0-8054-4365-3 page 114

Hoehner, Harold W (1978). Chronological Aspects of the Life of Christ. Zondervan. pp. 29–37. ISBN 0-310-26211-9.

Jack V. Scarola, "A Chronology of the nativity Era" in Chronos, kairos, Christos 2 by Ray Summers, Jerry Vardaman 1998 ISBN 0-86554-582-0 pages 61-81

Christianity and the Roman Empire: background texts by Ralph Martin Novak 2001 ISBN 1-56338-347-0 pages 302-303

Andreas J. Köstenberger, L. Scott Kellum, Charles L Quarles, The Cradle, the Cross, and the Crown (B&H Publishing, 2009), page 139-140.

Luke 1-5: New Testament Commentary by John MacArthur 2009 ISBN 0-8024-0871-0 page 201

Colin Humphreys, The Mystery of the Last Supper Cambridge University Press 2011 ISBN 978-0-521-73200-0, page 64

The Cradle, the Cross, and the Crown: An Introduction to the New Testament by Andreas J. Köstenberger, L. Scott Kellum 2009 ISBN 978-0-8054-4365-3 pages 140-141

Jesus and the Gospels: An Introduction and Survey by Craig L. Blomberg 2009 ISBN 0-8054-4482-3 page 224-229

Christianity: an introduction by Alister E. McGrath 2006 ISBN 978-1-4051-0901-7 pages 16-22

Who is Jesus? an introduction to Christology by Thomas P. Rausch 2003 ISBN 978-0-8146-5078-3 page

The building program of Herod the Great by Duane W. Roller 1998 University of California Press ISBN 0-520-20934-6 pages 67-71

The Temple of Jerusalem: past, present, and future by John M. Lundquist 2007 ISBN 0-275-98339-0 pages101-103

The biblical engineer: how the temple in Jerusalem was built by Max Schwartz 2002 ISBN 0-88125-710-9 pages xixx-xx

Encyclopedia of the historical Jesus by Craig A. Evans 2008 ISBN 0-415-97569-7 page 115

J. Dwight Pentecost, The Words and Works of Jesus Christ: A Study of the Life of Christ (Zondervan, 1981) pages 577-578.

 Andreas J. Köstenberger, John (Baker Academic, 2004), page 110.

Jesus in Johannine tradition by Robert Tomson Fortna, Tom Thatcher 2001 ISBN 978-0-664-22219-2 page 77

The new complete works of Josephus by Flavius Josephus, William Whiston, Paul L. Maier ISBN 0-8254-2924-2

Ant 18.5.2-4

Women in scripture by Carol Meyers, Toni Craven and Ross Shepard Kraemer 2001 ISBN 0-8028-4962-8 pages 92-93

Herod Antipas in Galilee: The Literary and Archaeological Sources by Morten H. Jensen 2010 ISBN 978-3-16-150362-7 pages 42-43

The Emergence of Christianity: Classical Traditions in Contemporary Perspective by Cynthia White 2010 ISBN 0-8006-9747-2 page 48

"Herod Antipas" by Harold W. Hoehner" 1983 ISBN 0-310-42251-5 page 131. Books.google.com. 1983-01-28. Retrieved 2012-07-18.

The relationship between John the Baptist and Jesus of Nazareth by Daniel S. Dapaah 2005 ISBN 0-7618-3109-6 page 48

bHerod Antipas by Harold W. Hoehner 1983 ISBN 0-310-42251-5 pages 125-127

International Standard Bible Encyclopedia: A-D by Geoffrey W. Bromiley 1995 ISBN 0-8028-3781-6 pages 686-687

Bromiley, Geoffrey W. (1995), International Standard Bible Encyclopedia. Wm. B. Eerdmans Publishing. vol. K-P. p. 929.

Matthew 27:27-61, Mark 15:1-47, Luke 23:25-54 and John 19:1-38

Theissen 1998, pp. 81-83

The Cradle, the Cross, and the Crown: An Introduction to the New Testament by Andreas J. Köstenberger, L. Scott Kellum 2009 ISBN 978-0-8054-4365-3 page 104-108

Evans, Craig A. (2001). Jesus and His Contemporaries: Comparative Studies ISBN 0-391-04118-5 page 316

Wansbrough, Henry (2004). Jesus and the oral Gospel tradition ISBN 0-567-04090-9page 185 James Dunn states that there is "broad consensus" among scholars regarding the nature of an authentic reference to the crucifixion of Jesus in the Testimonium. Dunn, James (2003). Jesus remembered ISBN 0-8028-3931-2 page 141

Skeptic Wells also states that after Shlomo Pines' discovery of new documents in the 1970s scholarly agreement on the authenticity of the nucleus of the Tetimonium was achieved, The Jesus Legend by G. A. Wells 1996 ISBN 0812693345 page 48: "... that Josephus made some reference to Jesus, which has been retouched by a Christian hand. This is the view argued by Meier as by most scholars today particularly since S. Pines..." Josephus scholar Louis H. Feldman views the reference in the Testimonium as the first reference to Jesus and the reference to Jesus in the death of James passage in Book 20, Chapter 9, 1 of the Antiquities as "the aforementioned Christ", thus relating the two passages. Feldman, Louis H.; Hata, Gōhei, eds. (1987). Josephus, Judaism and Christianity ISBN 978-90-04-08554-1 page 55

Van Voorst, Robert E (2000). Jesus Outside the New Testament: An Introduction to the Ancient Evidence Eerdmans Publishing ISBN 0-8028-4368-9 pages 39-42

Backgrounds of early Christianity by Everett Ferguson 2003 ISBN 0-8028-2221-5 page 116

Green, Joel B. (1997). The Gospel of Luke: new international commentary on the New Testament. Grand Rapids, Mich.: W.B. Eerdmans Pub. Co. p. 168. ISBN 0-8028-2315-7.

Flavius Josephus, Jewish Antiquities 18.89.

Pontius Pilate: portraits of a Roman governor by Warren Carter 2003 ISBN 0-8146-5113-5 pages 44-45

The history of the Jews in the Greco-Roman world by Peter Schäfer 2003 ISBN 0-415-30585-3 page 108

"Biblical Foundations". Google Plus. Archived from the original on November 5, 2013. Retrieved 25 January 2013.

Köstenberger, Andreas J. "Dossier (PDF)" (PDF). Southeastern Baptist Theological Seminary. Retrieved 15 January 2013.

Köstenberger, Andreas J. (2011). Excellence: The Character of God and the Pursuit of Scholarly Virtue. Wheaton, IL: Crossway. pp. 18–24. ISBN 978-1-58134-910-8.

"Köstenberger, Andreas Johannes". SEBTS Faculty Directory. Retrieved 22 March 2013.

"Publications". The Evangelical Theological Society. Retrieved 25 January 2013.

Works Cited: (additional research support material referenced)
I.   Holy Bible (NIV) and (NIV KJV) and other Holy Bible Versions
II.   Apostles Epistles
III. Scholars; Raymond E. Brown, Richard L. Niswonger, Andreas Köstenberger, Will Durant, H.D. Shively
IV.   Testimony of Witnesses
V.   Book of Mormon
VI.   Other Geographical, Historical, Biblical, Encyclopedic, Congressional Continental, Governmental Sources, World History International References Additional Copyrights and World Wide Web Hyper Linked References.

Reserved

Glossary

Appendix A
Covenant Scripture
Covenant Scripture Reading

Purpose:

(In joint being of Christian Practice in our homes, the Holy Trinity of Jesus Christ will flourish in abounding abundance.)

Objective:

- *I. Shared Reading of the Covenant Christ* (comfortably in living room)

Summary:

(Note: additional writing of the covenant reference Topical Ties: Genesis 17:4 "As for me, behold, my covenant is with thee, and thou shalt be a father of many nations." Covenant NIV Explained; Important in Genesis is God's covenant. A covenant is an agreement between God and humans which God initiates and upholds. God made a covenant with Adam in the Garden of Eden, in which the condition was obedience, the promise was life, and the penalty was death. Yet when Adam and Eve sinned, He did not abandon them, but remained the faithful, covenant God. God established a covenant with Noah before the flood and with all nature after the flood. He entered into a special covenant with Abraham and confirmed it by the right of circumcision. In this covenant God promised to make of Abraham a great nation, to give him the land of Canaan, and to bless all peoples of the earth through Him; this last promise was fulfilled in Jesus Christ. God repeated the Abrahamic covenant promises to Isaac and Jacob, Our covenantal God still pledges His love and faithfulness to us and calls us to believe in Him. To walk in obedience and to make Him our personal Lord.

Note: additional writing of the covenant reference Topical Ties: Genesis 17:7 "And I will establish my covenant between me and thee and thy seed after thee in their generations for an everlasting covenant, to be a God unto thee, and to thy seed after thee." Covenant NIV Explained; The family was the central unit of God's covenant in the old Testament, and the primary influence in the development of the personality and character of children. The father as the head of the family supervised all religious observances and education, and, until the establishment of the tabernacle, offered the sacrifices.

The Old Testament covenant provided a special relationship between God and the family unit. Some Christians believe that the same thing is true in the New Testament with regard to household salvation, stressing that God continues to operate in and through the family. Others see more emphasis placed on the individual and his or her personal belief, and less on the family. In any case, the New Testament has examples of both families and individuals coming to salvation in Christ and being baptized. Paul emphasized the necessity of a well-ordered family and established proper lines of responsibility.

Finally, God uses the concept of family to picture the church local and worldwide in the New Testament.

Note: additional writing of the covenant reference Topical Ties: Jeremiah 31:31 "Behold, the days come, saith the Lord, that I will make a new covenant with the house of Israel, and with the house of Judah:" Covenant NIV Explained; A covenant is an agreement or contract that God initiates with humanity; some have conditions some do not. For example, God's covenant with Adam before the fall required obedience to His commands, with the prospect of either life or death; the covenant with Abraham contained no conditions, but only promises of blessing to him and his descendants. These promises pertain to us as well, since those who love the Lord are children of Abraham through faith in Christ. Some see as many as nine separate covenants in the Bible: in Eden, with Adam, with Noah, with Abraham, with Moses and the Israelites at Sinai, with Israel in Palestine, with David, the new covenant in Christ, and the future covenant of peace. Others, preferring to emphasize only the division of old and new covenant Old and New Testament, see the other covenants on the same theme.

Note: additional writing of the covenant reference Topical Ties: Romans 4:11 "And he received the sign of circumcision, a seal of the righteousness of the faith which he had yet being uncircumcised: that he might be the father of all them that believe, though they be not circumcised; that righteousness might be imputed unto them also:" Covenant NIV Explained; Because God could not be seen, He often demonstrated His presence and power by visible signs, such as the miraculous signs done before the Israelites, Pharaoh, Gideon, Saul, Jeroboam, Ahaz, the crowds around Jesus and the crowds around the Apostles.

God used visible signs to remind His people of His covenant with them, the rainbow, the rite of circumcision, the blood of the Passover Lamb at the exodus, the Sabbath at Sanai, and the alter of the twelve stones at the crossing of the Jordan River. The New Testament uses the water of baptism and the bread and wine of the Lord's Supper as signs of our relationship with Jesus. Signs strengthen faith and draw us closer to God.

Note: additional writing of the covenant reference Topical Ties: Hebrews 7:27 "Who needeth not daily, as those high priests, to offer up sacrifice, first for his own sins, and then for the people's: for this he did once, when he offered up himself." Covenant NIV Explained; Christ came to fulfill the Old Testament, not so much in terms of specific prophecies, but as a better revealer of truth than what God employed in the Old Testament, Christ is better than the angels, Moses, Aaron and the Levitical priests. Christ's sacrifice, as a once for all sacrifice, is better than sacrifices of the Old sanctuary, and the covenant begun in Christ is superior to the covenant made through Moses at Mount Sinai. The blood of Jesus speaks a better word than the blood of Abel, for it guarantees forgiveness. Jesus, in other words, offers us a complete salvation for all eternity.)

- *II. Shared Reading of the HOLY BIBLE in Thanksgiving (Giving Thanks to Christ)* (comfortably in living room)

Luke 7 (a reading of Jesus Christ's miracles and glory)

John 6: 27 – 28

"27 Labour not for the meat which perisheth, but for that meat which endureth unto everlasting life, which the Son of man shall give unto you: for him hath God the Father sealed. 28 Then said they unto him, What shall we do, that we might work the works of God?"

John 6: 53 – 56

"53 Then Jesus said unto them, Verily, verily, I say unto you, Except ye eat the flesh of the Son of man, and drink his blood, ye have no life in you. 54 Whoso eateth my flesh, and drinketh my blood, hath eternal life; and I will raise him up at the last day. 55 For my flesh is meat indeed, and my blood is drink indeed. 56 He that eateth my flesh, and drinketh my blood, dwelleth in me, and I in him. "

Matthew 26: 26 – 28

"26 And as they were eating, Jesus took bread, and blessed it, and brake it, and gave it to the disciples, and said, Take, eat; this is my body. 27 And he took the cup, and gave thanks, and gave it to them, saying, Drink ye all of it; 28 For this is my blood of the new testament, which is shed for many for the remission of sins."

Luke 22:20

"20 Likewise also the cup after supper, saying, This cup is the new testament in my blood, which is shed for you."

- *III. Gather all at the supper table in prayer with Unleavened Bread and the Chassell in representation of Christ's body and blood.* (All standing honorably in dining room)

Shared Recital Prayer:

Bless us O Lord and these thy gifts, which we are about to receive, through the bounty of Christ our Lord. Please dear Jesus bless this food which we are about to eat all for the sacred heart of Jesus. Amen

Speakers Reading:

And we give special acknowledgement through you Lord in Giving Thanks to the beast and plants that have given their lives for us to be nourished with this food. And through you Lord we acknowledged all who work for You Lord and serve You Lord in the administration of the church. Angels, Prophets, Apostles, Saints, Popes, Bishops, Cardinals, Monseigneur's, Priests, Pastors, Ministers, Preachers, Monks, Deacons, and Nuns. The animals whom have befriended us, and the gathering of Believers in Faith of You Lord. Amen

(All drink of the Chalice and eat of the Unleavened Bread of Life in representation of the Body and Blood of our eternal Messianic King Jesus Christ.) All now feast! Amen

Appendix B
Thanksgiving Scripture
Thanksgiving Covenant Scripture Reading

Purpose:

In Christian Practice within our home, may the Holy Trinity of Jesus Christ reign with divine grace above and beneath the Canopy of Heaven in abounding abundance sayeth the Lord. Amen

Objective:

Shared Reading: Lead with the headship of Christ in this Christian Practice (Note: Recommended for better practice open the Holy Bible while gathered together in the unity of this Thanksgiving reading, form a prayer reading circle comfortably in the living room).

Introduction Narrative:

Note: additional writing of the covenant reference Topical Ties: Genesis 17:7 "And I will establish my covenant between me and thee and thy seed after thee in their generations for an everlasting covenant, to be a God unto thee, and to thy seed after thee." Covenant NIV Explained; The family was the central unit of Gods covenant in the old Testament, and the primary influence in the development of the personality and character of children. The father as the head of the family supervised all religious observances and education, and, until the establishment of the tabernacle, offered the sacrifices.

The Old Testament covenant provided a special relationship between God and the family unit. Some Christians believe that the same thing is true in the New Testament with regard to household salvation, stressing that God continues to operate in and through the family. Others see more emphasis placed on the individual and his or her personal belief, and less on the family. In any case, the New Testament has examples of both families and individuals coming to salvation in Christ and being baptized. Apostle Paul emphasized the necessity of a well-ordered family and established proper lines of responsibility.

Summary Reading:

1 Kings 19:16 New King James Version (NKJV)

"Also, you shall anoint Jehu the son of Nimshi as king over Israel. And Elisha the son of Shaphat of Abel Meholah you shall anoint as prophet in your place."

Anointing serves at least four purposes in the Bible: to make oneself beautiful, to promote healing, to prepare the dead for burial and to dedicate an object or a person to the service of God. Prophets, priests and kings were all anointed; one of the titles for a king was "the Lords anointed."

The most important anointing in the Bible is that of Jesus, the Messiah, the Christ. (the Anointed One). Jesus' anointing, prophesied in the Old Testament, was marked by the descent of the Holy Spirit on Him at His baptism. During His life He functioned as Prophet, Priest and King. (Acts 17:3 "explaining and demonstrating that the Christ had to suffer and rise again from the dead, and saying, "This Jesus whom I preach to you is the Christ").

Christians also are anointed with the Holy Spirit, suggesting that we must live in the power of the Spirit as prophets who boldly proclaim Gods message of grace and life, as priests who offer ourselves as "living sacrifices" committed to obedient service, and as kings who sensitively rule over creation on Gods behalf. (Romans 12:1-2 "I beseech you therefore, brethren, by the mercies of God, that you present your bodies a living sacrifice, holy, acceptable to God, which is your reasonable service. 2 And do not be conformed to this world, but be transformed by the renewing of your mind, that you may prove what is that good and acceptable and perfect Will of God").

Sanctification is closely allied to holiness (Leviticus 11:45 "For I am the LORD who brings you up out of the land of Egypt, to be your God. You shall therefore be holy, for I Am Holy"). And justification (Romans 3:24 "Being justified freely by His grace through the redemption that is in Christ Jesus,"). It expresses both a state in which Christians exist and a process of becoming holy that takes place throughout life. This process of sanctification, whereby we gradually become more holy, follows justification. Sanctification is possible only in the Father, in Christ and in Holy Spirit. These who are sanctified are called "saints."

Some feel it is possible for us to be fully sanctified in this life and so attain perfection. Others feel that our sanctification will not be completed until after death.

In passages referring to headship, there are two basic meanings to the word "head": (a) A source or origin; for example, Christ is the source (head) of all creation and of the church, and the source of spiritual growth in the church. (b) Particularly in dispute are those passages that compare the headship of Christ to the headship of male over female. Some interpret man's role as a loving servant of his wife, just as Christ lovingly serves the church. Others prefer to emphasize man's authority over woman, so that she must submit to him as Christ did to God. (Colossians 1:18 "And He is the head of the body, the church, who is the beginning, the firstborn from the dead, that in all things He may have the preeminence").

As well, in Genesis 17:7 conveying one of the nine covenants of God expresses the importance of salvation both individually for the family and household.

Conclusion Narrative:

As well, we are at the sixth millennia marked from the covenant with Noah. The Ark is located and under excavation proving the Bible is a true book. (According to the Bible, Noah was 9

generations after Adam 4004 B.C. – 3074 B.C. which is about 3500 B.C. and Jesus' resurrection sum 2017 A.D. years ago. Noah living to 500 years of age and Jesus' Ministry about 30 years of age at 33 trial, flogging, crucified and on the third day resurrected as written in scripture).

Henceforth, the headship of Christ and to institute good leadership with their voices restored, the men must accept King Christ as their "head" wherein the women can have faith restored in their men that they are men being led by the head of King Christ the Anointed One. This is the obligation of Men to bring salvation forward as head go before the alter of the Lord, bend your knee and bow your head, gather together share in reading scripture as it is written. The woman will have no fear of your headship in Christ. Therein, Christ the head your leadership will not stagger. Where brethren are brethren and sistren is sistren unified in fulfillment of the Lord. Drinketh His blood of the Holy Grail, this is good drink indeed. Eateth of His body the bread of life. This is good eat indeed. Share in the Eucharist. For His flesh is of our flesh and His blood is of our blood. Do all of this in Thanksgiving and in all that you do.

I. Practice Session of Faith:

Shared Reading of the Holy Bible in Thanksgiving (Giving Thanks to Christ) Lead with the Headship of Christ in this Christian Practice of Faith (Note: Recommended for better practice open the Holy Bible while gathered together in the unity of this Thanksgiving reading, form a prayer reading circle comfortably in the living room.)

- i. Saint John 11 (It is recommended read all of John 11 a reading of Jesus Christs miracles and glory.)

As well it is recommended to share in these readings of Christs last supper, John 6: 27-28, John 6: 53-56, and Luke 22: 20. Listed below.

- ii. John 6: 27 – 28

"27 Labour not for the meat which perisheth, but for that meat which endureth unto everlasting life, which the Son of man shall give unto you: for Him hath God the Father sealed. 28 Then said they unto Him, what shall we do, that we might work the works of God?"

- iii. John 6: 53 – 56

"53 Then Jesus said unto them, verily, verily, I say unto you, except ye eat the Flesh of the Son of Man, and drink His Blood, ye have no life in you. 54 Whoso eateth My Flesh, and drinketh My Blood, hath eternal life; and I will raise him up at the last day. 55 For My Flesh is Meat indeed, and My Blood is drink indeed. 56 He that eateth My Flesh, and drinketh My Blood, dwelleth in Me, and I in him."

- iv. Luke 22:20

"20 Likewise also the cup after supper, saying, this Cup is the New Testament in My Blood, which is shed for you."

- II. Practice Session of Faith:

Giving Thanks to Christ Lead with the headship of Christ in this Christian Practice gather together at the table (Tabernacle) in this prayer reading, present Unleavened Bread and the Chassell in representation of King Jesus Christs Holy Body and Blood of Eternal Life in Him. Note: For this encourage a standing of all honorably in the dining room with the Holy Bible open. Placed on the table (Tabernacle) present an offering of a single white candle representing the purity of the Holy Ghost, three small bowls one with grain (the Body) second with oil (the Anointing) third with wine (the Blood) and a fourth bowl to pore out the other three in combining the offering to one small bowl separate from the other three into one bowel. Also, a small plate with unleavened bread (Eucharist) placed upon the plate representing the Bread of Life, and Chassells (the Chassell represents the Holy Grail Christs Cup at the last supper) placed among for all present overflowing with the Living Water of Life and Wine the Blood of Messiah Jesus Christ. Also, place in alignment to this offering another plate for a burnt offering of Thanksgiving and Honor unto our living resurrected Messiah Jesus Christ. Do this with small written notes expressing what you personally and all who are present give unto God in this Thanksgiving Honor Burnt Offering. Amen

Continue this reading with the Holy Bible open with participation in a enactment of Giving Thanks an offering onto God for the divine grace and many blessings we have received.

- i. Matthew 18: 20

"20 For where two or three are gathered together in My Name, there am I in the midst of them."

- ii. Matthew 26: 26 – 28

"26 And as they were eating, Jesus took bread, and blessed it, and brake it, and gave it to the disciples, and said, Take, eat; this is My Body. 27 And He took the Cup (Holy Grail), and gave thanks, and gave it to them, saying, drink ye all of it; 28 For this is My Blood of the New Testament, which is shed for many for the remission of sins." Amen

- III. Practice Session of Faith:

Shared Recital Prayer:

- i. Bless us O Lord and these thy gifts, which we are about to receive, through the bounty of Christ our Lord.
- ii. Please dear Jesus bless this food which we are about to eat all for the sacred heart of Jesus. Amen

- IV. Practice Session of Faith:

Speakers Acknowledgement of the Administration of Christs Church Reading:

- i. And we give special acknowledgement through you Lord in Giving Thanks to the beast and plants that have given their lives for us to be nourished with this food. And through you Lord we acknowledged all who work for You Lord and serve You Lord. The Angels,

Prophets, Apostles, Saints, Popes, Bishops, Cardinals, Monseigneur's, Priests, Pastors, Ministers, Preachers, Reverends, Monks, Deacons, Nuns, Ushers, and Church Administrative Staff. The animals who have befriended us, and the gathering of Believers in Faith of You Lord. Amen

- V. Practice Session of Faith Conclusion:

(All drink of the Chassell the Cup overflowing with Him in eternal life and eat of the Unleavened Bread of Life in representation of the Body and Blood of thy eternal Messianic Lord King thine Savior Jesus Christ.) All now feast in Thanksgiving of our God given divine grace and many blessings. For we are the Unleavened the New Clump Risen in Him His beloved Church. Amen

- i. Feast Merrily
- ii. Eat of the Bread
- iii. Drink of the Chalice

Appendix C
Christmas Scripture
Christmas Covenant Scripture Reading

Purpose:

In Christian Practice within our home, may the Holy Trinity of Jesus Christ reign with divine grace above and beneath the Canopy of Heaven in abounding abundance sayeth the Lord. Amen

Objective:

Shared Reading: Lead with the headship of Christ in This Christian Practice (Note: Recommended for better practice open the Holy Bible while gathered together in the unity of this Christmas giving thanks reading, form a prayer reading circle comfortably in the living room).

Introduction Narrative:

Note: additional writing of the covenant reference Topical Ties: Hebrews 7:27 "Who needeth not daily, as those high priests, to offer up sacrifice, first for his own sins, and then for the peoples: for this he did once, when he offered up himself." Covenant NIV Explained; Christ came to fulfill the Old Testament, not so much in terms of specific prophecies, but as a better revealer of truth than what God employed in the Old Testament, Christ is better than the angels, Moses, Aaron and the Levitical Priests. Christs sacrifice, as a once for all sacrifice, is better than sacrifices of the Old Sanctuary, and the covenant begun in Christ is superior to the covenant made through Moses at Mount Sinai. The blood of Jesus speaks a better word than the blood of Abel, for it guarantees forgiveness. Jesus, in other words, offers us a complete salvation for all eternity.

Summary Reading:

The Birth of Our Messianic Christian King His Holy Royal Majesty King Jesus Christ Our Lord Our Savior The Lamb of Lambs the one time Atonement Blood Sacrifice for all of humanity.

Mass of Christ

The word "Christmas" means "Mass of Christ" or, as it later became shortened, "Christ-Mass." It came to us as a Roman Catholic Mass.

The historic record of the birth of Christ can be found in Matthew 1:18-25 and Luke 2:1-20.

Unlike any other baby, the one born that night in Bethlehem was unique in all of history. He was not created by a human father and mother. He had a heavenly pre-existence (John 1:1-3, 14).

He is God, the Son—Creator of the universe (Philippians 2:5-11). This is why Christmas is called the Incarnation, a word which means "in the flesh." In the birth of Jesus, the eternal, all-powerful and all-knowing Creator came to earth in the flesh.

His Majesty Our Holy Messianic King Jesus Christs Synopsis

Matthew 1

18-19 The birth of Jesus took place like this. His mother, Mary, was engaged to be married to Joseph. Before they came to the marriage bed, Joseph discovered she was pregnant. (It was by the Holy Spirit, but he didn't know that.) Joseph, chagrined but noble, determined to take care of things quietly so Mary would not be disgraced.

20-23 While he was trying to figure a way out, he had a dream. Gods angel spoke in the dream: "Joseph, son of David, don't hesitate to get married. Mary's pregnancy is Spirit-conceived. Gods Holy Spirit has made her pregnant. She will bring a Son to birth, and when she does, you, Joseph, will name Him Jesus— 'God saves'—because He will save his people from their sins." This would bring the prophets embryonic sermon to full term: Watch for this—a virgin will get pregnant and bear a Son; they will name Him Immanuel (Hebrew for "God is with us").

24-25 Then Joseph woke up. He did exactly what Gods angel commanded in the dream: He married Mary. But he did not consummate the marriage until she had the baby. He named the baby Jesus.

Summary Conclusion

Jesus Christ was born circa 6 B.C. in Bethlehem. Little is known about His early life, but as a Young Man, He founded Christianity, one of the world's most influential religions. His life is recorded in the New Testament, more a theological document than a biography. According to Christians, Jesus is considered the Incarnation of God and his teachings an example for living a more spiritual life. Christians believe He died for the sins of all people and rose from the dead.

I. Practice Session of Faith:

Shared Reading of the HOLY BIBLE in Thanksgiving (Giving Thanks to Christ) Lead with the Headship of Christ in this Christian Practice of Faith (Note: Recommended for better practice open the Holy Bible while gathered together in the unity of this Christmas reading, form a prayer reading circle comfortably in the living room.)

- i. Saint Matthew 2: 10-11 (It is recommended read all of Saint Mathew 2 a reading of Jesus Christs miracles and glory.)

As well it is recommended to share in these readings of Christs last supper, John 6: 27-28, John 6: 53-56, and Luke 22: 20. Listed below.

- ii. John 6: 27 – 28

"27 Labour not for the meat which perisheth, but for that meat which endureth unto everlasting life, which the Son of man shall give unto you: for Him hath God the Father sealed. 28 Then said they unto Him, what shall we do, that we might work the works of God?"

- iii. John 6: 53 – 56

"53 Then Jesus said unto them, verily, verily, I say unto you, except ye eat the Flesh of the Son of Man, and drink His Blood, ye have no life in you. 54 Whoso eateth My Flesh, and drinketh My Blood, hath eternal life; and I will raise him up at the last day. 55 For My Flesh is Meat indeed, and My Blood is drink indeed. 56 He that eateth My Flesh, and drinketh My Blood, dwelleth in Me, and I in him."

- iv. Luke 22:20

"20 Likewise also the cup after supper, saying, this Cup is the New Testament in My Blood, which is shed for you."

II. Practice Session of Faith:

Giving Thanks to Christ Lead with the headship of Christ in this Christian Practice gather together at the table (Tabernacle) in this prayer reading, present Unleavened Bread and the Chassell in representation of King Jesus Christs Holy Body and Blood of Eternal Life in Him. Note: For this encourage a standing of all honorably in the dining room with the Holy Bible open. Placed on the table (Tabernacle) present an offering of a single white candle representing the purity of the Holy Ghost, three small bowls one with grain (the Body) second with oil (the Anointing) third with wine (the Blood) and a fourth bowl to pore out the other three in combining the offering to one small bowl separate from the other three into one bowel. Also, a small plate with unleavened bread (Eucharist) placed upon the plate representing the Bread of Life, and Chalice (the Chalice represents the Holy Grail Christs Cup at the last supper) placed among for all present overflowing with the Living Water of Life and Wine the Blood of Messiah Jesus Christ. Also, place in alignment to this offering another plate for a burnt offering of giving thanks and Honor unto our living resurrected Messiah Jesus Christ. Do this with small written notes expressing what you personally and all who are present give unto God in this Giving Thanks and Honor Burnt Offering. Amen

Continue this reading with the Holy Bible open with participation in a enactment of Giving Thanks an offering onto God for the divine grace and many blessings we have received.

- i. Matthew 18: 20

"20 For where two or three are gathered together in My Name, there am I in the midst of them."

- ii. Matthew 26: 26 – 28

"26 And as they were eating, Jesus took bread, and blessed it, and brake it, and gave it to the disciples, and said, Take, eat; this is My Body. 27 And He took the Cup (Holy Grail), and gave thanks, and gave it to them, saying, drink ye all of it; 28 For this is My Blood of the New Testament, which is shed for many for the remission of sins." Amen

III. Practice Session of Faith:

Shared Recital Prayer:

- i. Bless us O Lord and these thy gifts, which we are about to receive, through the bounty of Christ our Lord.
- ii. Please dear Jesus bless this food which we are about to eat all for the sacred heart of Jesus. Amen

IV. Practice Session of Faith:

Speakers Acknowledgement of the Administration of Christs Church Reading:

- i. And we give special acknowledgement through you Lord in Giving Thanks to the beast and plants that have given their lives for us to be nourished with this food. And through you Lord we acknowledged all who work for You Lord and serve You Lord. The Angels, Prophets, Apostles, Saints, Popes, Bishops, Cardinals, Monseigneur's, Priests, Pastors, Ministers, Preachers, Reverends, Monks, Deacons, Nuns, Ushers, and Church Administrative Staff. The animals who have befriended us, and the gathering of Believers in Faith of You Lord. Amen

V. Practice Session of Faith Conclusion:

(All drink of the Chalice the Cup overflowing with Him in eternal life and eat of the Unleavened Bread of Life in representation of the Body and Blood of thy eternal Messianic Lord King thine Savior Jesus Christ.) All now feast in giving thanks unto our God given divine grace and many blessings. For we are the Unleavened the New Clump Risen in Him His beloved Church. Amen

- i. Feast Merrily
- ii. Eat of the Bread
- iii. Drink of the Chalice

Appendix D
Easter Scripture
Easter Covenant Scripture Reading

Purpose:

(In joint being of Christian Practice in our homes, the Holy Trinity of Jesus Christ will flourish in abounding abundance.)

Objective:

- I. Shared Reading of the Covenant Christ (comfortably in living room)

Summary:

Easter: The fulfillment of scripture the Resurrection of His Holy Royal Majesty Our Christian King Jesus Christ Our Lord

Christians believe, according to Scripture, that Jesus came back to life, or was raised from the dead, three days after his death on the cross. As part of the Easter season, the death of Jesus Christ by crucifixion is commemorated on Good Friday, always the Friday just before Easter. Through his death, burial, and resurrection, Jesus paid the penalty for sin, thus purchasing for all who believe in him, eternal life in Christ Jesus.

In Western Christianity, Easter marks the end of Lent, a 40-day period of fasting, repentance, moderation and spiritual discipline in preparation for Easter. Lent begins on Ash Wednesday and ends on Easter Sunday. Eastern Orthodox churches observe Lent or Great Lent, during the 6 weeks or 40 days preceding Palm Sunday with fasting continuing during the Holy Week of Easter. Lent for Eastern Orthodox churches begins on Monday and Ash Wednesday is not observed.

The biblical account of Jesus' death on the cross, or crucifixion, his burial and his resurrection, or raising from the dead, can be found in the following passages of Scripture: Matthew 27:27-28:8; Mark 15:16-16:19; Luke 23:26-24:35; and John 19:16-20:30.

The well-known Old Testament Passover story centers on God's deliverance of Israel from Egypt through ten miraculous plagues. These included how the death angel would "pass over" all the houses where the Israelites lived. They were instructed to put blood over their doorposts to ensure that only the firstborn of Egypt would die. In this first Passover, it was only the blood of the slain lamb that protected each Israelite home.

While Egypt suffered the plague of death, the Israelite firstborn were delivered by blood. By obeying God's command and by faith in His promise to protect them, they were spared from death.

The Passover account is found in Exodus 12:12-14. Verse 14 states that the Passover ceremony was commanded by God to be an annual memorial feast to be kept by Israel "forever." (This command is repeated in Leviticus 23:5.) Exodus 12:15 introduces the seven-day festival called the Days of Unleavened Bread (also repeated in Leviticus 23:6-8), which was to immediately follow the Passover feast each year.

This is why Acts 12:3 states, "Then were the days of unleavened bread," before mentioning the Passover in the next verse. These days were always kept in conjunction with one another.

If the Passover was instituted forever, then New Testament instruction for its observance should be clear. This instruction is found in I Corinthians 5:7-8: "Purge out therefore the old leaven, that you may be a new lump, as you are unleavened. For even Christ our Passover is sacrificed for us: Therefore let us keep the feast (of unleavened bread, which always followed Passover, as explained above) …"

Christ, as the Lamb of God (John 1:29; Acts 8:32; I Peter 1:19; Rev. 5:6), replaced the Old Testament lamb eaten on Passover evening each year.

The New Testament symbols of the bread and wine were instituted so that Christians could eat the body and drink the blood of Christ, the true Lamb of God. Jesus' sacrifice replaced the need to kill a spring lamb. Luke 22:19 shows that Jesus substituted the bread and wine to be taken annually in commemoration of His sacrifice for the remission of our sins—both spiritual and physical.

- II. Shared Reading of the HOLY BIBLE in Thanksgiving (Giving Thanks to Christ) (comfortably in living room)

Saint John 14 (a reading of Jesus Christ's miracles and glory)

John 6: 27 – 28

"27 Labour not for the meat which perisheth, but for that meat which endureth unto everlasting life, which the Son of man shall give unto you: for him hath God the Father sealed. 28 Then said they unto him, what shall we do, that we might work the works of God?"

John 6: 53 – 56

"53 Then Jesus said unto them, Verily, verily, I say unto you, except ye eat the flesh of the Son of man, and drink his blood, ye have no life in you. 54 Whoso eateth my flesh, and drinketh my blood, hath eternal life; and I will raise him up at the last day. 55 For my flesh is meat indeed, and my blood is drink indeed. 56 He that eateth my flesh, and drinketh my blood, dwelleth in me, and I in him."

Matthew 26: 26 – 28

"26 And as they were eating, Jesus took bread, and blessed it, and brake it, and gave it to the disciples, and said, Take, eat; this is my body. 27 And he took the cup, and gave thanks, and gave it to them, saying, Drink ye all of it; 28 For this is my blood of the new testament, which is shed for many for the remission of sins."

Luke 22:20

"20 Likewise also the cup after supper, saying, this cup is the new testament in my blood, which is shed for you."

- III. Gather all at the supper table in prayer with Unleavened Bread and the Chalice in representation of Christ's body and blood. (All standing honorably in dining room)

Shared Recital Prayer:

Bless us O Lord and these thy gifts, which we are about to receive, through the bounty of Christ our Lord.

Please dear Jesus bless this food which we are about to eat all for the sacred heart of Jesus. Amen

Speakers Reading:

And we give special acknowledgement through you Lord in Giving Thanks to the beast and plant's that have given their lives for us to be nourished with this food. And through you Lord we acknowledged all who work for You Lord and serve You Lord in the administration of the church. Angel's, Prophet's, Apostle's, Saint's, Pope's, Bishop's, Cardinal's, Monseigneur's, Priest's, Pastor's, Minister's, Preacher's, Chaplain's, Rabbi's, Imam's, Monk's, Deacon's, and Nun's. The animals who have befriended us, and the gathering of Believer's in Faith of You Lord. Amen

- IV. (All drink of the Chalice and eat of the Unleavened Bread of Life in representation of the Body and Blood of our eternal Messianic King Jesus Christ.) All now feast! Amen

Appendix E
Holy Bible
Books of the Holy Bible Old and New Testament

Old Testament

The Old Testament (also known as the Jewish Tanakh) is the first 39 books in most Christian Bibles. The name stands for the original promise with God (to the descendants of Abraham in particular) prior to the coming of Jesus Christ in the New Testament (or the new promise). The Old Testament contains the creation of the universe, the history of the patriarchs, the exodus from Egypt, the formation of Israel as a nation, the subsequent decline and fall of the nation, the Prophets (who spoke for God), and the Wisdom Books.

Genesis
Genesis speaks of beginnings and is foundational to the understanding of the rest of the Bible. It is supremely a book that speaks about relationships, highlighting those between God and his creation, between God and humankind, and between human beings.

Exodus
Exodus describes the history of the Israelites leaving Egypt after slavery. The book lays a foundational theology in which God reveals his name, his attributes, his redemption, his law and how he is to be worshiped.

Leviticus
Leviticus receives its name from the Septuagint (the pre-Christian Greek translation of the Old Testament) and means "concerning the Levites" (the priests of Israel). It serves as a manual of regulations enabling the holy King to set up his earthly throne among the people of his kingdom. It explains how they are to be his holy people and to worship him in a holy manner.

Numbers
Numbers relates the story of Israel's journey from Mount Sinai to the plains of Moab on the border of Canaan. The book tells of the murmuring and rebellion of God's people and of their subsequent judgment.

Deuteronomy
Deuteronomy ("repetition of the Law") serves as a reminder to God's people about His covenant. The book is a "pause" before Joshua's conquest begins and a reminder of what God required.

Joshua
Joshua is a story of conquest and fulfillment for the people of God. After many years of slavery in Egypt and 40 years in the desert, the Israelites were finally allowed to enter the land promised to their fathers.

Judges
The book of Judges depicts the life of Israel in the Promised Land—from the death of Joshua to the rise of the monarchy. It tells of urgent appeals to God in times of crisis and apostasy, moving

the Lord to raise up leaders (judges) through whom He throws off foreign oppressors and restores the land to peace.

Ruth

The book of Ruth has been called one of the best examples of short narrative ever written. It presents an account of the remnant of true faith and piety in the period of the judges through the fall and restoration of Naomi and her daughter-in-law Ruth (an ancestor of King David and Jesus).

1 Samuel

Samuel relates God's establishment of a political system in Israel headed by a human king. Through Samuel's life, we see the rise of the monarchy and the tragedy of its first king, Saul.

2 Samuel

After the failure of King Saul, 2 Samuel depicts David as a true (though imperfect) representative of the ideal theocratic king. Under David's rule the Lord caused the nation to prosper, to defeat its enemies, and to realize the fulfillment of His promises.

1 Kings

1 Kings continues the account of the monarchy in Israel and God's involvement through the prophets. After David, his son Solomon ascends the throne of a United Kingdom, but this unity only lasts during his reign. The book explores how each subsequent king in Israel and Judah answers God's call or as often happens, fails to listen.

2 Kings

2 Kings carries the historical account of Judah and Israel forward. The kings of each nation are judged in light of their obedience to the covenant with God. Ultimately, the people of both nations are exiled for disobedience.

1 Chronicles

Just as the author of Kings had organized and interpreted Israel's history to address the needs of the exiled community, so the writer of 1 Chronicles wrote for the restored community another history.

2 Chronicles

2 Chronicles continues the account of Israel's history with an eye for restoration of those who had returned from exile.

Ezra

The book of Ezra relates how God's covenant people were restored from Babylonian exile to the covenant land as a theocratic (kingdom of God) community even while continuing under foreign rule.

Nehemiah

Closely related to the book of Ezra, Nehemiah chronicles the return of this "cupbearer to the king" and the challenges he and the other Israelites face in their restored homeland.

Esther
Esther records the institution of the annual festival of Purim through the historical account of Esther, a Jewish girl who becomes queen of Persia and saves her people from destruction.

Job
Through a series of monologues, the book of Job relates the account of a righteous man who suffers under terrible circumstances. The book's profound insights, its literary structures, and the quality of its rhetoric display the author's genius.

Psalms
The Psalms are collected songs and poems that represent centuries worth of praises and prayers to God on a number of themes and circumstances. The Psalms are impassioned, vivid and concrete; they are rich in images, in simile and metaphor.

Proverbs
Proverbs was written to give "prudence to the simple, knowledge and discretion to the young," and to make the wise even wiser. The frequent references to "my son(s)" emphasize instructing the young and guiding them in a way of life that yields rewarding results.

Ecclesiastes
The author of Ecclesiastes puts his powers of wisdom to work to examine the human experience and assess the human situation. His perspective is limited to what happens "under the sun" (as is that of all human teachers).

Song of Songs
In ancient Israel everything human came to expression in words: reverence, gratitude, anger, sorrow, suffering, trust, friendship, commitment. In the Song of Solomon, it is love that finds words–inspired words that disclose its exquisite charm and beauty as one of God's choicest gifts.

Isaiah
Isaiah son of Amoz is often thought of as the greatest of the writing prophets. His name means "The Lord saves." Isaiah is a book that unveils the full dimensions of God's judgment and salvation.

Jeremiah
This book preserves an account of the prophetic ministry of Jeremiah, whose personal life and struggles are shown to us in greater depth and detail than those of any other Old Testament prophet.

Lamentations
Lamentations consists of a series of poetic and powerful laments over the destruction of Jerusalem (the royal city of the Lord's kingdom) in 586 B.C.

Ezekiel

The Old Testament in general and the prophets in particular presuppose and teach God's sovereignty over all creation and the course of history. And nowhere in the Bible are God's initiative and control expressed more clearly and pervasively than in the book of the prophet Ezekiel.

Daniel

Daniel captures the major events in the life of the prophet Daniel during Israel's exile. His life and visions point to God's plans of redemption and sovereign control of history.

Hosea

The prophet Hosea son of Beeri lived in the tragic final days of the northern kingdom. His life served as a parable of God's faithfulness to an unfaithful Israel.

Joel

The prophet Joel warned the people of Judah about God's coming judgment—and the coming restoration and blessing that will come through repentance.

Amos

Amos prophesied during the reigns of Uzziah over Judah (792-740 B.C.) and Jeroboam II over Israel (793-753).

Obadiah

The prophet Obadiah warned the proud people of Edom about the impending judgment coming upon them.

Jonah

Jonah is unusual as a prophetic book in that it is a narrative account of Jonah's mission to the city of Nineveh, his resistance, his imprisonment in a great fish, his visit to the city, and the subsequent outcome.

Micah

Micah prophesied sometime between 750 and 686 B.C. during the reigns of Jotham, Ahaz, and Hezekiah, kings of Judah. Israel was in an apostate condition. Micah predicted the fall of her capital, Samaria, and also foretold the inevitable desolation of Judah.

Nahum

The book contains the "vision of Nahum," whose name means "comfort." The focal point of the entire book is the Lord's judgment on Nineveh for her oppression, cruelty, idolatry, and wickedness.

Habakkuk

Little is known about Habakkuk except that he was a contemporary of Jeremiah and a man of vigorous faith. The book bearing his name contains a dialogue between the prophet and God concerning injustice and suffering.

Zephaniah

The prophet Zephaniah was evidently a person of considerable social standing in Judah and was probably related to the royal line. The intent of the author was to announce to Judah God's approaching judgment.

Haggai

Haggai was a prophet who, along with Zechariah, encouraged the returned exiles to rebuild the temple. His prophecies clearly show the consequences of disobedience. When the people give priority to God and his house, they are blessed.

Zechariah

Like Jeremiah and Ezekiel, Zechariah was not only a prophet, but also a member of a priestly family. The chief purpose of Zechariah (and Haggai) was to rebuke the people of Judah and to encourage and motivate them to complete the rebuilding of the temple.

Malachi

Malachi, whose name means "my messenger," spoke to the Israelites after their return from exile. The theological message of the book can be summed up in one sentence: The Great King will come not only to judge his people, but also to bless and restore them.

New Testament

The New Testament is a collection of 27 books, usually placed after the Old Testament in most Christian Bibles. The name refers to the new covenant (or promise) between God and humanity through the death and resurrection of Jesus Christ. The New Testament chronicles the life and ministry of Jesus, the growth and impact of the early church, and instructive letters to early churches.

Matthew

Matthew's main purpose in writing his Gospel (the "good news") is to prove to his Jewish readers that Jesus is their Messiah. He does this primarily by showing how Jesus in his life and ministry fulfilled the Old Testament Scriptures.

Mark

Since Mark's Gospel (the "good news") is traditionally associated with Rome, it may have been occasioned by the persecutions of the Roman church in the period c. A.D. 64-67. Mark may be writing to prepare his readers for such suffering by placing before them the life of our Lord.

Luke

Luke's Gospel (the "good news") was written to strengthen the faith of all believers and to answer the attacks of unbelievers. It was presented to debunk some disconnected and ill-founded reports about Jesus. Luke wanted to show that the place of the Gentile (non-Jewish) Christian in God's kingdom is based on the teaching of Jesus.

John

John's Gospel (the "good news") is rather different from the other three, highlighting events not detailed in the others. The author himself states his main purpose clearly in 20:31: "that you may believe that Jesus is the Christ, the Son of God, and that by believing you may have life in his name."

Acts
The book of Acts provides a bridge for the writings of the New Testament. As a second volume to Luke's Gospel, it joins what Jesus "began to do and to teach" as told in the Gospels with what he continued to do and teach through the apostles' preaching and the establishment of the church.

Romans
Paul's primary theme in Romans is presenting the gospel (the "good news"), God's plan of salvation and righteousness for all humankind, Jew and non-Jew alike.

1 Corinthians
The first letter to the Corinthians revolves around the theme of problems in Christian conduct in the church. It thus has to do with progressive sanctification, the continuing development of a holy character. Obviously, Paul was personally concerned with the Corinthians' problems, revealing a true pastor's (shepherd's) heart.

2 Corinthians
Because of the occasion that prompted this letter, Paul had a number of purposes in mind: to express the comfort and joy Paul felt because the Corinthians had responded favorably to his painful letter; to let them know about the trouble he went through in the province of Asia; and to explain to them the true nature (its joys, sufferings and rewards) and high calling of Christian ministry.

Galatians
Galatians stands as an eloquent and vigorous apologetic for the essential New Testament truth that people are justified by faith in Jesus Christ by nothing less and nothing more—and that they are sanctified not by legalistic works but by the obedience that comes from faith in God's work for them.

Ephesians
Unlike several of the other letters Paul wrote, Ephesians does not address any particular error or heresy. Paul wrote to expand the horizons of his readers, so that they might understand better the dimensions of God's eternal purpose and grace and come to appreciate the high goals God has for the church.

Philippians
Paul's primary purpose in writing this letter was to thank the Philippians for the gift they had sent him upon learning of his detention at Rome. However, he makes use of this occasion to fulfill several other desires: (1) to report on his own circumstances; (2) to encourage the Philippians to stand firm in the face of persecution and rejoice regardless of circumstances; and (3) to exhort them to humility and unity.

Colossians

Paul's purpose is to refute the Colossian heresy. To accomplish this goal, he exalts Christ as the very image of God, the Creator, the preexistent sustainer of all things, the head of the church, the first to be resurrected, the fullness of deity (God) in bodily form, and the reconciler.

1 Thessalonians

Although the thrust of the letter is varied, the subject of eschatology (doctrine of last things) seems to be predominant in both Thessalonian letters. Every chapter of 1 Thessalonians ends with a reference to the second coming of Christ.

2 Thessalonians

Since the situation in the Thessalonian church has not changed substantially, Paul's purpose in writing is very much the same as in his first letter to them. He writes (1) to encourage persecuted believers, (2) to correct a misunderstanding concerning the Lord's return, and (3) to exhort the Thessalonians to be steadfast and to work for a living.

1 Timothy

During his fourth missionary journey, Paul had instructed Timothy to care for the church at Ephesus while he went on to Macedonia. When he realized that he might not return to Ephesus in the near future, he wrote this first letter to Timothy to develop the charge he had given his young assistant. This is the first of the "Pastoral Epistles."

2 Timothy

Paul was concerned about the welfare of the churches during this time of persecution under Nero, and he admonishes Timothy to guard the gospel, to persevere in it, to keep on preaching it, and, if necessary, to suffer for it. This is the second "Pastoral Epistle."

Titus

Apparently, Paul introduced Christianity in Crete when he and Titus visited the island, after which he left Titus there to organize the converts. Paul sent the letter with Zenas and Apollos, who were on a journey that took them through Crete, to give Titus personal authorization and guidance in meeting opposition, instructions about faith and conduct, and warnings about false teachers. This is the last of the "Pastoral Epistles."

Philemon

To win Philemon's willing acceptance of the runaway slave Onesimus, Paul writes very tactfully and in a lighthearted tone, which he creates with wordplay. The appeal is organized in a way prescribed by ancient Greek and Roman teachers: to build rapport, to persuade the mind, and to move the emotions.

Hebrews

The theme of Hebrews is the absolute supremacy and sufficiency of Jesus Christ as revealer and as mediator of God's grace. A striking feature of this presentation of the gospel is the unique manner in which the author employs expositions of eight specific passages of the Old Testament Scriptures.

James

Characteristics that make the letter distinctive are: (1) its unmistakably Jewish nature; (2) its emphasis on vital Christianity, characterized by good deeds and a faith that works (genuine faith must and will be accompanied by a consistent lifestyle); (3) its simple organization; (4) and its familiarity with Jesus' teachings preserved in the Sermon on the Mount.

1 Peter
Although 1 Peter is a short letter, it touches on various doctrines and has much to say about Christian life and duties. It is not surprising that different readers have found it to have different principal themes. For example, it has been characterized as a letter of separation, of suffering and persecution, of suffering and glory, of hope, of pilgrimage, of courage, and as a letter dealing with the true grace of God.

2 Peter
In his first letter Peter feeds Christ's sheep by instructing them how to deal with persecution from outside the church; in this second letter he teaches them how to deal with false teachers and evildoers who have come into the church.

1 John
John's readers were confronted with an early form of Gnostic teaching of the Cerinthian variety. This heresy was also libertine, throwing off all moral restraints. Consequently, John wrote this letter with two basic purposes in mind: (1) to expose false teachers and (2) to give believers assurance of salvation.

2 John
During the first two centuries the gospel was taken from place to place by traveling evangelists and teachers. Believers customarily took these missionaries into their homes and gave them provisions for their journey when they left. Since Gnostic teachers also relied on this practice, 2 John was written to urge discernment in supporting traveling teachers

3 John
Itinerant teachers sent out by John were rejected in one of the churches in the province of Asia by a dictatorial leader, Diotrephes, who even excommunicated members who showed hospitality to John's messengers. John wrote this letter to commend Gaius for supporting the teachers and, indirectly, to warn Diotrephes.

Jude
Although Jude was very eager to write to his readers about salvation, he felt that he must instead warn them about certain immoral men circulating among them who were perverting the grace of God. Apparently, these false teachers were trying to convince believers that being saved by grace gave them license to sin since their sins would no longer be held against them.

Revelation
John writes to encourage the faithful to resist staunchly the demands of emperor worship. He informs his readers that the final showdown between God and Satan is imminent. Satan will increase his persecution of believers, but they must stand fast, even to death. They are sealed

against any spiritual harm and will soon be vindicated when Christ returns, when the wicked are forever destroyed, and when God's people enter an eternity of glory and blessedness.

Appendix F Reserved

Appendix G
Prayer of Faith
Additional Reading "Prayer of Faith"

As Wise Old Confucius stated within the fortune cookie scroll: Improve yourself each year, visit the earth, make love and cooking with reckless abandonment. Through a process of self-improvement, a more proper gentleman has evolved than the previous year as another year has passed.

I have grown stronger, faster, greater agility, more educated, better equipped, another year wiser, more cunning, improved more developed technique with better abilities, a gentleman and a scholar, more handsome, a stronger relationship with Christ greater faith in the Lord our God. Again, no fear of change always improving each day and advancing.

After enduring a multiple of spinal injuries in early 2009 that slowed me down in all aspects of my most treasured things of my life's experiences, I had made it to my feet in 2013 after four years of medical assistance in aid to recovery. I stood at the base of a mountain still in spinal discomforts and my physical coordination still effected – I understood my father's teachings, "keep your faith," "where there is a will there is a way" I chose a combination of healthy body, healthy mind, healthy soul. I am now recovered, and it has been four years ago that I combined this healthy recipe.

James 5:15 "And the Prayer of Faith shall save the sick, and the LORD shall raise him up; and if he have committed sins, they shall be forgiven him"

The only verse in Scripture that contains the phrase, "Prayer of Faith," is James 5:15. Though spoken of only once, the prayer title conveys an assurance of success in prayer. The conviction that life, if lived with Faith in God, rewards with an Eternity spent in God's presence, encourages us to believe that Faith accomplishes whatever it sets out to do. "For whatsoever is born of God overcometh the world: and **this is the victory that overcometh the world, even our Faith**" (1 John 5:4).

With the Promise of victory beforehand, prayer linked by Faith that is founded in God assures itself to be both rewarding and exciting in "exploits" for God. "The people that do **know** their God shall be strong and do exploits" (Daniel 11:32).

Many times, prayer does not yield the desired results we yearn for. "Hope deferred maketh the heart sick" (Proverbs 13:12). Hope precedes all prayer, but only when the answer comes do, we recognize the difference that Faith makes in praying. "But when the desire cometh, it is a Tree of Life" (13:12).

Picture lightning. When God's will makes contact with our hope, Faith is established and grace races down the lightning rod of experience. Faith is the way you use God's grace. It's our part to exercise the Faith God authors, but it's God's part to finish it.

Index:

A.

About the Author:

Entering the world from the mother's womb into Roman Catholicism Orthodox Christianity, attending school of the Catholic Archdiocese. Thereafter, general public-school education, evolving theretofore postproduction production in film and media editing as a major. Along the way engaging in aviation piloting rotor wing flight missions for a duration. Also, information technology cyber forensics as a minor.

Again, returning, to the root core pages with both thumbs thumbing through much text of the Holy Bible in attending Temples, Mosques, Cathedrals, Chapels, Churches, and Universities of the Crafts. Consisting of interviewing with many persons of these organizational administrations of faith.

Again, evolving forward into an ascension of faith. There is only one Divine and Greater Being Creator of all.

Again, advancing in degrees of knowledge, Masonic Jr. Chaplain Master Mason, author Verwalter des Umhangs – custodian of the cloak presents the first of a feature undertaking in the creating of the LAMB OF GOD. This author brings forward thousands of years of combined knowledge objectively.

(ob·jec·tive·ly /əbˈjektivlē,äbˈjektivlē/ adverb

in a way that is not influenced by personal feelings or opinions.

"events should be reported objectively"

in a way that is not dependent on the mind for existence; actually.

"the physical world we think of as objectively true.")

Reserved

Lightning Source UK Ltd.
Milton Keynes UK
UKHW051532190221
379006UK00002B/55